T0313263

The Facility Manager's
GUIDE TO SAFETY
and SECURITY

The Facility Manager's
GUIDE TO SAFETY
and SECURITY

John Henderson, CPP

CRC Press
Taylor & Francis Group
Boca Raton London New York

CRC Press is an imprint of the
Taylor & Francis Group, an **informa** business

CRC Press
Taylor & Francis Group
6000 Broken Sound Parkway NW, Suite 300
Boca Raton, FL 33487-2742

Library of Congress Cataloging-in-Publication Data

Names: Henderson, John W. (Security consultant), author.
Title: The facility manager's guide to safety and security / author, John W. Henderson.
Description: Boca Raton : Taylor & Francis, CRC Press, 2016. | Includes bibliographical references and index.
Identifiers: LCCN 2016000434 | ISBN 9781498737722 (alk. paper)
Subjects: LCSH: Security systems. | Public buildings--Security measures. | Commercial buildings--Security measures. | Emergency management--Planning.
Classification: LCC TH9705 .H465 2016 | DDC 658.3/82--dc23
LC record available at http://lccn.loc.gov/2016000434

Visit the Taylor & Francis Web site at
http://www.taylorandfrancis.com

and the CRC Press Web site at
http://www.crcpress.com

CONTENTS

PREFACE

The Facility Manager's Guide to Safety and Security came about as an idea following my ten-year tenure as a facility security manager in several facilities of critical importance and my roles as a consultant and security planner. There seemed to be a lack of such material for managers new to the role of looking after facilities, either from the facility or security perspective. A guide, complete with real anecdotes of what happens inside larger buildings, can be an invaluable tool for people taking on such roles for the first time so that they can get some idea of what to expect as their role evolves.

ACKNOWLEDGMENTS

The Facility Manager's Guide to Safety and Security is the second book written by John Henderson. There are several influential people that contributed significantly to John's experience, making it possible for this book to be written and published.

The first and most important person is his beautiful wife, Nicole, who has supported everything John has done through the years and who has been there for him without fail when times were tough. Her own example of perseverance in the face of adversity and of demonstrated strength when the outlook was grim have been inspirational. *Forever...*

Others of positive influence include John's favorite manager, Darylene Foster, who confirmed by example that remaining true to yourself and others in the face of corporate politics by those who seemed able to park their ethics at the curb as they reached for success is the only way to go. Being able to live with one's decisions and actions of the past, present, and future is the greatest gift.

Science fiction author Don Perrin is an old friend of many years who selflessly toiled in assisting John with his first book *The Family Guide to Home and Personal Security*. Don's patience in helping to edit John's first book has contributed to the writing of this second book in numerous ways.

John would also like to extend his thanks to the following for their support and/or kind assistance by allowing permission to access reference material.

- Jason D. Reid, Life Safety Systems, http://www.nationallifesafety group.ca
- Fire Chief Trent Elyea, Collingwood and the Blue Mountain Fire Department
- CPTED Ontario, http://cptedontario.ca
- Taylor & Francis Group

AUTHOR

John Henderson, **BA**, **CPP**, is a 51-year-old Canadian whose early life was a mix of experiences from living in Lahr, Germany as a Canadian army brat and serving with the Royal Canadian Army Cadets, and later with the Canadian Army Reserves, to working his way through university as a gas station attendant, short-order cook, shopping cart returner, dish washer, and security guard. He graduated from Carleton University in Ottawa, Ontario with a bachelor's degree in sociology/anthropology, and took police sciences courses in preparation for his career in policing.

John has served with a large police force in Canada for the past 29 years and holds the rank of sergeant. He not only accumulated nearly a decade of street-level policing experience, but also served in corporate human resources, policy development, and conducted research before taking command of the headquarters physical security unit for a decade. He developed as a facility security manager by taking numerous courses, joining the American Society of Industrial Security (ASIS International), and later attaining the accreditation of certified protection professional (CPP). He served the government as a security consultant during the initial period following the 9/11 attacks and helped develop business continuity planning for government to the cabinet level. He also led teams of facility reviewers to assess security in over 55 government and private facilities in the space of a two-year period and served on the Occupational Health and Safety Committee.

John has a great deal of experience leading large-scale facility evacuations and in developing and revising fire safety and evacuation policies in cooperation with local fire services. He has routinely organized large facility events featuring the influx and movement of thousands of people and vehicles, while working with public and government agencies.

He has taught many sessions covering a variety of topics in human resources and safety/security to match his extensive experience leading employees and keeping facilities running under all conditions.

John is a recipient of the Canadian Police Exemplary Service Medal and has been awarded several commendations including a life saving award when a colleague's airway became blocked, requiring a quick administration of the Heimlich maneuver.

John is very happily married to the greatest woman in the world, and they are raising two wonderful children in southwestern Ontario.

1

Introduction

Facilities around the world are found in a variety of types, shapes, and sizes and are built for differing purposes as human need arises. The main reason for building a facility is to provide a safe, contained location for people, assets, information storage and processing, manufacturing, or a combination of all of those. As such, there are basic similarities throughout all facilities that allow facility managers to operate with similar skill sets.

To be more specific, there are facilities and buildings all over the world that serve as single residences, multiunit residential buildings, retail stores and shopping malls, offices, warehouses, factories, sports stadiums, museums, and public service facilities such as hospitals and government services entities. Each type of facility always has one person in charge of operations and safety/security; although that person may not carry such a title as a full-time endeavor, the function remains the same. In the case of a large factory or other large complex, there may be an identified security and/or facility manager, while in a small residential building, the manager may simply be an occupant that looks after any problems and is usually known as the building superintendent.

What I have found in my many years of public service, but more specifically in my years as a security manager and facility threat and risk assessor, is that most buildings have many commonalities despite their different shapes, sizes, and functions. These commonalities derive from the basic requirements of any facility and the nature of the construction and occupants, as well as the intended use of the facility. In other words, a basic building is designed to hold occupants, furniture, items of value, or, in the case of a factory, machinery and workers, for example. The main objective of any building is not only to keep people, assets, and information secure but also to keep the weather and natural elements out, forming a basic part of the need for humans to remain safe and secure, consistent with Maslow's Hierarchy of Needs.

The commonalities are basic in nature and indicate a common set of regular human functions in each facility, regardless of the size and nature of the facility, that lend to a common set of methods to run and maintain each facility. Although the complexity of managing and maintaining different facilities will vary widely with purpose and function, buildings still have common human functions and resulting issues that should be managed in a consistent manner to ensure the success of the facility, as well as the success of the activity within the facility, by addressing safety and security.

Simply explained through example, a family home is intended to shelter a family from the elements and keep them and their possessions secured against the outside world. Inside the average home, we find access and egress points; access controls; a small furnace or heating plant, and perhaps air conditioning; an electrical power panel; water sources and drains; a hot-water tank; common areas; a kitchen that is full of electrical and perhaps even gas appliances; bathrooms with a sink, bathtub/shower, and toilets; and private areas such as the bedrooms and perhaps an office. Compare this to an apartment building that has numerous self-contained units containing all of the aforementioned aspects, but also a general facility-level heating plant, water source, drainage system, electrical power facility, and access/egress to the entire building, as well as to each individual unit. There may also be an elevator system in addition to the stairs and a multispace parking garage as opposed to the household one- or two-car garage. Although on a much greater scale, the apartment building still has the same kind of basic services and hardware as the single family home.

Securing and managing both these types of facilities and others requires a person or team of people with identified responsibilities toward managing and maintaining the facility to support the intended function. In the case of the family home, the homeowner and/or spouse (if there is one) usually handles all of the responsibilities, or he or she will hire persons to perform maintenance and cleaning functions. In an apartment building, most often there is a hired building superintendent, while a large factory might have a security and/or facility manager and a facilities team to handle security, cleaning, and maintenance. However, the most basic human functions remain the same as those in the family home.

TYPES OF FACILITIES

The range of facilities in the world is huge, but most have basic functions common to the comfort and physical needs of people. As described, the most basic of facilities is the family home that supports the life of a family. It is this comfort and physical security that create commonality in most buildings, but the following are descriptions of different types of facilities, all of which require human comforts, security, and management by a designated person or team of individuals whose sole purpose is to keep the facility running in its intended manner.

The following are descriptions of typical facilities in cities and towns across the world including their uses, functions, and management requirements. The commonalities in each facility type will stand out. The list does not account for combination facilities where more than one type of facility has been built with the purpose of effective planning and convenience. The list is not exhaustive and is not intended to reflect facilities in totality. It is general in nature and intended to illustrate the commonalities in facilities for the purposes of this book.

Residential Facilities

Family home: This is a private dwelling.
> Use: It provides a safe and secure base for a family.
> Functions: It contains sleeping quarters; a heating, ventilation, and air conditioning (HVAC) system; power and fuel supply; water and drainage; a kitchen with cooking and food-storage appliances; personal assets; furniture; tools and vehicles.
> Management: Management is handled by the homeowner and perhaps contractors for upkeep.

Apartment building: This is a common building containing multiple dwelling units.
> Use: It contains multiunit dwellings for individuals and families and a garage and/or parking facilities.
> Functions:
>> Building level: HVAC, including chillers, boilers, furnaces, power supply and uninterruptible power supply (UPS); fire annunciation panel and subpanels; maintenance equipment and storage.
>> Individual dwelling: HVAC; power and fuel supply; water and drainage; kitchen with electric appliances and cooking facilities; personal assets; tools; furniture.

3

Management: Management is handled by the owner; a building superintendent/manager and contractors take care of maintenance.

Commercial Facilities

Office building: This is a common building containing multiple units for business purposes.
Use: It contains multiunit offices and common areas, boardrooms, reception stations, kitchenettes, lunchrooms, and media rooms/auditoriums.
Functions: It contains HVAC, including chillers, boilers, furnaces, power supply and UPS; fire annunciation panel and subpanels; maintenance equipment and storage; water and fuel supply; drainage; and designated parking in a lot or garage.
Management: Management includes a facilities manager and/or security, a maintenance contractor, and subcontractors.
Commercial retail store: This is a storefront business operation for retail sales and trade.
Use: It is used for retail sales of goods and services to the public, storage of assets, shipping and receiving, and office space.
Functions: In a stand-alone building these include HVAC, including chillers, boilers, furnaces, power supply and UPS; fire annunciation panel and subpanels; maintenance equipment and storage; water and fuel supply; and drainage.
Part of a mall system: All the aforementioned functions are supplied to the tenant business by the mall building operation, but the store may still have washroom facilities and change rooms, a kitchenette, cooking appliances, cash registers, and a stand-alone alarm system.
Management: Store managers usually handle everything and work through mall management/maintenance and security for particular issues.
Restaurant: This is a professional kitchen for the preparation and sale of meals and alcohol.
Use: Restaurants provide a service and an experience to customers who order food and drink, wait for the preparation, and then consume the meal. The in-house experience often lasts one to two hours.
Function: Industrial kitchen setup is led by a professional chef; it contains multiple cooking appliances using electricity and

fuel and multiple cold storage units, as well as restroom facilities, power and water supplies, drainage, cash registers, and ATM machines. Sometimes recreational facilities are present.

Management: Management consists of a restaurant manager, head chef, owner/operator, and contractors.

Research facilities: Research facilities are proprietary and information driven and can be for cognitive research or for researching technology, medicine, goods, or food.

Use: These facilities will be tailored to the type of research being performed but all will be high-security entities.

Function: Research facilities will contain all typical functions of large facilities such as office space, HVAC, UPS, hydropower (hydro), fuel supplies, water and drainage, and human comforts such as kitchenettes and restrooms; they will also contain specialized testing equipment, laboratories and facilities, either indoor or outdoor as the functions require. Laboratories contain special environmental equipment, specialized alarms, and chemical fire suppression; special exhaust facilities and incineration may be present as well for disposal of toxic and biological waste.

Management: Some research entities are private consortiums, while others are public and funded/managed by government agencies. Regardless, management is tight on research facilities as the accountabilities are usually quite high. Most staff and management are in house; contractors must undergo rigorous clearance processes.

Manufacturing facilities/factories

Use: Factories are generally designed as large boxes of aluminum containing the equipment needed for manufacturing a wide range of goods. Older factories are often standard bricked buildings with timber or metal shells, constructed with rooftop ventilation, but this style is falling out of use as time progresses.

Function: Factories house the machinery and equipment, often in mass-production lines requiring a large supply of hydro and gas/oil/diesel, as well as water and drainage, and waste-holding and disposal facilities. They will still have offices and boardrooms, and restrooms, change rooms, kitchens, and common rooms for workers, as well as boilers, chillers, and

HVAC, including special HVAC for the manufacturing line to vent dangerous fumes from manufacturing processes.

Management: Most often factories are privately owned, reporting to boards of directors or to an owner. They have professionals managing day-to-day operations through which the buildings are run by in-house facilities management and security and/or contracted management, security, and maintenance.

Storage facilities: Storage facilities exist for the storage and movement of manufactured goods and food supplies or for long-term storage of information.

Use: There are active supply chains of storage facilities in all countries where goods are stored prior to moving to retail locations and cold storage of food items to prevent spoilage during transit and delivery to grocery stores. Information storage exists mostly for government, where massive warehouses may contain decades' worth of files and information for the population.

Function: Storage facilities have offices and boardrooms; restrooms and change rooms; hydro, gas supply, water supply and drainage; and kitchens and common rooms for workers, as well as boilers, chillers, HVAC, including special HVAC and chilling/heating equipment for the cold and warm storage facilities. Security systems and transportation are important for storage and supply systems.

Management: Government information storage will be run by government managers reporting to a chain of command with in-house facilities management/maintenance/security or contracted services. Commercial storage will be privately owned or reporting to a corporation and/or board of directors. There can be in-house facilities and maintenance management and employees or contracted services.

Gas stations/garages: These are most often private, for-profit corporations delivering gasoline, diesel, and mechanical services to consumers at small vending stations across each community.

Use: Gas stations most often have a small storefront building where transactions are made for the vended gasoline and some minor vending of goods with available public restrooms and, sometimes, also small restaurants. Outside are separately located gas pumps where the fuel is delivered. Some gas stations have car wash facilities while mechanic shops have several bay garages within which to safely do mechanical work with their specialized tools.

Function: Gas stations require the same HVAC, hydro, fuel supplies for heating, water and drainage, and maintenance as other facilities but they also have special fuel storage requirements for the fuels being sold, which are located in underground tanks on the property. Car wash facilities will have more complicated plumbing, water supply, and extra drainage requirements, subject to environmental regulations.

Management: There is a gas station manager who could also be the owner of the independent business, which is also a franchise of a larger corporate structure that supplies the fuel from storage and refining plants. The corporation dictates the price and the owner/operator is contracted to take a small percentage of the income from the gasoline sales.

Critical Infrastructure Facilities

Banks: Banks are financial institutions within the community.

Use: They serve as financial centers for the local community where savings and valued assets are kept as well as offer an array of financial services for the community.

Function: A bank contains customer service stations, secured bank vaults, office space, restrooms, kitchenettes, hydro with UPS, water and drainage systems, and automatic cash machines.

Management: Management comprises a bank manager as a franchisee and contracted maintenance and security.

Airport: An air transportation hub for people and commerce/goods, this is a facility of critical importance with unique security requirements.

Use: Persons/goods are transported by air to multiple destinations; aircraft are stored and air traffic control is present.

Function: This includes aircraft takeoff and landing; aircraft maintenance and storage; aircraft loading and unloading, passenger screening; and baggage handling, as well as retail shops; restaurants and bars; restrooms; entertainment; water and drainage, hydro and UPS; heating fuel and aircraft fuel, including storage and refueling stations; customs booths; police; car rental agencies; fire and emergency medical services and other services.

Management: A management team will include airport authorities, government officials, police and fire command, security, and business leaders. Maintenance and security services are contracted.

Government buildings: These facilities house the hubs of government activity organized by respective ministries and departments. Some government buildings are facilities of critical importance with unique security requirements.

Use: These offer administrative functions and government service delivery to the population.

Function: Government facilities function in a similar manner to other office buildings; they have office and boardroom space, reception stations, loading docks, mail facilities, kitchenettes, restroom facilities, self-contained power and fuel supplies, HVAC, UPS, water, and drainage.

Management: Political leaders, facilities managers, maintenance and security, and contracted and subcontracted maintenance services can be involved.

Military: Military facilities house the equipment and operations/training of personnel dedicated to the service to and protection of the citizens, assets, and interests of the nation. Many of these are facilities of critical importance with unique security requirements.

Use: Operational, training, and administrative functions of all types will be incorporated into these facilities from offices to armories, fleet storage, armed forces bases, headquarters and detachments, airports, sea ports, and heliports.

Function: All functions will be present such as HVAC, power supply and UPS, fuels of all types, ammunition and firearms storage, fleet vehicles and aircraft maintenance garages and storage, restrooms, classrooms, parade spaces, gymnasiums, retail sales, quartermaster supply warehouses, and residential buildings.

Management: Management consists of command ranks, lower level managers, civilian specialists, contracted maintenance, contracted and/or in-house security, and military police.

Police/fire/ambulance: Police, fire, and ambulance are the three tiers of first-response in Western society for communities and typically each is structured in much the same manner.

Use: Police and fire departments and ambulance services typically have headquarters facilities and operational detachments

8

that are scattered throughout communities, including at the state/provincial and national level. This is for localized service delivery featuring efficient response times and localized relationship building. Headquarters buildings will be larger self-contained facilities holding administrative offices, boardrooms, common areas, public reception, training facilities such as firearms ranges for police, treatment rooms for ambulances, and perhaps fire simulation facilities for fire services. All facilities will have HVAC, hydro, boilers and chillers, water supply and drainage, fuel supply, and UPS. The detachment levels will be smaller and focused primarily on local service delivery such as common office space, management offices, reception, holding cells for police, fleet service and loading bays, and multipurpose rooms, including lockers, restrooms and change rooms, kitchenettes, and common rooms.

Management: Management of police/fire/ambulance facilities is typically by a local commander for the service combined with facilities management from the organization with some in-house maintenance combined with contractors for specific tasks.

Pipelines: Pipelines are facilities of critical importance that transport oil and gas over long distances and have unique security requirements.

Use: Pipelines are large steel hollow pipes that are typically thousands of miles in length and are designed to bring oil and gas from sources to market or refinery. Pipelines have buildings along the way to maintain flow rates and perform other tasks for the maintenance of the system.

Function: Pipeline buildings provide protection from the elements for workers but are mainly there to house machinery, equipment, and electronics to maintain or change flow rates, stop or start the flow, and provide facilities and remote abilities for companies to troubleshoot the pipeline. The buildings will contain all of the comforts of other facilities for the times when people do visit, such as HVAC, water and drainage, sewer, kitchens, hydro, boilers and chillers, UPS.

Management: These facilities are typically company-owned entities reporting through private corporations and are accountable to boards of directors. Security and maintenance can be contracted.

Prisons: Prisons are used to warehouse persons convicted of offenses and sentenced to serve time by the justice system. There are minimum-, medium-, and maximum-security prisons based on the severity of the offense. These are facilities of critical importance with unique security requirements.

Use: Prisons function as self-contained, secure residences with the main facility encompassing numerous smaller facilities and prisoner cells.

Function: Function includes HVAC, water and drainage, hydro and fuel supplies; secure cells, common areas, restroom and change room facilities, gymnasiums, libraries, educational facilities, industrial sized kitchens, laundry, and other services to avoid risk of using outside services.

Management: Management consists of government oversight, prison executives/commanders, lower level managers, and contractors for maintenance.

Hospitals: These are facilities of critical importance with unique security requirements and critical supply needs.

Use: Hospitals house the community functions of health care and treatment. They are required to function in good working condition 24 hours a day, every single day of the year without fail and remain accessible to all citizens.

Function: These are the most complicated facilities in most communities but still have the typical HVAC, water and drainage, hydro and fuel, and communications wiring. Uninterrupted power supply is a critical function at a hospital, usually consisting of several large diesel generators, depending on the size of the facility and an accompanying fuel supply that must last sufficient time for government infrastructure to provide assistance. The UPS must be kept in a reliable, functioning state. There are many specialized gases plumbed throughout hospitals that require special delivery, handling facilities, and storage. There are industrial sized kitchens and laundry facilities for the hospital population. Significant plumbing exists to service treatment and operating rooms, patient rooms, employee change rooms and lunchrooms, kitchenettes, restaurants and retail, and for maintenance requirements. Hospitals also contain office space, boardrooms and space for general administration, as well as loading docks for supplies and mail receiving and processing facilities. For transportation and receiving of patients, hospitals have loading bays and ambulance storage and maintenance; some feature heliports or helipads for rapid delivery of critical patients by helicopter. Biohazard disposal facilities also exist in many hospitals.

Management: Reporting to either government or a private board of directors, hospitals have highly accountable executives and facility management/security, supplemented by in-house workers and contracted service providers as well as teams of volunteers for various functions.

Parliament/Legislature: This is a facility of critical importance with unique security requirements. This is the seat of democracy at either the federal or state/provincial level, where elected officials gather to conduct the business of government decision making and debate.

Use: The buildings house elected members' offices, political party meeting spaces, and a legislative hall, with hundreds of seats for sitting elected members, where political debate and voting take place.

Function: These buildings are secured access for authorized people and contain offices, meeting rooms, restrooms and change rooms, kitchenettes, a large multiseat hall for political debate and voting, security offices, and access control stations. Legislative buildings also usually contain a reference library, media rooms, and in-house printing services. Typical of large facilities, legislative buildings have centralized HVAC, hydro with UPS, water and drainage, fuel supplies for heating water and boilers, and office supply storage. They will certainly have extensive security systems, including closed circuit television, electronic access control, alarms, and security services personnel on duty 24/7.

Management: Legislative facilities will be run by an impartial government ministry or department with local officials appointed to run the buildings and direct either in-house or contracted maintenance/security. Legislative facilities containing state secrets and vast amounts of personal information will also have the protection of federal, provincial/state, or municipal police depending upon the level of legislative facility.

Educational Institutions: These are elementary and high schools, colleges, and universities. Also included are privately run schools and colleges.

Use: In essence, schools, colleges, and universities are large, Multiuse facilities intended for the educational needs of the population. Like theatres, educational campuses have become frequent targets for shooters/attackers, given the target-rich environment of populated classrooms and slow egress.

Function: These facilities contain office space/boardrooms for administration, classrooms and auditoriums for instruction, common rooms for individual study, gymnasiums, change rooms and libraries, and numerous restroom facilities; many contain cafeterias and lunchrooms. Typical of large facilities, schools have centralized HVAC, hydro, water and drainage, fuel supplies for heating water and boilers, and school supply storage.

Management: Schools of varying types can report to boards of directors, government, and/or elected school trustees. There is usually a president in larger entities or a principal in charge of administering the school with a management team and in-house maintenance as well as subcontractors for various tasks.

Railroads: These are facilities of critical importance and have unique security requirements.

Use: Railroads are part of the vital transportation hub that moves commerce across countries and continents.

Function: Railroads feature thousands of miles of track interconnecting cities and remote locations. There are railroad terminals for passenger service and commercial movement of goods and there are railroad yards that store and maintain/repair train engines and cars, as well as provide loading and unloading services to get goods and raw materials to market. The buildings all contain the typical human comforts such as HVAC, water and drainage/sewer, hydro, gas and oil supply, and often stored chemicals. Terminals will contain retail, restaurants, restrooms, office space, and boardrooms as places of business for the movement of people and goods.

Management: Management is by corporate structure with a mix of in-house management and contracted services for maintenance and security. As unique service providers, some railroads have their own police services.

Port Facilities: These are of critical importance and have unique security requirements.

> Use: These are complex entry points to countries on a shoreline, mainly for people and goods, as well as for the administrative processing of people and imports/exports for entry to and exit from the country.

> Function: Ports will have complex docking systems for ships of all sizes for the massed loading and unloading of people and shipments of commercial goods. The buildings may have all of the human comforts, including HVAC, water and drainage/sewer, restrooms, retail and restaurants, hydro, gas supply, boilers and chillers, repair and maintenance facilities, storage of commercial containers and cold storage for perishable goods, and access to transportation systems such as rail, air, and road. A customs presence is also on site for international traffic.

> Management: Management will be a mixture of government and private enterprise and contain border screening services, police, government and corporate managers, and a mix of in-house and contracted maintenance and security services.

Border Stations: These are facilities of critical importance and have unique security requirements.

> Use: Border stations are formal entry points to countries through which all persons should be screened for identity, nationality, and purpose.

> Function: These are self-contained facilities designed to receive walk-ins and road traffic at international border points. Rail, fort, and air traffic may be screened at border services offices inside larger facilities such as ports, airports, or rail terminals. The border point offices contain HVAC, hydro, restrooms, office space and screening kiosks, water, drainage/sewer, gas supplies, hydro, and UPS. Some border points may have retail and restaurants, garages for vehicle searches and containment, and holding cells.

> Management: Management will be through government border services and whatever commercial and privately owned interests exist. Maintenance and security will be a mix of in-house and contracted services, while police and border guards may also be present.

Entertainment Facilities

Sports Arenas and Stadiums: These are outdoor and domed stadiums of varying size, with indoor arenas and sport venues for competition and training. These are also used for large events such as music concerts, political rallies, and religious events.

Use: Sport venues such as indoor track and field, swimming, speed skating and other Olympic sports have specialized facilities. Professional and amateur football, baseball, and hockey will use indoor or outdoor stadiums based on need and attendance. In community, state/provincial, or national emergencies, stadiums can become shelters for displaced people.

Function: Specialized playing surfaces are central in these facilities, requiring special care for grass or ice and to be able to transform the shape of playing surfaces depending upon what the event requires. Seating is accessed by numerous entry points, and restroom facilities, vendors, office space, and team dressing rooms are strategically placed. Parking of user vehicles requires specialized and well-maintained lighting. Significant plumbing exists to service dressing rooms, ice surfaces, kitchenettes, restaurants, and retail, and for maintenance requirements.

Management: Building ownership or executives will have a management team and in-house maintenance/security combined with outside contractors for event days.

Multiuse Community Centers: These are community-funded centers of activity and recreation with multiple uses.

Use: Community centers most often contain gymnasiums and amateur sports facilities and sometimes ice rinks, common rooms for events and meetings, office space, rest and change rooms, and sometimes retail stores and restaurants. These facilities are meant for the recreation and general use of community members as needed.

Function: Complicated functions can resemble those of a sports stadium in that the main building will have HVAC, water and drainage, fuel supply, hydro, UPS, and requirements to clean and repair gymnasium and arena facilities; parking of user vehicles requires specialized and well-maintained lighting. Significant plumbing exists to service dressing rooms, ice arenas, kitchenettes, cafeterias, and maintenance requirements.

Management: Usually funded by the municipality, facility managers will report to the governing body, usually a municipal council. The facility manager will have a team of maintenance personnel and contractors for varying functions.

Theatres: There are two common types of theatres in most communities: (1) the multiple-screened movie theatres that play current motion pictures for paying audiences, and (2) live, performance-oriented venues with a set stage and actors appearing live for performances in plays. Unfortunately, theatres have become frequent targets for solitary attackers wanting to cause havoc and death randomly as they are rich targets of opportunity. As anonymous people are drawn to theatres, they are packed tightly into rooms with seats that provide attackers with easy massed casualties if they open fire into a theatre during a show. Escape from these rooms is not easy for the victims, who must line up and move slowly through perhaps two or three doors to the outside. The attacker, on the other hand, can blend into the crowd and has a reasonable chance of escape.

Use: Live theatres typically have reception areas where tickets and refreshments are sold; access to the seating area is controlled as the audience is admitted by paid ticket stub to a prearranged seat. Movie theatres are similar in structure but seats are usually not reserved in advance: the first come, first served approach sorts out seating.

Function: Similarly to other public facilities, theatres contain a full range of functions and require the comforts that paying customers expect. Theatres contain retail and ticket sales stations, food vendors, restrooms, office space, change rooms for employees, carpentry shops, screening rooms, and sometimes arcade games. HVAC is present, hydro, water and drainage, fuel for heating and cooking, UPS, and a significant parking area.

Management: Management is usually by owner/operator and a professional management team with contracted maintenance and security.

Museums: Museums of various types warehouse items of value and historical/cultural significance for public examination and the preservation of history. The museums also preserve artifacts and repair damaged items with the expertise and specialized equipment on hand.

Use: Museums are most often self-contained facilities with office space and restrooms and change rooms for the public and employees, with eating facilities/restaurants, retail sales, and tickets sales counters. Beyond access-controlled doors are exhibit storage and preservation rooms where work is done to maintain exhibits in good repair. Also access controlled are the exhibit rooms for public viewing. The exhibits and general areas are mostly monitored by security guards, closed circuit television, and intricate alarm systems, as well as environmental/humidity controls to maintain preservation of the artifacts and displays. The goal of the museum curator is to balance the positive experience of the visitor with security and preservation of the displays by letting people get close enough to enjoy the experience, but not too close to damage or steal anything.

Function: Museums have HVAC and specialized environmental controls, hydro and sophisticated security systems, fuel supplies, water and drainage, typical restrooms, change rooms, kitchen and eating facilities, and storage and restoration facilities with specialized environmental controls.

Management: Museums can have large organizations involved in management of the contents/exhibits that are separate from the facility itself, but similarly accountable. A board of directors or something similar will be operating the museum, under which a facilities management and security team will operate to secure and manage the building(s) on a daily basis. Maintenance functions are usually in house but can be subcontracted.

Other Facilities

Religious Worship Buildings: These are traditional church buildings but include community centers, other buildings converted to religious use, and special auditoriums constructed or renovated specifically for worship activities.

Use: Religious worship buildings and churches have offices, restrooms and change rooms, great rooms and kitchens for activities, and either a stage or presentation area with audience seats for religious services and rituals.

Function: These buildings remain nearly vacant during the week with the exception of the office staff and religious leaders.

Events are scheduled such as worship times during the week or on a Sunday morning for some religions, or during special holidays where masses of people attend services. Events beyond worship can also occur, such as meetings, fundraising events, educational and counseling sessions, and others. Typical of large facilities, churches/worship buildings have centralized HVAC, hydro, water and drainage, fuel supplies for heating, water and boilers, kitchens and eating facilities, and church supply storage.

Management: Management can be of a variety of styles from owners of an evangelical church, to a local rabbi for Jewish worship, to a local priest/minister on behalf of a larger formal religious organization such as the Catholic Church, Protestant Christian denominations, Sikh, Hindu, and Muslim, amongst other world-wide religious. The buildings are usually maintained by contracted maintenance.

Tourist Attractions/Historical Buildings

Use: These are cultural and historic institutions designed to educate the public and provide income for profit and for maintaining the sites and exhibits as cherished assets for the nation.

Function: As attractions to be visited, these facilities must contain human comforts such as HVAC, restrooms, retail and restaurants, water and drainage/sewer, hydro, gas supply, security systems and UPS, and parking. There are also specialized environmental controls and fire suppression systems.

Management: Management can emanate from various levels of government, depending on the type and nature of facility, or they can be entirely private enterprises for profit, reporting to boards of directors or owners/operators. Maintenance and security can be contracted, in house, or a mixture.

Municipal/State/Provincial/National Parks

Use: These are nature reserves for the protection of natural habitat for animals and vegetation, and for the controlled enjoyment of citizens.

Function: Parks contain expanses of natural wilderness and a wide variety of wildlife. They typically feature controlled access to certain areas, while other areas remain protected and access is prohibited to avoid human-caused damage to ecosystems and wildlife populations. There are warden and visitor facilities with human comforts such as HVAC, water and drainage/sewer, hydro, gas supply, restrooms, kitchens, restaurants, retail, and sometimes commercial campgrounds.

Management: Management can be a variety of government, private interests, and for-profit corporations. Maintenance and security can be in house, contracted, or combined.

CONCLUSION

Managing a small facility versus a larger one of complicated, multiple functions is a matter of experience and specialized training and development; however, the basic functions remain the same in supplying the facility with water, drainage and sewer, hydro, and fuel for the furnaces, boilers, and chillers. This is to ensure that proper maintenance and cleaning of the facility occurs to keep equipment running and the physical environment in a clean and mechanically optimal condition so that the human comforts are maintained at an acceptable and standardized level.

While keeping these commonalities in mind, this book is intended to guide facility owners and managers in successfully securing and maintaining their facilities to ensure a safe and secure environment for occupants and visitors. This approach will afford facility owners the confidence that they are doing everything they can to ensure that the basic safety and security for occupants is actively managed, thereby reducing the likelihood of crime, injury, or death, which should also significantly reduce the liability risk of any facility owner.

There is so much common sense that is applicable in facilities management that managers simply have to think of what is reasonable and what they would expect if they walked through the door. Cutting corners to save money and trim budget expenses is a trap that so many facility managers fall into, but it is never worth it in the end to compromise on safety and security, or on the human comforts that people expect. In the end it is more sensible to spend the money up front to avoid complaint, as well as the increased risk and liability that may, in the end, wind up costing far more through mishaps, injury, and death, and the resulting litigation, than would be saved by cutting corners on maintenance and service.

2

Safety and Security: Maslow's Hierarchy of Needs and How It Applies to Your Facility

FEELING SAFE AND SECURE

Abraham Maslow's Hierarchy of Needs is an excellent way to illustrate how facilities should be designed in regard to safety and security because they are the building blocks of a person's sense of self and ability to succeed with safety in the world. If buildings are not designed with these needs guiding the architect's direction, it is up to the facility manager to instill this sense of security and safety through policy, procedure, and a good security program.

People walk into different kinds of facilities every day. Some facilities make them feel welcomed and give them an instantaneous idea of where to go or what to do, while others make people feel trapped and/or insecure the moment that they enter, leaving them wanting to remove themselves from that location to restore that feeling of safety and security. It is this sense of safety and security that is the unspoken mission of every facility owner, operator, and maintenance manager. Once this aura of safety and security is achieved, the benefits will cascade over time with happy tenants and customers, less crime in the facility, and a lower risk of liability simply because the facility looks professional and is being run in a manner that will discourage mischief and crime, as well as having an environment capable of responding positively and effectively in an emergency situation. This philosophy ties in well with *Crime Prevention Through Environmental Design*, discussed later in the book.

MASLOW'S HIERARCHY OF NEEDS

The author first came across the theory from Maslow while studying for promotion to the first line of supervision in his police force [1]. It had been thoughtfully included in the study material by the force's Human Resources Bureau as a method of explaining how people feel about safety and security, and how they react in different stages of life based on their personal circumstances. It also explains how to appeal to this sense of safety and security that people feel as they progress through life. Readers can be immediately drawn to the solid logic of the theory and how it seems to explain the many and varied human experiences people encounter and how the basic sense of safety and security can affect behavior in dramatic ways (Figure 2.1).

To briefly explain the pyramid model, people are concerned with satisfying each need or level, starting at the bottom with *physiological* and progressing to the top as they move through their circumstances. Maslow suggested that it is not likely that an individual can progress to the next rung or level on the hierarchy without satisfying the one before and that with which the person is concerned. The two bottom rungs—*physiological* and *safety*—are basic needs concerning being adequately fed and sheltered (having a safe place to live where the simple act of sleeping does

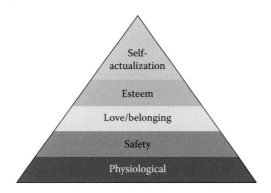

Figure 2.1 Maslow's Hierarchy of Needs pyramid.

not place one's life in danger due to the unstable social surroundings and constant exposure to people of ill intent). It is quite reasonable to see that people who are concerned daily with struggling to have enough food to eat and a safe place to sleep are not going to be concerned with love, self-esteem, and self-actualizing activities. However, once a person's food sources and accommodation have been secured on an ongoing basis, the person can and will shift his or her focus to higher level, self-actualizing activities such as finding a mate and starting a family, going to university, or starting a career.

Safety and security in the facilities context belong in the bottom two rungs of Maslow's model, being basic needs of keeping oneself alive and sheltered securely to be able to sleep without constant fear of compromise. The theory suggests that without satisfying natural impulses such as fear and hunger, humans cannot move on to any other aspirations such as relationship building, ego satisfaction, or reaching goals and dreams. When this theory is applied in the context of facility management, the success of any facility, regardless of the function, begins with establishing a sense of safety and security, where the occupant, tenant, or user does not feel threatened or unsafe enough to not pursue the reason he or she entered the facility. As users get their bearings and feel safe enough to enter, they will seek their destination and purpose. If they fail to attain that sense of security or well-being, most people would simply leave, if they even entered at all. This natural sense of foreboding and lack of safety and security can be felt in many facilities all over the world. Well designed and effectively managed facilities have managed to turn that sense of foreboding into a sense of comfort and security, which is a highly valued feeling in a building where one has to spend time either at work or living as a resident.

Facility managers have a responsibility to establish that sense of comfort and security while discouraging criminal intent and the trespass or presence of undesirable persons. There is a process involved in first finding out what is really going on in your facility as opposed to what you are guessing is going on or have been told by other people. From experience, the author has discovered that most facility owners, managers, or operators actually have little accurate knowledge of *what is really going on* in a multiuser building, which makes it extremely inefficient and ineffective to properly secure the site and suggest that it is safe for users. In the end, the lack of a safe and secure environment is a liability issue for the manager and owner of the facility—not to mention that the foreboding environment will naturally deter users and visitors anyway. As the manager, one needs to be able to actually show an investigator or a court that everything possible was done within reason to improve safety and security, which in turn will reduce the percentage of responsibility assigned to a facility manager or owner/operator.

REFERENCE

1. Maslow, A. 1943. "A Theory of Human Motivation." *Psychological Review* 50 (4): 370–396.

3

What Is Really Going On in the Building?

WHAT IS REALLY GOING ON INSIDE YOUR BUILDING? WHY SHOULD YOU CARE?

That is the main question: What is *really* going on in your facility? One cannot possibly know what is going on without asking the everyday users and occupants/tenants. Maintenance workers often know what is going on because of their ongoing duties throughout the entire facility at all hours of the day, but lack channels of communication and even motivation to send the message to the right listeners. Further, other occupants only see what is in front of them as they come and go and many problems remain hidden from most of the occupants; tenants may see more because they are present in and around their dwellings at all hours. On the other hand, owners/operators often have no idea what is going on inside the facility as the chain of command, although designed to feed information from maintenance worker or employee upward to the executive level, can also inadvertently filter out critical information. This will occur in organizations that do not expect or predict certain kinds of activities and it leaves the organization blind to what is really going on beyond the formal structure of management in a facility.

As the author was completing one facility security review after another, it became very clear, very quickly that most of the owners and managers really had no idea what was going on inside their buildings. This was also particular to buildings that had a lot of turnover, such as government buildings and office towers. Of course, most managers had their assumptions based on whatever limited safety and security measures they had installed and their own perceived but limited experiences; however, it became evident that one of the first things that the review team needed to do was talk to the maintenance workers and as many occupants of all levels as could be found, to find out what was really going on inside the building.

For example, in office buildings, the team began by interviewing the receptionists and mail clerks on each floor and in each different organizational entity. Team members began to piece together information that painted a very different picture of activity from what was described to the review team by the management group briefing before entering the facility. Examples of unknown problems included rampant cases of individual managers turning off or disabling the access control system for their own convenience and thereby leaving the facility wide open to the uncontrolled entry of unauthorized persons. In one particular facility of critical importance, there were persons of a supervisory level in a highly secured area, taping the door hardware open on a particular locked door out of convenience to access a bathroom outside their secured area. These supervisors could have still reached the bathroom by going through the front door but the aim of their breach of security was to reduce their walking distance to the bathroom by about fifty feet! This so-called minor breach actually compromised the security of the entire section, the workers therein, and the valuable assets on site consisting of proprietary information and critical organizational files. The employees, who should have known better, were deliberately bypassing the section's electronic access control, meaning that unknown persons from the main hallway could access critical, top-secret files without a card swipe and therefore no alert arriving at the reception desk and no electronic record of the egresses and accesses being recorded.

Stories such as the two aforementioned incidents began emerging out of these interviews as the review team were finding basement doors being propped open with blocks of wood and other objects when the building manager counted on those particular doors being secured at all times, again usually being compromised out of convenience. The two main purposes of these breaches were for smokers to sneak out to the back compound for a quick smoke, or for employees and managers to unload cargo and personal items out of cars, bypassing access controls. This not only opened the entire building up to potential theft or damage, but it also exposed any building occupants to the potential of violence or sexual crimes and theft occurring under the responsibility of the facility manager and owner. Other issues uncovered through facility occupant interviews were loss of key control, unpracticed or underdeveloped fire evacuation procedures, unwanted access of persons soliciting business, blocked fire doors and evacuation routes, improper parking practices, underage drinking, sex, drug use, and even drug deals occurring inside the buildings, as well as homeless squatters—not to mention inadequate maintenance practices and complaints about how the building was being operated. When laid out in this manner, it is easy to see how the compromised facilities lose the safety and security level that they thought was in place, taking on a foreboding feeling and actually becoming tragedies waiting to unfold in many cases. The occupants also see one or more of these disastrous scenarios happening right in front of them and they either have no awareness of what to do or lack good policies that would support their ability to recognize and report the incidents effectively. The occupants actually begin to lose their sense of safety and security without realizing the extent of decline in the building and surroundings. This decline can happen subtly over time and, once it takes hold, if it is not recognized and steps are not taken to fix it, it will snowball as more and more deterioration occurs requiring more and more money to fix it and stop the decline.

THE BROKEN WINDOWS THEORY

In *Crime Prevention Through Environmental Design*, the Broken Windows Theory suggests that this kind of pattern can actually spread when minor deficiencies are not repaired and a building is allowed to deteriorate in a number of ways. Neglected buildings occur when an owner does not take security seriously and fails to put money and resources into maintenance, or the situation has simply gone too far and the owner cannot afford to bring it back. Neglect includes situations such as not repainting a building in need, not painting over graffiti, ignoring broken windows, allowing flyers and newspapers to accumulate, not replacing burnt out light bulbs, and not maintaining landscaping (Figure 3.1). These signs of neglect can actually attract more crime and misbehavior as persons of ill intent will be attracted to a facility that appears to be neglected because the likelihood of their shady activity being detected is reduced (CPTED Ontario).

The point is that if an owner or manager gives the Maintenance Department the financial resources required to make basic building repairs and they keep the facility operating in an acceptable state of maintenance and repair, it will look as though the building is being looked after by

Figure 3.1 Papers collecting on a doorstep. As innocent as this collection of papers appears, it is a definite sign to a person of ill intent that people are not currently populating this building. Counting four weekly flyers would suggest the building has been unoccupied for at least a month. This is a sign of neglect under the Broken Windows Theory and makes this building a prime target of low risk for a criminal searching for opportunities to commit property crimes. (Photo by J. Henderson.)

responsible management who care about the state of the facility, and persons of ill intent will actually look elsewhere to perform their shady and illicit activities for fear that they will be disrupted or even caught as their comfort zone is altered. The Broken Windows Theory also suggests that the state of poorly maintained buildings can actually spread through a neighborhood, leading to a general deterioration of the area as the more desirable, law-abiding people move out and are replaced by persons that thrive in insecure and crime-ridden neighborhoods. This is precisely what is behind the revitalizing strategy being employed by many municipalities as they engage in downtown revitalization projects. The whole idea is similar to reversing the Broken Windows Theory in the effort to bring positive, law-abiding citizens back to the downtown core and chase away the criminals, drug dealers, and persons of ill intent by making the area unpleasant and uncomfortable for them, while raising their risk level of detection.

CLANDESTINE LABORATORIES

Clandestine laboratories are another aspect of *what is really going on in the building*. These criminal enterprises can pop up in apartment buildings, condominiums, private homes, and abandoned facilities. They are amateur chemical processing labs set up by criminals for the production and sale of illicit drugs. These inherently dangerous operations bring large amounts of dangerous chemicals and fuels and the ongoing potential for explosions involving property, assets, and, most importantly, innocent victims caught up in the effects of a chemical or fuel explosion caused by unskilled and unprofessional criminals cooking up drug recipes in anonymity. Other significant damage to the facility may include mold from high humidity caused by growing marijuana and chemical contamination of the building as these criminals do not use professional equipment and storage containers to maintain integrity of the chemicals.

Jason D. Reid of Life Safety Systems has compiled the following list of tip-offs that might indicate a clandestine criminal drug operation is functioning in a facility. The list is used with permission:

- Smell of chemicals or other unusual odors
- Unusually large amounts of waste being disposed of through regular garbage collection, or disposal of apparent waste through methods other than regular garbage collection
- Window coverings drawn closed at all times, or windows opened at times to vent unusual odors
- Occupants arriving and leaving at late hours of the night, apparently to avoid contact with other residents, or a high volume of traffic in and out at all hours of the day and night
- Unusual concerns for security exhibited by occupants; surveillance equipment possibly installed outside windows or doors
- Occupants paying rent in cash and possibly paying for a number of rental payment periods in advance
- Occupants unwilling to entertain inspections of the premises by building staff and possibly changing locks in order to prevent entry in emergent situations
- Upon inspection, staff noticing unusual equipment, including large plastic buckets; plastic or metal drums; containers with apparent chemicals; chemistry equipment such as glass vessels, burners, stands, hoses, batteries, acetone; large amounts of matches; and empty blister packs of cold medication (pseudoephedrine). In this case it is recommended to immediately evacuate the unit and call emergency responders

The activities on Mr. Reid's list are the kinds of things that will be seen by facility managers and employees, as well as the building occupants. It is extremely important for the facility management team to ensure a constant easy flow of information from building occupants, who often will be the eyes of the building when the employees are not there. When a building occupant reports something suspicious, it is important for the facility manager to take it seriously and investigate as much as possible without placing himself or herself in danger, and to call the police if necessary. The police will investigate based on suspicion for something as dangerous as a drug operation.

Marijuana production also requires a large ongoing supply of water to keep plants growing and huge amounts of hydropower (hydro) to keep hydroponic equipment functioning. Criminals may even resort to hydro theft by connecting to building electrical line feeds. Facility managers noticing any of these suspicious activities or signs of drug production should **immediately call the police and not investigate themselves** because criminals involved in drug production may be armed and dangerous, and they might violently attempt to protect their interests. The responding police will assess the situation with public safety as the primary consideration, and they will bring in necessary resources to deal with suspects and then the explosive or contamination risk before facilities management is allowed in to start cleaning up. If there is any perceived danger to people from possible explosion or chemical contamination, the facility will be evacuated and closed until either a determination has been made that no unsafe chemicals or activities were present, or the site has been thoroughly cleaned and is deemed safe by fire department hazardous material technicians for people to return. The all-clear will be determined by the fire chief in cooperation with the police before anyone can return to the building. The entire investigative process may involve the facility manager and employees who have intimate knowledge of the building(s) and can assist investigators immensely.

REFERENCE

CPTED Ontario on March 31, 2015, through CPTED Ontario website internal e-mail form (http://cptedontario.ca/contact/).

4

Access Control

LOSS OF KEY CONTROL

Key control is a basic requirement in every facility around the world. By effectively controlling keys, access to facilities is limited to those who are actually supposed to be there and have an interest in maintaining the safety and security of the facility. Losing key control is, unfortunately, a common and rampant phenomenon that is caused by management ignorance of the issues of key control. There is often misunderstanding of the level of accountability that may exist if a tragedy occurs in a facility directly relating to the loss of key control. This is a hidden issue that many facility managers postpone due to cost, but one that can result in an unauthorized person entering the facility and performing criminal or terrorist acts with a found, borrowed, or copied key.

Key control in a private household is easily maintained and will serve as basic strategy in explaining key control theory. For example, in a family with two spouses and two children, there will be a set number of keys (probably four). There should be one master key and the rest will be copies. The head of the household will determine who has legal access to the building and issue keys to trusted people and/or family members, usually with the strict instruction, "Do not lose this key." Those authorized and trusted with a key should keep that key to themselves and use it as intended. If they lose their key, they should immediately report the lost key to the person that issued the key. Now a determination of risk must occur about whether to accept that a key has been lost and simply replace it, or to rekey the building by replacing the locks and issuing new keys copied from a new master key to ensure that key control is maintained.

If the person that lost the key was anonymous in a large crowd of people and there are no identifying features on the key or key chain, perhaps the risk can be accepted. If a purse was lost containing the address and other identifiers, then the key controller should decide to rekey the house and issue new keys in a different configuration to those authorized, because whoever has the key also has the address and, if so inclined, will be able to enter the building at will without detection. In this scenario, key control has been lost and the house is now wide open to whoever might have the key and the address together.

NEW HOME? WHAT ABOUT THE KEYS...?

When a house purchase occurs and the door keys are turned over to the purchaser on closing day, the recipient should immediately purchase a new lock set and rekey the home. The reason is that there is no way to know who had copies of the keys previously and who might have access to the house without the new owner's knowledge. Although the real estate agent may hand over an envelope of keys and say, "Here are all the keys," this is not a chance that any family should ever take and it is relatively inexpensive to buy a new lock set and keys for the exterior doors of the house.

KEY CONTROL AND LARGER FACILITIES

In larger facilities and commercial buildings, key control is much more difficult and complicated, but accountability is just critical as, or even more critical than, in a private home toward maintaining safety and security. It starts with a master key that opens everything, followed by the subkeys that are copied from the master. This master key is critical and if it is lost or copied, the entire system will be compromised as unknown people will have access to any door in the facility. This risk extends to people inside the organization that could access highly secured areas to which they are not authorized, or it could allow outsiders to access nonpublic areas where sensitive information and assets could be located.

Large facilities should therefore have a planned and organized approach to key control using an electronic key control cabinet that is programmed and maintained by the master key holder. Each key is locked in the cabinet and signed out by an individual for a specified time period. If the key is not returned and reinserted into its spot in the cabinet, an alarm sounds, prompting the master key holder or accountable manager to investigate. These keys should be marked to indicate that they are not to be copied, and only the master key holder should be able to make a copy, make a subkey, or authorize either to be done.

A state-of-the art alternative to a master key system is to go completely electronic with a computerized access control system operated by swipe card and a system of turnstile portals that allow one person at a time to enter. These systems can get quite expensive, given the technology and hardware involved. Some newer systems feature iris and/or fingerprint recognition technology but they remain exorbitantly expensive and out of reach for most businesses and governments for a wide scale of use. Most facilities use a traditional master key system or a combination of master key and computerized access control. In these systems, master key control and secure database integrity are essential for maintaining security and control over who enters the space in question.

Any manager of a large facility should have an experienced and certified security consultant or locksmith brought in to assess the locking strategy of the facility and to find the existing holes or problems for immediate reparation. Overall, such a consultant can help the facility owner/operator with improving key control or even with planning a system replacement. Ignoring key control is a huge mistake for a facility manager to make and a potentially costly error in the long run.

Apartment Buildings

Apartment buildings have a constant turnover of tenants and key control is therefore very difficult to maintain in such buildings. As individual apartment units have a separate key that is part of the master key system, a building superintendent can maintain key integrity without replacing the whole system by rotating the apartment unit locks as people move in and out. This cancels the advantage of people holding keys for certain apartments if the lock has been exchanged with that of another apartment somewhere else in the building. It is certainly reasonable to expect that tenants will give keys out to whomever they wish to allow into their apartment, and the landlord or building superintendent will just never know who has copies of the keys for each apartment as tenants come and go. It is prudent to eliminate this problem by rekeying each apartment, which will remove the onus on the facility manager as being responsible for a break-in or home invasion because unknown people had keys.

Electronic Access Control

Electronic access control is perhaps one of the greatest advances in facility management and security to come along in the modern age. Not only does a centrally managed access control system have the ability to let only authorized people into certain locations at certain times, but it also adds accountability by recording who entered at what time. Marry this data with closed circuit television imagery, and investigations become much easier when proprietary items or information is stolen, or vandalism and other crimes have occurred. It must be remembered, however, that access control data collected for the purpose of access control should not used as a method of attendance keeping or for other purposes by management. Such other uses can be construed as privacy violations since the information was not collected for attendance management. Management, however, can potentially release the access control data in the case of a formal investigation by police where a serious crime has occurred.

Where electronic access control is not practicable or even possible for outbuildings or deployed locations, a good alternative is to use mechanical combination locks. These units feature a key pad connected to the door knob, that opens only with the correct five-number combination that should only be given to a small number of employees (Figure 4.1).

Definition: Security Breach

Before describing electronic access control in detail, it is important to define *security breach* as a term that defines nonadherence to the published and practiced access policies of a facility and any activity in the facility that goes against the interests of the corporation or entity in control of the facility. Security breaches may also include criminal activity and trespass or unauthorized access of persons without accountability or the proper access privilege to certain areas within the facility. Security breaches should always be identified and rectified by whatever action is deemed necessary by the entity controlling the facility. Sometimes security breaches can be dealt with from within by the facility or applicable manager with sanctions, including immediate ejection from the premises; at other times, for more serious security breaches, the local police should be called. Insurance claims by the organization may require an incident number from a police report before insurance will cover any loss or damage resulting from a security breach. Failure to deal with security breaches can cause serious long-term damage and loss of information security and proprietary information and assets. Security gaps only get wider over time

Figure 4.1 Mechanical combination lock. This combination lock requires a five-number code to be entered before it will open. It is great for outbuildings and other facilities not part of the main access control system. (Photo by J. Henderson.)

and people will inevitably exploit them as the biggest risk always comes from within. Any security breach data or information should be captured in a formal reporting process and stored for future reference, which could include analysis of building activity for security review purposes and upgrades. This relates directly back to the notion of understanding what is really going on in your facility. The timely collection and proper storage of accurate information is powerful and allows for the proper analysis of a situation and planning of security measures based on real threats as opposed to perceived threats.

Electronic Access Control Systems

Electronic access control is simply a modern version of the old key systems, combined with guard service. The advent of electronic controlling access very much more efficient, effective, and accountable, as well as convenient, because doors can be locked, unlocked, and opened remotely. Electronic access control has its drawbacks, which will be discussed a bit later on, but overall it has made security planning much more effective and facilities much easier to control.

Electronic access control in a facility usually consists of a series of access and egress points in a facility connected electronically to a central database of access cards assigned to holders, which is often combined with closed circuit television and intrusion alarms. The database is the nerve center containing all of the names of the cardholders, who should each have been screened for employment, as well as background checked for reliability and determining criminal records and intelligence flagging. Each person's profile is set up to specific access privileges based on what areas the person needs to access and what his or her clearance level is for accessing low-, medium- or high-security areas. Each door or turnstile has an electronic lock controlled by the main computer and operated by a card reader beside the door that is communicating with the main computer, drawing from the database. The person requesting entry must be authorized with that particular access level programmed into his or her profile for the card to be read and unlock the door. When the person swipes the access card on the reader, the computer will recognize that the person is authorized to go through that door and it will signal to the magnetic lock on the door to open. The time and identity of the person are recorded on the database and the door should lock behind him or her automatically after entry. The computer will also record unsuccessful access requests where the access level required for entry did not match the authorized access levels assigned to the cardholder. Figure 4.2 shows an example of an access card.

The card has a microchip inside it and copper wiring that follows the outside contours of the card. This is what the card reader magnetically reads when the card is swiped on the reader. If a card is damaged, it will only stop working if the wire inside has been broken or severed. Each access card has a number assigned to it, which connects the card to the profile in the database. The profile is programmed with access privileges

Figure 4.2 Typical plastic access card with microchip inside. This is an access card that contains a programmed microchip and wires lining the edges of the card. The chip contains the access profile information of the cardholder that is read by the card reader to activate the door latch. (Photo by J. Henderson.)

by manager authorization. The manager of a particular area in the build-ing will give permission for the individual to access the area, usually by need and security clearance. The programmer then can program that access code to the card so that the area door will open when that card is swiped and the database recognizes the programming. The main issue is that whoever holds the card can access that area, so it is critical to get employees to hold onto their access cards, not to lend the cards to other people, and to report lost or missing cards to the Access Control Manager as soon as possible (Figure 4.3).

Access cards can be programmed with multiple access levels for the same facility from one simple access privilege for common doors and areas all the way up to and including all-access cards that can open every door in the facility. One card may also contain access levels for other buildings in other locations as long as they still function from the same database.

One strategy to improve the integrity of the access card swipes is to use closed circuit television. Closed circuit television (CCTV) can be placed and aimed at the door area to record the image of the person requesting access by swiping the access card. The central system can be programmed to pull up the photograph of the cardholder, which can be compared to the person swiping the card. If the photograph does not match the person swiping the card, it is most often considered a security breach in secure facilities. Both the cardholder and the person swiping the card can be held accountable for violating access regulations if the cardholder allowed the other person to use that card. It is further cause of great concern if the cardholder did not know the person swiping the card, in which case this may be a theft of an access card for illicit purposes.

Another main weakness of this type of access control is that one person can swipe his or her card at a door and multiple persons can enter, with the database recording only one entry when actually a number of

Figure 4.3 Card reader and steel strike guard. The photo shows an access card reader beside a secured door and plate that prevents someone from getting at the door strike. The cardholder simply has to hold the access card by the reader so that the card chip is read by the system. When the data in the chip match the system information, the door latch will open, allowing access. (Photo by J. Henderson.)

unknown people entered the space behind the cardholder. Yet another weakness, already alluded to in the previous example, is that if a cardholder lends his or her card to another person, the card will enable entry to that person but record the cardholder's name instead of the person that entered. Policy should prohibit the lending of access cards as a security breach and require cardholders that have lost their access cards to report the lost card immediately to security or building management.

The best way to ensure proper access control is to install pod-style turnstiles that only allow one cardholder at a time to pass through. This is the only way, other than having the post staffed by a security officer, to ensure that one person enters at a time. Having turnstiles going in and out would provide a true record of who has entered the building and who has exited and when, but without exiting turnstiles activated by card swipe, it is not possible to track people leaving. This kind of information is useful in a high-security location as it provides accuracy and continuity of data about facility access; however, it is quite expensive to install such a system and may double the number of doors or pods required because it necessitates both in and out turnstiles. To stop multiple entries on one card swipe, policy could also require a card swipe for each person through each door but this is unreliable and impossible to enforce. It is comical to think of policy requiring one person to swipe, enter though the door, and then close it again for the next person to repeat the process. It is simply not going to happen and as the door is opened the first time, all the people standing there will go through it.

Electronic access depends highly on the accuracy of the database content from which the system functions. As each cardholder is set up as a profile for identification purposes, the profile should also contain a recent photograph for accuracy. As the management-approved access levels are assigned to the profile based on need and security clearance level of the person in question, a photograph is the only way to quickly ascertain that the card and holder match. When the photograph pops up beside the profile on the security control room computer, it gives the security officer the ability to remotely ensure that card and person match, without the officer having to leave the camera monitors. This CCTV evidence is also useful in an after-the-fact investigation in asserting who swiped the access card on a particular reader.

Magnetic Locks

Magnetic locks are found in most large facilities controlling the main access and egress doors from a central fire evacuation system and/or a security system. These are blocks of magnets at the top of the door that connect to another block of magnets on the door frame. A signal from the central computer simply tells the magnets to either lock or release and the magnets are strong enough that people cannot pull them apart. The system gives the central controller the ability to lock or unlock specific doors or the entire building at the same time. The system can also be programmed to lock and release on schedule through an access control system or as a result of fire and intrusion alarms. As an example, a scheduled lock opening could be a secured office floor that is locked off the elevator lobby during the night or nonbusiness hours but opens to common traffic during the day between 0800 hours and 1600 hours, after which it locks again on schedule. This might be done in concert with the scheduled appearance of section receptionists who will take over screening responsibilities during the day, allowing easier and personalized access flow to people using the common walkways and halls, but requiring security screening to access higher security areas (Figure 4.4).

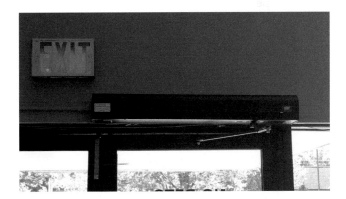

Figure 4.4 Magnetic lock and opener system on an exterior door. Above is a combination automatic door opener and magnetic lock system connected to a handicapped button at a medical facility. As a bonus is the exit sign in plain view. These door combinations work well and will open automatically; however, the drawback that a facility manager must keep an eye on is the fact that people will push the handicapped button when the building is closed, which will activate the mechanics of the door opener, but since the door remains physically locked, it does not open fully and reset to shut off. It could remain powered up all night if no one is checking. That can cost considerable money in extra hydro and result in premature hardware burnout. (Photo by J. Henderson.)

In an apartment block, magnetic locks could be used for fire evacuation but also on the front door. Access requesters buzz an apartment to request access, which could then be given by the person receiving the access request, with the intent being that the receiver knows the requester as a method of maintaining general security in the building by giving access only to people that know someone inside. Most apartment buildings employ electronic strike locks on their doors, but the effect is similar.

Push Bars

Another aspect of electronic access control may be out of the database loop and not controllable, yet highly relevant. Many egress doors are installed in large facilities for fire and/or emergency evacuation and open only to exit the building, while remaining locked from the outside. These doors, once opened from the inside and allowed to latch shut, will automatically lock and remain locked unless someone from the inside opens the door. There is no mechanism on the outside of the door to unlock or open the door, which is by design in order to prevent outside people from entering the facility unscreened.

Most of these types of doors are opened from the inside by a push bar, where the simple act of pushing will release the mechanism and allow the door to swing open. This style of door is ideal in the application of an organized emergency evacuation program whereby the group can evacuate with an exit supervisor holding the door open until all of the group have left the building; the supervisor can count people as the leave. The exit supervisor then can close the door without fear that someone will reenter the building without authorization.

The weakness of this type of door comes from the fact that anyone can open it from the inside without accountability, and what develops are habits of people opening the doors and using whatever material is handy to pin or prop the door open, as discussed elsewhere in the book. Depending on what is used, the item may actually permanently damage the door hardware, as a typical metal door can bend over time, leaving gaps in the seal or the door or preventing the door from closing properly, prompting a service call or possibly even a costly replacement. Further, many of these people do not remove the item used to pin or block the door open, leaving a security breach and a source of power loss as hot air escapes in the winter and, conversely, cool air escapes in the summer. This causes the heating, ventilation, and air conditioning (HVAC) system to continually work hard to cool or heat the escaping air and wastes enormous amounts of energy, costing considerable money needlessly.

One way to alleviate this risk is to install local alarms in the doors, if it is not possible or practical to wire the door to the electronic access control system. Local alarms will ring if the door is opened and will keep ringing until the alarm is reset by someone with a key—either a facility technician or a security officer, who should respond if he or she hears it or if called by a worker that has to listen to the annoying alarm signal. The ringing will draw unwanted attention to the person opening the door for any reason other than emergency evacuation and will assist with stopping the problem of people propping the doors open to access their cars for easy unloading or stopping smokers from using the doors to slip outside for a smoke.

Push-bar doors must be tested as an ongoing part of the entire life safety system because it is essential that they open during an emergency to let people escape. A failure of one of these doors to open essentially turns the egress point into a wall, forcing evacuees to find another way out in the midst of the chaos of an emergency. Facility managers will assume responsibility for ensuring these doors function properly and, where there are security officers assigned in a facility, it is good practice to have the doors checked for security and the push bars tested several times a day as part of the regular patrols of the security officers. The officers should be documenting the checks and taking action if a problem is noted, as these doors are the outer skin of the building.

ACCESS CONTROL POLICY

Card access databases are critical pieces of the system and must be maintained on a daily basis, supported by strict policy. New assignments, resignations/firings, and any relocation in a facility should be reported to the access control manager immediately so that the proper access level(s) can be programmed to the person's profile. Old and unneeded access levels should be removed from the profile to ensure data integrity and security of locations. Failure to maintain an accurate database eventually results in chaos with all sorts of people being able to access secure locations that they do not require for any purpose. This destroys any notion of continuity and being able to investigate any security breaches.

Another problem that often develops is the political and peer pressure on the security and facilities managers to add access levels to certain profiles for convenience or other reasons without the knowledge and clearance of the authorizing managers in those areas. Some managers will also wave people through without following the procedures, based on *it's ok, he's a good guy….* Security and facility managers must resist the temptation to ruin the integrity of their own databases. There are always individuals that will take advantage of the manager, who could be held accountable once an investigation determines that the security or facility manager, who should have known better, facilitated a serious breach of security and caused financial and asset loss and/or a data breach. It is not up to the database programmer or manager accountable for access control as to who gets what access level. Authority comes from the manager in charge of each area in the building.

Periodic reviews of cardholders and access levels should be completed to ensure that ghost cards are not in circulation still and potentially in the hands of someone that has already left employment. It is also important to ensure that employees who merely transferred from one location or function to another have only the access levels needed by their positions. Reviews will catch errors and the failure of a manager to report a transfer, retirement, or firing of a cardholder.

All-access cards are access cards programmed to open all doors in the facility. These should be issued only as needed to people that hold account-ability for the entire facility. Most often, the people getting all-access cards are the facility and security managers and maintenance workers with sufficient security clearance. Security officers should be issued the all-access card only when they are on duty and it should be retrieved at the end of the shift. This card for security officers is generally attached to the master keys they require to perform their tours of duty. It is critical to restrict access levels to people that need them to avoid destroying continuity in high-security facilities. Only the authorized people should be entering these areas. Anyone else must be able to provide a legal reason for entering to be considered reasonable. For example, it could be deemed reasonable for the security officer to enter at 0100 hours to check the refrigerators in the evidence room of a police facility. It would not be reasonable for the superintendent from Human Resources to enter the evidence room at 0100 hours and this could spoil a court case as continuity of evidence is called into question.

The integrity of the database is critical in electronic access control, as is the discipline of issuing access levels to profiles and only allowing authorized people access to the locations for which they have authorization. Otherwise, they must be escorted by someone with the authorization.

Visitors

Visitors to facilities should be treated with a consistency contained in the policy. As parts of a facility become more secure, visitor access must be contained and accountable by placing visitors under escort by a person accountable to the organization that is occupying or has control of the space. Accountable visitor access control requires identification of the visitor by photo identification, the signing of an access log by the visitor with the time in and time out recorded as they occur, the wearing of a visible visitor identification tag programmed only to a general access level to public areas, and finally, but not least, escort by an accountable person. Any time that a visitor is in a secure space, he or she should be escorted, even to the bathroom. The failure to escort visitors consistently can open an organization up to security breaches and possibly even a future attack as most visitors simply do not have any accountability to the organization and may choose to operate against it if an opportunity presents itself.

Visitor access can be assigned and tracked through visitor access cards with a generic access level to main doors only. Secure areas should always have visitors escorted by building sponsors from within the organization with accountability to the organization. Requiring visitors to wear a visitor access tag is very important as it allows employees and people with access privileges to know when a nonaccountable person is among them. Policy should direct employees and all persons with access privileges to report visitors who

- Do not have an escort in a secure area
- Do not have a visible visitor access tag
- Are in an area to which they should not have access
- Are behaving in a suspicious manner

Policy should direct the security breach reports to security if there is a security unit, or to the facility or access control manager as decided in advance and published in the policy. Security and/or the applicable manager can decide how to handle the breach up to and including ejection from the premises or calling the police if necessary. If there is no security unit or designated person, the section manager must assume this role or delegate it to someone in the section. There are many organizations where this does not occur, and it is a problem waiting to happen when a security breach takes everyone by surprise and chaos ensues because these procedures and assignments were not worked out in advance.

Employee buy-in to the access control policies is critical in maintaining access control integrity and in ensuring that the facility remains safe and secure. Without buy-in, gaps begin to appear as employees allow unauthorized persons to access secure areas and do unauthorized activities against the interest of the corporation or entity. In facilities, human nature always seems to push the boundaries of what is acceptable behavior in regard to security and visitor access. Policy and procedure must contain this natural penchant for human mischief and convenience seeking, and the managers must take it seriously and be consistent in its application for it to work effectively. The policies and procedures are only as good as those using and enforcing them.

Open-Access Schools

Schools are a particularly vulnerable class of facility as they have been by nature traditionally open to the public and recognized universally as a trusted and safe environment for our children. Schools therefore present a very complicated problem with the ever-increasing active shooter events taking place at public schools. Although many jurisdictions have experienced or at least observed armed attacks on the target-rich environment of a school by a shooter, many of these jurisdictions across North America and Europe fail to take action in making schools more secure, and access remains open to anyone that wishes to walk into a school. The issue impeding progress on more secure schools is that some school and community leaders/politicians do not want to be associated with an image that they are supporting or operating an *armed camp* instead of a school. It is in this kind of environment that our leaders willfully neglect to install access controls, or fail to maintain, upgrade, or replace a secured master key system. There are jurisdictions where substitute or replacement teachers arrive at the school to fill in for an absent teacher but are never given a key to lock their assigned classroom if the school goes into a lockdown. This is in complete contradiction to the rules that all teachers are supposed to follow in a lockdown procedure. The usual reason given by school management is that the supply or replacement teachers might lose the key. This scenario leaves these schools at risk of being unable to complete a lockdown because the teachers replacing ill or otherwise absent teachers cannot possibly fulfill their mandated responsibilities of locking classroom doors. If an active shooter arrives at such a school, it is unknown what these teachers are supposed to do: They will move the children as directed by the plan to a location, but be unable to lock the door.

This simple problem could be the difference between an attacker entering a target-rich classroom or moving on down the hall because the door was locked. After a tragedy occurs because these teachers did not have access to the keys to lock down the classroom, someone is likely going to be held accountable and, logically, it will be the person of responsibility that failed to make the key available to the substitute or replacement teacher. It seems, given that this reality still exists in places, that many people still suffer from the "it won't happen here" mentality. This is a very dangerous attitude, given that governments all over North America have been systematically closing mental health facilities due to budgetary cuts and putting the residents, who used to be classified as needing to be in secure facilities, back into communities. This situation makes every community a risk for a school attack if the leaders do not take a more serious look at changing access privileges to allow entry only to screened individuals.

It is known that most parents do not like the idea of not being able to attend a school and access their children whenever they need or want, which is the issue to which politicians and school administrators will react in banning access controls. However, contrary to the arguments of many that oppose such access controls, *screened access does not block access* into the school for parents or the general public. It merely means that each access request to a school in session will be subject to access screening where the requester will be identified by photo identification and asked what the purpose of the visit will be. This simple screening procedure will deter many attackers, who will seek a softer target, and it will enable the school authorities to view and assess anyone trying to access the facility. Such an access control procedure will also serve to reduce the risk of child abduction by forcing undesirable people or those that have lost custody rights to declare themselves before they enter the school. It allows school officials a moment to decide if they wish to grant access to someone and it will also provide a moment to check a list of banned persons or to ask a colleague what to do in a particular situation rather than just allowing people direct entry into the school without screening.

In the meantime, until access control is taken more seriously and implemented into more schools, it is not unreasonable to implement a procedure that will add accountability where replacement or substitute teachers must sign a key out with a responsibility to return it at the end of the day. It is simply unacceptable to assume that a professional teacher cannot be trusted with a key to allow him or her to fulfill a mandated responsibility that could potentially save the lives of the group of children entrusted to his or her care for the day. This is a topic of discussion that a facility manager should consider having with school administration if the school is one that ignores access control during school hours. Before having the conversation, though, it is advisable for the facility manager to fully research the topic and potential application at the school before approaching school officials.

Proprietary Information and Security

Many workplaces contain sensitive information that is either proprietary or considered secret and highly accountable for the success of the business or government or simply contains the private information of customers and employees. Most jurisdictions have privacy legislation protecting this information, which in turn requires the business owner or government manager to secure and protect this information. For facility managers, this means ensuring the safe storage and handling of sensitive information by ensuring that it is kept locked in a proper container such as a locking filing cabinet in a secured room to which only a small number of precleared people have access. There must be policies and procedures implemented surrounding the storage and use of the information, as well as to ensure that the information is not left out in a vulnerable situation or copies made of certain information leave the secure site. Electronic information must also be considered for policy protection, as it must be made clear to employees that they are being trusted with the information and that it is not proper to remove thumb drives or DVDs containing sensitive or proprietary information from the workplace.

Facility managers using computers can easily protect information stored on computers by using p-drive folders with limited access privileges. Only certain people by selection or need would be able to open these electronic files, which, because they are on the p-drive, will be available anytime they are needed by those with the access privilege. It remains important, however, that people with access privileges do not leave their computers open when they are not present. This enables anyone to go in and use that person's profile to access whatever is there. It is necessary to remember to lock up the computer before leaving for any period of time or simply program it so that it automatically shuts off after several minutes of inactivity. Computer users at work are responsible for what is done under their profiles on the computer and people must be more cognizant of their responsibility to protect proprietary and personal information.

Disposal of sensitive and/or proprietary information should be done with care and accountability as well. Documents should be shredded

45

before disposal either by employees or by a bonded shredding company that will collect and process secured document containers from the workplace by contract. Committing breach of trust by either negligence or by doing something on purpose is not something with which a facility manager wants to be involved. Not only does it create vulnerabilities for individuals but it can also affect future employment of the person committing the breach of trust—not to mention possible prosecution depending on the severity of the breach or what legislation covered the breach of trust.

The security of information remains a critical aspect in any corporation as privacy laws continue to be strengthened in developed countries. When proprietary information is present in an office setting, managers must be aware of the possibility of electronic theft of information. As most people carry highly capable cellular telephones that can snap quality photographs and record conversations without detection, personal and proprietary information collected or developed by corporations and government must be used in an environment designed to secure that information. Information should never be left on tables or desks, but rather filed in secure locking cabinets or in staffed file rooms that remain under lock and key, where documents and files must be signed out and returned at a particular time. Organizations should have policies concerning the use of cell phones in the work area to avoid the photographing and theft of proprietary information that could damage the corporation or private information that could constitute a breach of privacy. Managers must also be aware of thumb drives and the possibility that someone with access to a computer could also download proprietary or private information from a company computer to a thumb drive and remove it from the workplace. Provisions for firing and possibly prosecuting individuals must be included in hiring contracts so that employees know up front that copying and/or removing information from the workplace could cost them their jobs; local policies should require secure storage of information at all times and ban or at least limit the use of cell phones and thumb drives. Policies communicated up front to new employees should include a notice that work computers and the information contained therein belong to the company or government entity and that computers may be audited for unauthorized use. It should be made clear that unauthorized use of a computer may trigger accountabilities up to and including dismissal and/or breach of trust charges. Facing lawsuits for lost proprietary and personal information can be a very expensive and embarrassing situation for a manager or corporation and a little accountability communicated up front can go a long way toward protecting proprietary information.

5

Performing Safety and Security Audits

WHY SHOULD MONEY BE SPENT ON AN AUDIT?

Performing safety and security audits is an important step in facility management that often is overlooked, ignored, or continually delayed because it is viewed as an inconvenient exercise and an extra financial burden. The audit, however, is a critical component of an owner's or operator's activity because it protects against liability as well as providing a safer and more secure property. Those that ignore it or cut corners to save money are asking for trouble as everything is always fine until something goes wrong. The second that something goes wrong, everything the owner/operator did to manage or make the property safer may come under the microscope and he or she may be appearing as a witness in a coroner's inquest to explain his or her actions or nonaction in regard to upgrading safety and security. In an inquest hearing, an owner/operator appearing as a witness had better be able to honestly say words to the effect: "I had a safety and security audit performed and had begun a multiyear implementation as budget restrictions allowed, but in the meantime had this policy and that procedure to compensate for the shortfall." That shows the courts that you took safety and security seriously and took *reasonable* steps to achieve a safer space. On the other hand, owners/operators that cannot offer any explanation to a court for the poor condition of a building or property, and for whom saving money appeared to be the main focus instead of providing a safe and secure location, can be held liable as well as possibly even face criminal prosecution for making decisions in their own financial interest rather than making an effort to improve safety and security. Making that effort and commitment to providing a safe and secure property will in the long run make good business sense and offer financial stability as insurance costs may be lower and the risk of being held liable for not providing a safe and secure location drops dramatically. Having a safe and secure location will also attract a more professional class of clientele and occupant, which in turn will make persons of ill intent feel threatened and under constant risk of being caught. They will find another place to practice their misdeeds and crime as the Broken Windows Theory suggested earlier.

CRIME PREVENTION THROUGH ENVIRONMENTAL DESIGN

Before we examine the safety and security audit, a lower level strategy is going to be explained for its value as a stand-alone program or as an information-gathering tool for a bigger security audit that actually has proven solutions that make properties safer. *Crime Prevention Through Environmental Design*, or CPTED, is an excellent program developed initially as a tool for police officers to introduce to businesses that have been victimized by crime or as a proactive crime prevention tool. As previously mentioned, CPTED is based on the Broken Windows Theory, where a police service has an interest in assisting a business district, a specific business, or a residence by introducing a series of recommendations to upgrade safety and security by adapting the environment into natural security measures in a cost-effective manner. Properly executed, CPTED can draw the expected clientele into a business location, discourage undesirable persons, and reduce corporate liability simultaneously without visitors realizing that they have entered an organized, secured space. Effectively executed CPTED spaces will discourage undesirable people and welcome desirable people, directing them subtly toward a celebrated entrance and wherever else they are supposed to go, often without their knowing that they are being psychologically led by well designed landscaping and effectively planned and installed flooring and lighting into a safe and secure location.

CPTED auditors approach a property with a critical eye, looking for a *celebrated entrance, natural surveillance, lighting,* and problems such as a lack of maintenance, shadows, and places for concealment.

A celebrated entrance is simply the most obvious entry point into the facility and is usually an oversized door with extra lighting or signage and the spot where the sidewalk leads, perhaps with bushes on either side. It is a natural way of directing people to the correct door psychologically so that they automatically know where to go and be welcomed. The use of a celebrated entrance can actually separate law-abiding citizens from those with criminal intent, as the criminal element will avoid the celebrated entrance, lest he or she be easily recognized for his or her intent.

Natural surveillance is simply explained as the ability of people to see outside or inside a building by design. Good natural surveillance will consist of well-lit, unblocked sight lines from inside the building leading out, or from the outside leading in. Criminals like to work in shadow and obscurity where they can isolate their victims and prevent detection and/or interference from another person. An example of good natural surveillance would be a late-night variety store whose sole employee is actually protected by excellent lighting, large unobscured windows with shelving placed perpendicular to the large windows so that people outside the store can easily see the employee at the counter, and see almost every section of the store and up and down the aisles without any difficulty. A person of ill intent who is looking for a target of opportunity will likely move on somewhere else as the natural surveillance makes it too risky that he or she will be detected or spotted from outside the store and get caught. This fish-bowl effect provides a measure of protection by removing the opportunity afforded by obscurity and isolation.

LIGHTING

The International Facility Management Association (IFMA) supports the notion that an organization can actually save substantial money with the installation of modern, attractive-looking, and energy-efficient lighting that will also improve the interior environment of the building and perhaps even improve productivity among the employees. Facility managers should consult professional bodies such as IFMA for such guidance as a method of not only improving the aesthetic look and feel or the facility but also lowering operating costs in a meaningful way (http://www.ifma .org/know-base/how-to-guides#sthash.o8J05Fh3.dpuf).

In the world of CPTED, lighting has six basic functions:

1. Safety
2. Identification
3. Environmental integration

4. Beautification
5. Attraction
6. Recreation

These six functions are the reasons that well planned lighting is essential when a facility is upgraded for safety. Upgrades should be focused on improving safety by increasing the power and coverage of lighting; it should be strategized to assist occupants with identifying people attempting to enter or those already inside; it can be used to integrate the environment by guiding people to where they should be going, such as an elevator lobby or bathroom or even a main hallway. Lighting can also be used to display art and plants and in other ways to make the space more attractive; lighting can also attract people as a form of advertisement or simply guide people to where the host wants them to go. Lighting is also used extensively for recreational purposes to extend business hours into the darkness of night by providing as much light as there is at noon on a sunny day. The improved human manipulation of artificial light over the past 200 years has certainly extended the ability to function productively well past sunset and all night as necessary.

Different types of lighting can be chosen for different applications in any environment. General lighting, such as street lights, is most often low-pressure sodium (LPS) that exudes that common orange-tinged appearance. The reason that municipalities use this type of lighting in a general application is that it costs the least of all types of lighting and provides less impact on a municipal budget, which is quite important when the streets of a town or city can be lit up for upwards of eight or nine hours per day. The disadvantage of LPS lighting is that color rendition is very poor and people cannot see the difference between greens, reds, and grays, as everything takes on a gray shade of varying degrees. Witnesses cannot make good descriptions in LPS light, which is why LPS is a poor choice for a variety store or gas station that remains open all night. In contrast, fluorescent lighting provides excellent color rendition and detail, making it ideal for retail applications, but it uses more power and tends to cost more over time. LED lighting can be used as well in commercial applications as it uses less power than traditional incandescent bulbs, lasts longer, and has a convenient smaller size. People can see real color and better detail with fluorescent and LED lighting, making them ideal for the variety store and gas station applications. Employees are able to see well at night and make excellent, real color descriptions when a person of ill intent commits a crime.

Emergency Lighting

One often ignored aspect of lighting in facilities is emergency lighting. These tend to be those boxes with an odd looking round light sticking out of the top. The box is actually the battery and the light should be aimed at a doorway, hallway, or stairwell to provide guiding light in a power failure (Figure 5.1). Due to this function, emergency lights are not used often and can be neglected in facilities that do not have a formalized inspection process that causes regular inspections to occur.

Emergency lights are installed by building and fire code requirements in critical areas and are designed to ease evacuation of the building when the main power and lighting have failed. Emergency lights are designed to come on immediately when the main power disconnects and will light up hallways, stairwells, and doorways to ease the movement of people during an emergency. Neglect of emergency lighting can occur particularly in buildings where the maintenance budget is too small to maintain the facility and, unfortunately, some owners and managers may stop or delay regular maintenance of some items to save money. Contracted maintenance companies have been known to cut corners when budgets are stretched and one of the areas that may suffer is the lighting budget, where light replacement is delayed and the money goes elsewhere. This

Figure 5.1 Emergency battery-operated light system. The photo shows a typical battery-operated emergency light unit in a basement office. It is plugged into a power socket to maintain charge. When the lights go out, this unit automatically comes on and lights up a hallway and doorway as the lights are pointed there for a reason. Where there is UPS, these units come on instantly, bridging the gap until the UPS generator kicks in and begins supplying power. (Photo by J. Henderson.)

is not acceptable as the emergency lighting forms part of the life/safety system of the building and high accountability can be laid at the feet of someone in a position of responsibility who is found guilty of failing to ensure that emergency lighting worked properly before an evacuation event occurred, resulting in injury or death.

Even when uninterrupted power supply (UPS) has been installed in the facility, it is still critical for emergency lights to be in functioning condition for several reasons. Although UPS is intended to keep the power in the facility flowing through a hydropower disruption or other power-disrupting event, there is still a power bump and a pause before UPS kicks in and the generator starts to function. If this bump happens when people are in a stairwell or some other area of passage, injury can result in the middle of an evacuation event. A second reason is that emergency power still represents a backup to UPS if it fails because of a generator running out of fuel or UPS batteries failing.

Emergency lighting is not something to ignore or fail to maintain as it is a critical part of the life safety system in the building. If the emergency lights fail or simply do not illuminate as expected during a real fire event, people may get injured or even die when they are suddenly trying escape a burning building in the dark as panic is setting in. A postevent inquest will determine that emergency lighting failed to work and it will seek to determine the cause. An investigation will reveal whether reasonable efforts were made to maintain emergency lighting and/or repair faulty lighting. Accountability will be assigned when it is found that maintenance was not prioritized and it failed when it was needed most.

Although people rarely notice emergency lighting until it is used, the system must be tested regularly and repaired or replaced as soon as it is noticed not to be functioning as intended. Not having emergency lights available in the middle of a facility evacuation where power has failed may turn out to be a tragedy with inevitable accountability assigned to those that failed to spend the few dollars on maintenance when it could have been easily done. Those odd-looking lights that never seem to turn on in normal situations are actually critical to any facility, and facility managers must prioritize them as essential life safety equipment by testing them regularly and repairing or replacing them as soon as they are found to be less than 100% effective. To do otherwise risks lives unnecessarily and puts the manager and the facility owner in peril of being held responsible for a tragedy.

As always with life safety systems, local fire codes should be consulted for the specific requirements in the area of the facility and the advice of the local fire department should be sought and followed.

CPTED IMPROVING PROPERTIES

As an example of using CPTED principles to improve properties, if we examine a business owner/operator that has already been victimized by local gang members who skateboard along the sidewalk near the entrance to the business at night, the CPTED auditor may recommend that the lighting not simply be repaired, but also improved to a white light source such as fluorescent or LED, which, as explained earlier, provides excellent color rendition and brightness of detail. The reason for choosing fluorescent lighting in this case is that, when identification and descriptions become important not only for the investigation but also for court processes and trials, it allows for witnesses to see true color as opposed to the standard yellow street lighting that shows shades of gray and black. There may be other recommendations, such as removing coverings from the windows and turning shelving so that the ends of the rows face the windows to allow onlookers to see what is going on inside the store, thereby removing the comfort zone of physical cover for the criminal by improving the natural surveillance. The auditor can also recommend changing smoothly paved sidewalks to smaller individual block or slightly uneven stone sections to remove the ability of people to skateboard in front of the store by making the surface rougher and bumpier for the skateboards, yet still functional and safe for walking and attractive to see.

CPTED can be used to move people along intended paths by manipulating the environment with sightlines, flooring materials, walls and fencing, different leveled and textured walkways, lighting changes, and anything that subtly directs people along an intended path. It is the effort to cater to everyone's need for comfort and desire to seek it in a space.

In museums, CPTED concepts can be used in conjunction with other security hardware to achieve the desired balance between allowing visitors to experience the exhibits or art as directly as possible while still being able to protect the item from being touched or otherwise damaged by enthusiastic, curious, or ill-intending people. An example of this can be with a piece of art, where the flooring in front of the artwork has been differentiated with off-colored stripes parallel to the wall containing the item, but at a 90° angle to the walking path toward the item. This creates a psychological barrier in front of the item that tells the visitor's brain that he or she is not welcome to proceed past that spot on the carpet. For those that still wish to proceed, museums can add a motion-controlled chirp alarm that alerts the visitor that he or she has moved too close to the exhibit and also alerts security to a potential threat developing. Most often, the visitor is startled by the chirp and moves back, but the security guard response should also be on the way just in case the visitor has more on his or her mind than accidently getting too close to an exhibit. Even better is to have a physical barrier or attractive guide rope in front of the exhibit to stop people from getting too close. Measurements of barriers should always be overestimated to account for someone falling forward or sideways just to ensure that no one can impact the exhibit with a falling action.

Responses in facilities such as museums will be layered in this manner, where defeating one measure will almost certainly cause the person to encounter and have to defeat another measure as they effectively overlap. The following anecdote illustrates the concept.

News broke in August 2015 of a young boy of 11 years of age that was visiting a museum in the Philippines. There was a painting on display that was worth over US$1,000,000. As the boy casually approached the painting from the side, the safety barrier in place was not sufficiently planned or installed; the boy stumbled across the front of it, and in an apparent natural reaction, braced his hand outward to the left, where he inadvertently punched a fist-sized hole in the canvas near the bottom of the work. This demonstrates the necessity of physically testing and examining these sorts of safety measures for effectiveness. Overplanning is necessary to ensure that expensive works of art remain safe in museum settings when school age children come along. In the case illustrated by the example, the box in front of the painting was the same length as the painting and only jutted out in front by about two feet. This allowed the boy to enter from the side and, as he tripped over the box, it was not long enough to prevent the boy from impacting the painting as he fell, causing major damage to it. Thankfully, reports indicated that the boy was not blamed and no attempt was made to hold him accountable. However, it is quite conceivable to guess that the security or facilities manager accountable for the security of the museum pieces would be held accountable in some manner for this monumental failure of not finding the correct balance between allowing guests to experience the art and yet preventing them from touching and damaging the artwork. This situation will also trigger an investigation and perhaps an insurance claim and payment or litigation between the painting owner and the museum. It becomes easy to see what a small amount of good security planning might have avoided.

The situation in the anecdote, of course, was deemed an accident and not an ill-intentioned act. Good CPTED planning by overestimating the size of the barrier in front of the exhibit might have prevented it at no cost to the museum.

The aforementioned and other CPTED strategies can be very effective in making a business more customer friendly and welcoming, while making unwanted persons feel uncomfortable enough to find another place to commit their crimes and misdeeds. The bottom line is that criminals do not want to be caught and they need to feel comfortable about the space within which they operate. If they feel uncomfortable in a particular space, they will move on to another target where they can perform their misdeeds without fear of being seen or apprehended. Well-designed CPTED spaces can remove that comfort level from the criminal and give it back to the business owner/operator and, most important of all, the paying client.

6

Fire Safety in Facilities

Fire safety in facilities is often the topic that people do not want to talk about or be bothered with in their day-to-day lives in the workplace. It is the inconvenient and time-consuming activity for which some people will even make themselves absent from the workplace to avoid participation. That is an unfortunate view of a critical aspect of the life/safety system in a building. This unpopular topic is also an essential aspect of facilities that most often falls into the lap of facilities management and maintenance personnel, but can also find its way into the responsibilities of the building security personnel.

Every building, including private homes, is mandated to have some kind of fire and smoke detection device, but in business facilities, it is very serious to get it right and do it properly. There is high accountability attached to poor management of the fire safety program in a building if something happens and the system fails to work as designed—particularly if it is due to the neglect of those that carry the responsibility of ensuring that equipment functions properly and is tested regularly and that the building population are educated and practiced in evacuation.

It is imperative to advise any facility manager to remember to plan for evacuation and fire events during regular business hours and also to ensure that nonbusiness hours and night-time are covered as well because different people may be staffing the facility and performing different functions in different areas. Appropriate off-hours planning must be conducted with the same importance as the business-hours planning.

Every facility beyond a private residence is going to have a fire panel that centralizes all of the functions and signals. This panel will alert building occupants by sounding the alarm and it will send alarm signals to alarm monitor stations that in turn will call the fire department.

Figure 6.1 shows a typical fire panel in a modern business facility. It has warning lights that will pinpoint the source of alarm, and it connects to all vital electronics and alarmed areas in the facility. It is the central nervous system of the fire protection program in the building and must be in a protected location where vandalism is unlikely but where it can be accessed quickly and easily by firefighters at a main entry point into the building. It is this panel that firefighters will seek as they arrive on a fire alarm call to get information about the alarm before they enter the building. These panels are installed and maintained by contract to an alarm installation company, which may also monitor the system off-site. It can also be a different contractor that monitors these signals, but the contracts are important for facility managers to periodically review and ensure that they are up to date.

These modern panels are mostly single stage and function in a rather simple manner, as they are connected to sensors throughout the building that monitor specific areas for smoke, fire, and noxious fumes such as carbon monoxide. The panels will detect trouble in certain circuits and ring a local alarm by sounding a buzzer without activating the evacuation tone throughout the facility. In these cases, employees that know what they are doing can observe the panel indicator and verify physically by visiting the area to determine that, yes, in fact there is no fire and a sensor or other electronic component has likely burned out. Where an

Figure 6.1 A typical fire panel in a modern business facility. (Photo by J. Henderson.)

actual fire has occurred and or smoke has reached the sensor, the building will go into general alarm, sounding the evacuation tone. This tone will compel all building occupants to immediately evacuate by following their established and, hopefully, well practiced fire evacuation plan. Building occupants should immediately leave the building and leave firefighting to the professionals, although it is possible for a skilled building occupant to grab a fire extinguisher and attempt to extinguish a small fire. If this is an option, it should be stated in the fire plan and approved by the local fire department. Anyone touching a fire extinguisher should be trained in advance.

Some larger facilities have two-stage alarm systems that will sound slow warning tones for alarms that compel occupants to ready themselves for evacuation and stand by for further instruction. The facility or security manager then has five minutes to send a runner to verify visually whether or not there is a fire, allowing the manager to make a decision to drop the building into general evacuation alarm or to shut the tone off, pending investigation by the fire department when they arrive. If the five-minute time period has passed and there has not been a decision and/or action to shut off the tone, the fire panel will drop into automatic evacuation and sound the much quicker evacuation tone, compelling all occupants to immediately evacuate. The two-stage systems will also pinpoint trouble alarms in the facility for maintenance employees to check and repair without sounding any tones throughout the building.

Two-stage alarm systems can give more flexibility in larger, multi-building or multitower and interconnected buildings to manage the fire event and prevent a general shutdown of the entire facility and the business being conducted therein. In other words, if a small fire event occurs in a three-tower building, with a two-stage system, you could have one tower evacuate while the other two towers wait for further instruction. If the fire event is extinguished quickly, the other two towers can get back to work without too much delay, while the tower where the event happened will lose time from the cleanup, the investigation, and the time it takes to repopulate the building once the all-clear is given by the fire chief. All of these possibilities, however, must be worked out in advance by the facility manager with the approval of the fire department and must form part of the published fire plan before it is legal or advisable to attempt.

Part of an established fire safety plan should include annual inspections of all buildings in the facility. Commonly, these inspections should be conducted with the facilities management team, the fire department, and any contractor involved, such as maintenance or alarm companies.

This work should consist of the testing of pull stations, smoke detectors, and sprinkler heads, along with fire extinguishers that should be getting checked every month anyway. These inspections should include any electrical and communications closets, wiring in the ceilings, and the functioning of the main fire and any subpanels should be included. Audible testing of all of the alarm areas should also be done to ensure that alarm tones reach the areas they were meant to reach and that there are no dead signal zones. Where strobe lights have been installed in replacement of, or in addition to the audible alarms, the light signals should be checked. It is also a great idea to have an actual building-wide fire drill, particularly if the local fire chief or a fire captain/fire prevention officer is present, as this cooperation and relationship is so important to facilities managers.

If there is one note of caution to make for facility and security managers entrusted with fire evacuation responsibilities in a building, it is to *know, understand, practice, and follow the approved fire plan in the facility precisely during evacuation events.* Failure to do so could result in serious charges against the manager and high accountability if people are injured or killed during any evacuation, particularly if the manager deviated in an unapproved manner from an established procedure. Every action taken must have been previously vetted and approved in the published fire plan with the endorsement of the local fire department.

EVACUATION ALARMS

Alarms in facilities are the emergency communication method to tell people in the facility what to do when facility-wide emergencies occur. Fire codes require the installation of an approved fire detection system that is connected through a central fire panel, often referred to as a fire annunciation panel. This panel is the brain of the system and must have a contracted ongoing maintenance schedule from the installer or a certified alarm services company. The contract must stipulate precisely what the alarm company must do to keep the alarm in working order at all times and it should also describe in detail what the alarm company will do when the system breaks down or some other unexpected situation unfolds. The response by an alarm company to system breakdowns must be addressed in the contract as an immediate response by technicians, as the loss of evacuation alarms in a facility generally means a cessation of business and the mandatory evacuation of people as fire coverage would now be lost. This situation can be very expensive for a business owner/ operator and extremely disruptive to tenants or facility users.

The Fire Alarm Panel and Fire Annunciation Panel

The fire annunciation panel, as indicated earlier, is the brain or central computer of the system and has a verbal communication system often confused by building occupants as a public announcement system. An annunciation panel often will have subpanels in other connected facilities that communicate with each other electronically to manage coverage of different wings of a building or different floors/areas. The main panel is generally located in a central part of the building under the control and monitoring of either the facility manager, maintenance manager, or security manager, with proper training to monitor and/or operate the system. When alarms are triggered by a stimulus, a signal will travel to the central panel and raise an alarm for the manager to examine. The signal should tell the manager the location and what type of alarm has occurred— smoke, fire, or simply a trouble signal for an HVAC system or within the branch panel.

Fire annunciation panels in large facilities are excellent systems but can be constantly in demand by building occupants to disseminate building-wide communications. There is no room for compromise on this for the facility manager. The verbal communication capability of the fire annunciation panel should never be used for any communication other than for a bona fide emergency. Even when explanation is provided, building occupants constantly push managers for use of the fire annunciation panel to announce bake sales, public events, travel instructions, and myriad other bits of corporate information that should be sent through e-mail and other manners of communication. When use of fire annunciation panels is allowed to happen for nonemergencies, people stop listening to the warning tones and become disinterested in the system, which can be very dangerous in a real emergency. Although most people will likely continue to listen to the evacuation directions, there will be others that are perhaps in the washroom and simply did not hear enough of the message to realize that an evacuation is at hand. Occupant familiarity with hearing the annunciation system used for other purposes on a regular basis can actually cause many of the people to begin to disregard or to pay less attention to the specific message of that particular alarm, resulting in possible future tragedy as some people may have failed to evacuate when it was possible, simply because they did not take the annunciation panel message seriously.

FIRE EVACUATION PROCEDURES

Fire and emergency procedures are an often overlooked aspect of buildings and facilities of every size and shape. Everyone despises the news that a fire drill will be occurring sometime during the business day and some people deliberately do not cooperate and do not follow the procedures. The reasons for this attitude are unknown but appear to be anti-establishment or anti-authority, as though the employee feels it is a way to strike back for frustrations in the workplace. However, it is an attitude that does not do anyone any good, particularly the people with the attitude, as they will not know what to do when the emergency evacuation tone sounds and they must quickly exit the building. These nonconformists could even become a dangerous hindrance to those taking the drills seriously.

Fire and emergency evacuation procedures form part of every fire code in every municipality, township, county, and state or province. They are a critical part of facility and building management that, if not handled properly, can land facility owners/operators in serious trouble. In most cases, a local fire chief can actually lay charges against a person who purposely disrupts a drill or fails to evacuate a space as required.

Fire code regulations are there for a very good reason. In most cases, the regulations have evolved over many years of trial and error—sometimes as a result of coroner inquests stemming from building fire tragedies— and are the most important safety regulations enacted across the board in every jurisdiction. It is absolutely critical for all building owners/operators to review their fire and emergency evacuation procedures on a yearly basis and to consult with their local fire department if they feel the procedures need revising or they simply wish to conduct a drill to improve evacuation skills. Practice reduces the likelihood of panic as people faced with an evacuation will have some idea and practiced skill level of what they are supposed to do when the evacuation tone sounds. Panic and chaos can result when many of the occupants have no idea what the fire plan consists of and what their responsibilities are, or even how to exit the building. Building operators/owners must be able to explain to a judge, post-tragedy, that they had an active fire plan in place that complied with the fire code and had been endorsed by the local fire department. Further, they should be able to advise with written records when the building population had evacuation training and when there were evacuation drills to test the procedures and further educate building occupants. Failure to do this can land a facility owner/operator in deep trouble through the law and with potentially huge liability. It is advisable for facilities to include evacuation drills in their general incident reporting system to ensure the information is searchable and available quickly if needed.

Owners/operators may be able to get away with not doing evacuation drills and/or training for some time; however, if a fire event does eventually happen in the building, and particularly if someone is injured or killed, every action and nonaction will come under a microscope and the owner/operator and building management will be answering tough questions from authorities. A quick Internet search using the term *nursing home fire* will reveal multiple recent stories about tragic fires that have ripped through long-term care residences and nursing homes. These stories are also full of information about owner/operator negligence as determined by courts and inquests in regard to failure to prepare residents for evacuation through updating procedures and conducting real fire drills, to owner/operator negligence in not having proper equipment, such as sprinkler systems, installed or repaired, resulting in multiple deaths. Management that elects to take shortcuts and save money may be doing so as a convenience or as a money-saving tactic, and all is fine until something serious happens. This type of management is irresponsible and takes people's lives for granted when the primary responsibility of facility owners/operators and managers is to safeguard the lives of the people that pay to live in those buildings. Short-term cutbacks and risky decisions can backfire and get people killed—not to mention ruin the career of the manager responsible for the situation. Long-term planning and active inclusion of safety regulations and equipment save money over the long run and prevent tragedies from happening (Figure 6.2).

As mentioned previously, the fire and emergency evacuation plan must be created with the advice and support of the local fire department that has responsibility for the local fire code requirements in that particular jurisdiction. It is essential to have the fire department's approval on your plan and its participation in fire drills for several reasons. First of all, it means that your planning is in compliance with fire code regulations and, second, employees will have a reference point, some training, and hopefully an active drill to experience the plan in action before it is needed in a real scenario. Third, emergency first-responders get critical experience responding to alarms in a particular facility and get to know the interior building plan, how to get to the heating plant or boilers, where

Figure 6.2 A large residential complex on fire. From this perspective, the complexity of residential buildings and fire evacuation become painfully clear. Regular fire drills are essential to ensure the building population knows what to do and that any physically challenged people have evacuation plans tailored to their abilities and the capabilities of rescuers. (Used by permission from Jason D. Reid.)

the gas shutoffs are, where the main hydropower panel is located, and other critical areas in which quick access can help stop a fire from progressing. It also identifies choke points in the evacuation planning where too many people may be trying to use a particular door or evacuating people actually block firefighters from entering the building to do their jobs. These potential situations need to be identified up front, solved with effective solutions, and rectified in the published plan (Figure 6.3).

A common sense way to support the fire evacuation program is to have the building fire program connected to health and safety, as well as to have the group looking after first aid and fire extinguishers and being connected to the training of Fire Wardens and Exit Supervisors. The idea is to create a group of skilled people looking after these similar themed activities and equipment, which widens the number of people formally involved and creates redundancy when people move in and out of the building or get promoted and leave their responsibilities. There will always be someone to take over a position and the more people involved means there will be skilled people in the midst of more evacuating groups providing guidance and support.

In a large facility, the plan should be organized to effect an efficient, safe, and rapid exit of all persons. There must be a verification exercise by building and fire officials to ensure that everyone has left as required. When the building population is larger, the evacuation team should be

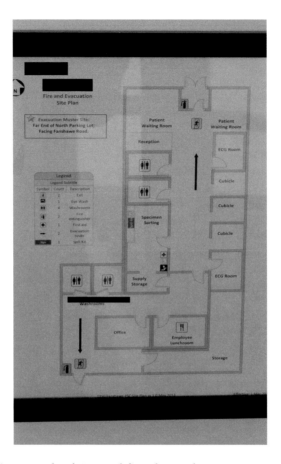

Figure 6.3 An example of a posted fire plan at the entrance to a public health facility that has heavy traffic of persons not familiar with the facility. It publicizes the fire plan for whoever will read it and provides evacuation information. In this case the people entering the facility have a responsibility to look at the plan and know what to do. (Photo by J. Henderson.)

organized by an appointed building fire chief into Exit Supervisors and Fire Wardens. These people should be volunteers selected from every department and every area of the building, and this must be a live list with attention paid to the natural organizational movement of personnel and vacancies, which should always be filled immediately when volunteers move on, in order to maintain this critical function to each work area.

Backup volunteers should be designated in each area, as well, to account for absences and training to ensure there are always trained Exit Supervisors and Fire Wardens in every work area of a facility during each business day. Only willing and interested volunteers should be used because many people want no part of the extra duties and responsibilities involved with being a warden or supervisor, and this responsibility requires motivated and interested people to keep it relevant and up to date. Employer incentives, good training, and recognition go a long way in motivating employee participation in the facility evacuation plan.

What Do the Evacuation Volunteers Do?

The *Exit Supervisor* leads the predesignated group of evacuees, usually ten to twelve people, along a designated, previously practiced route to their designated exit. Having designated exits should help prevent overstacking of people trying to leave through the same door and it will raise evacuees' confidence in knowing where they are supposed to go. Alternates are worked out in advance as well, in case the main exit for that group has been blocked. At the exit, the Exit Supervisor opens and stays at the door until that group has passed and then leads them to a predesignated meeting spot safely away from the building.

The *Fire Warden* does the interior sweep and clearance of the work area for that group. He or she checks all desk locations, offices, meeting rooms and even bathrooms for people that either did not hear the evacuation tones or misinterpreted them. The Fire Warden then follows the evacuation route with anyone found during the sweep and, once reunited with the Exit Supervisor, goes to the predetermined meeting spot safely away from the building. The Fire Warden takes names and numbers from the group and makes a report as soon as possible to the fire department. It is the duty of the Fire Warden to ensure that no one is missing from the work area and declare it cleared.

Evacuation of the Physically Challenged

A separate but no less important duty before emergencies occur is to ensure that the needs of all employees have been considered and addressed in the evacuation plan. Specifically, this is in relation to persons with physical or mobility issues that may not be able to use the stairs or cannot hear the tones. Planning in advance must be done in consultation with in-house security or facilities managers and the local fire department's Fire Safety

Officer, who can strategize what that mobility or sensory-impaired person is to do in an evacuation. Instructions could include that the person and a guide be designated to wait in a certain area for a fire employee to come and get them out of the building another way. Other upgrades to the system may require the installation of alarm signal strobe lights to accommodate the hard of hearing. Failure to plan for the blind and hearing impaired and to get a mobility-impaired person out of the building, or at least out of danger, could result in a significant tragedy involving loss of life and the resultant severe legal ramifications for the operator/owner and managers.

Along these lines of activity comes the advice that any facility manager must establish good relations and excellent communication with the local fire department and, in particular, with the fire safety or prevention officer. These professionals will always work enthusiastically with someone that shows the forethought and interest in ensuring that the facility is safe and that the evacuation procedures are current and staff trained properly to use the procedures.

After leading safety and security review teams on multiple site surveys and assessments, it became very clear to the author that many facilities either had outdated and neglected fire safety plans, or that they had not been practiced in years. There were also locations that had experienced significant renovations without altering the fire plans and maps. Examination of this problem showed, in some cases, plans that actually directed evacuating persons to newly installed walls or doors that had been permanently sealed.

The advice given was to quickly call the fire department and have the fire safety officer come to examine the evacuation plan, check it for fire code compliance, and ensure that the plan details were relevant to the facility at this point and did not place occupants in danger. Testing the plan was also part of the advice as it does not do any good for the population to be panicked and unsure of what to do in the middle of a real evacuation alarm, even if that plan is functional, up to date, and approved. Panic causes chaos and can lead to serious injury and death. Having the fire evacuation plan signed off by the fire department will ensure that the plan is current, approved by the authorities, and effective, but it will also protect the owner/operator from liability if tragedy does strike.

Evacuation Obstructions

Facilities suffer from the ever ongoing problem of obstructions in passageways, stairwells, or just about anywhere that space exists. As facilities and in particular office buildings, are places of business, there always

67

exist issues of space whereby deliveries are either coming in or going out or the growth of a company or business unit causes the inevitable subdivision of space through wall additions as boardrooms disappear and offices multiply to accommodate more employees. People always run out of room to store equipment, deliveries, and just about anything that is relevant in an office setting. When room becomes scarce, people do whatever they can to achieve their short-term goal of convenience, which results in the storage of equipment and deliveries in hallways, on loading docks, and even on stairwell landings. What happens, however, is that mandated and measured minimum clearance found in fire plans and fire codes is being ignored in the effort to *just put the stuff somewhere*. When this occurs, fire evacuation routes are inadvertently affected to the point where any number of people will not be able to use escape routes and responding fire personnel with their equipment may experience serious difficulty in reaching the areas within which they need to perform their services. These situations are code violations and, when tragedy strikes, can cause people to be injured or killed. The tragedy will happen, for example, because someone in the advertising department had a pallet of pamphlets delivered and stored in the basement hallway, thus blocking the exit, simply because he or she had the pallet delivered before figuring out where to store the delivery. There are cases where these people even know that they are violating fire code requirements to achieve their short-term goals of convenience but feel that nothing will happen and that they "have no choice." This is a dangerous game to play over time as, at some point, a real evacuation event will happen and, even if it turns out not to be a serious incident, chances are that a fire department official may stroll through the facility during or just after the evacuation and discover the violation, whereby the perpetrator may be facing fire code violation fines. The point is that most people in large facilities simply do not take these regulations and mandated fire drills seriously and view them as inconvenient and unnecessary. The challenge for building life safety supervisors is to change the prevailing noncompliant and ignorant attitude into a well-versed building population that buys into the fire evacuation and life/safety programs.

"It Won't Happen Here..."

Murphy's Law is alive and well, and much stronger in reality than the notion of "it won't happen here...." There is nothing like real experience to drive this point home. As a security manager, the author was facilitating a public event in cold winter weather at a facility of critical importance that contained numerous buildings and fleet storage. Of course, as he battled for the resources he knew were needed to handle the inevitable and unexpected, he was told, "No, we don't need extra personnel, nothing will happen here." As the event continued to unfold on a particular Saturday, several thousand people were strolling up and down the main halls of the main building and several hundred children had gathered in the cafeteria for special children's events. The security and support personnel were stretched thin, of course, by design from the nonapproval of resources by executives and the failure of one organizer to deliver his promised and much-needed volunteers. The security staff were therefore being run off their feet trying to close all the gaps. But there was little to worry about because, as a higher placed manager told the security manager, "It won't happen here." All of a sudden in midafternoon, the warning tone of the two-stage evacuation system began to sound, much to everyone's amazement. The system advised that it was in the area of the cafeteria and there were a short five minutes to confirm that the alarm was either real or not a threat before the system kicked into the full evacuation tone. A runner was sent, who confirmed it was not a fire event but a little extra smoke from a grease trap draining out of the kitchen. With the fire department rolling up to the front of the building, the decision was taken to shut down the alarm tone to avoid throwing several hundred children into frigid −20° weather. As fate can have it, though, within minutes a full evacuation tone began sounding from another of our buildings across the street. Although all the security staff were already occupied with necessary work, the previous time and effort in ensuring excellent relations between security and facilities maintenance came to fruition as a maintenance worker instantly stepped up and said, "I'll go." Off he went to see what was going on in the other building.

Murphy's Law had provided a unique and unexpected situation with two major alarm tones in two different buildings within ten minutes of each other and not enough staff to handle them, with several thousand guests in the main building. The second building was a dormitory that happened to be vacant only because it was Saturday, so as a little bit of luck would have it, nobody was in the building at the time. This alarm sounded because of a dramatic spike in temperature in the basement when insulation on some steam pipes was removed for replacement. The temperature soared unexpectedly high, causing the sprinkler heads

> in the basement fire sprinkler system to blow off, spraying the basement with water. Everything turned out fine with cooperation between Security and Maintenance and a very patient fire captain, but it demonstrates very clearly that "yes, it can happen here" and likely will some time in the future when you are least expecting it, due to Murphy's Law!

This example clearly helps to demonstrate that the best advice for facility managers in event planning is to overplan with Human Resources and ensure that emergency services are aware of the event and to even have them physically on site and participating if possible. Most often, the event will not need the extra people for the planned activities during the event but one can always use them for various tasks anyway. It is when the unexpected happens that the extra people become a necessity, and that time always comes at some point in a facility manager's career. It would not be a good thing to be pointed out as the manager or executive that said "No, you can't have those resources because *it won't happen here*...." That manager or executive would have many tough questions to answer in the event of a tragedy, and it may well be in front of a court or an inquest where the answer, *"I was trying to save the company some money,"* would have to be explained and justified to a very tough audience who want to know why people died or were seriously injured.

MAKING A FACILITY SAFER

As safety and security programs continue to develop, wonderful items can be added to facilities that can save lives and add to the feeling of safety in the workplace. Ideas to install such items or develop specialized training often come from difficult and sometimes traumatic experiences that facility and security managers go through, followed by the inevitable question during debrief of "How can we make this safer?"

Automatic External Defibrillators

The automatic external defibrillator is more commonly known as the AED. It is a compact, battery-operated electric stimulus intended to stop a person's heart from defibrillating so that it can start beating properly again. The moment to use one is when a person has collapsed and no pulse is detected, but always in accordance with the manufacturer's instructions and training (in advance) and after the 911 call has been placed to get emergency responders on their way as quickly as possible. Once connected to the victim with the supplied special paddles, the AED will automatically detect the pulse rate and rhythm and audibly instruct the operator on what to do next, including exactly when to deliver an electric shock to the heart to stop defibrillation and restart the heart following a coronary event if needed. Use of an AED does not cancel summoning an ambulance. Even if the person responds to the shock and gets back up and walks around talking, it is imperative that the 911 call not be cancelled and that paramedics still come to check the patient, provide treatment, and ensure that everything is fine. Further treatment and medical tests may be needed and the minutes following the collapse of a person are not the time to cancel emergency response, even if the person appears to recover.

An AED can be used by anyone that can follow direct instructions, as most commercial models feature step-by-step recorded verbal commands that tell the operator exactly what to do. Facility owners/operators can and should consider installing such devices that are government approved in high-traffic areas such as lobbies, sports arenas and stadiums, office buildings, apartments, and shopping facilities to improve the chances of saving a heart attack victim's life by starting response in the precious time before paramedics arrive. As time counts in these situations, having such devices readily available can make a difference and demonstrate to a facility population that the owner/operator is invested in health and safety.

AEDs are commercially available and, through experience, an AED company can be selected by tender with the facility's needs and cost factors addressed. The winning company should send a representative to work with facility management to discover the precise needs in the building(s) and plan accordingly as to how many units are needed, how far apart they should be located, and where exactly they should be placed for effective coverage and security of the units. Reputable companies will offer professional training; maintenance instructions, battery replacement schedules, and other support that should be automatically included in any contract to ensure continuity of an AED program. Some AEDs are designed to be operated only by trained persons, such as the one in Figure 6.4, and this must be a subject of discussion during the formation of the business case. These considerations should be included in any proposal and cost estimates should be realistically configured, including any renovation requirements. This is important before a proposal goes forward

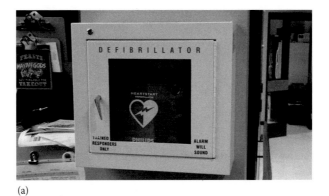

(a)

(b)

Figure 6.4 (a) Installed automatic external defibrillator in a busy office with many employees of all ages and varying levels of health. (b) AED/fire extinguisher installed together at a major grocery store. (Photos by J. Henderson.)

to management to secure the funding before a tender is even considered. Designated persons in the organization should also be appointed to maintain the program, train users, and ensure batteries are kept charged and schedules maintained. Such programs are appreciated by building populations as they are a relatively low-cost but highly visible sign that management takes safety and security seriously.

7

Incident Response

DETER, DETECT, AND REACT

An effective way to organize the security and incident response system in a facility is to engage the philosophy of *deter, detect,* and *react.* Such a layered strategy makes for the efficient use of resources in a structured environment where the person of ill intent determines how far the response will go by his or her own actions. As the level of activity increases past initial deterrence, the detection of activity through layered security begins, which then should trigger a measured reaction from the facility.

To Deter: To start, any security program should have deterrent strategies that can be seen from the outside and experienced by visitors to the inside. The deterrents in a facility often will create a public sense or reputation that a building has effective measures in place and that persons of ill intent may as well just move along and find another, less daunting target.

Deterrents consist of many-layered measures that indicate that an organized security program is present. On the facility perimeter, deterrents begin with fencing and gates, which indicate clearly to persons of ill intent that their presence is not desirable at the facility. Signage such as "No Trespassing" and "Visitors Must Report to the Security Office" are examples of directional signage designed not only to give instructions, but also to instill a sense of structure and accountability into anyone entering the space. The presence of uniformed security guards provides more visual deterrence as the uniform suggests authority and professional incident response capability. Access control procedures, such as signing in and identifying oneself at an exterior security kiosk, add accountability once again and remove the anonymity so craved by persons of ill intent.

To Detect: The activities of detection should dovetail with the deterrent measures as the detection measures must be visibly aligned with the deterrent measures. If someone goes beyond a deterrent measure, the detection system should pick up the intrusion and trigger an alarm of some kind that alerts responders.

Detection can come in the form of vibration detection wiring on fence lines, infrared detectors that trigger audible alarms, closed circuit television with live monitoring or motion triggering alarms, security officer patrols, motion-triggered lighting, and even reports from engaged employees at the facility who are part of a security culture that challenges those that may not be authorized to be in certain locations.

To React: Reaction comes in response to the detection of improper activity. As the security measures have detected the activity, procedures ensure that preselected resources react to the situation in order to resolve it in the interest of the facility and the employees.

Reaction often comes in the form of an employee challenge of the presence of an individual or, if security is in use, a security officer confronting the person. Other reactions can include the locking of doors or gates, use of audible warning, lighting, or even calling local police, who will come and make arrests if needed. They can also otherwise solve the situation in the interest of the facility and its occupants.

Reaction closes the loop of *deter, detect*, and *react* upon which analysis can occur. Upgrading of security measures and policies, hardware, and personnel can be considered to close any gaps exposed during an incident.

INCIDENT RESPONSE

Incident response in large facilities begins with building management and security, and the tenants or occupants. As incidents occur and are detected, occupants that participate, are victimized, or simply witnessed the event occur have a moral responsibility and should have policy-driven responsibility to report the incident to building management and/or the police or appropriate emergency service. Facility managers have a critical responsibility to ensure that rapid response occurs to any incident in order to maintain order, maximize safety, and minimize liability in their properties. They also must record such incidents for internal purposes such as liability protection and for crime/incident analysis. As mentioned in Chapter 3, recording data and incident details is very important in being able to take proper security measures in making a facility a safe place to be, which in turn makes the area a more desirable place to be and less attractive to persons of ill intent.

Incidents can be grouped according to the response required but may include one or all emergency services for the same event. Police incidents would be for anything requiring police response such as violence, sexual attacks, theft, trespass, vandalism, disturbances, or anything requiring police to deter activity, remove persons of ill intent, or intervene in making the site safe again. Fire department incidents would be anything where smoke or actual fire is present and may include hydropower incidents, poison gas, or fuel leaks, among others. Ambulance response will be required for any injury, serious sickness, or death incidents that require a medical response. A good example of all three emergency services being required at a scene would be a motor vehicle collision between a car and a tanker truck carrying gasoline. Police are required for traffic control, investigation of the incident, and possible enforcement action; the fire services may be required to extinguish a gasoline fire and to extricate a victim from a vehicle; while paramedics can perform advanced lifesaving procedures and then transport the victims to hospital. Before the paramedics arrive, however, fire and police personnel can provide lifesaving first aid and/or CPR to injured victims. These overlapping abilities from the emergency providers can also translate into facility incidents such as fires, floods, or even ambulance assist calls for occupants in distress where fire or police happened to be closer than an ambulance and arrive first. The responsibility of facility and security managers in these instances is to facilitate response by having someone meet the responders by an entry point and escort them as directly as possible to the location of the incident, as well as offering crowd control services and anything else required by the responders.

Most municipalities are now using 911 systems for tiered response of emergency services; although one service may be required or requested initially, one, two, or all three services may end up responding depending upon the need. These services work together on a daily basis and a responsible facility manager will see the value in calling these services when they are required as quickly as possible when a situation demands their response. Failing to respond erodes the sense of safety and security in a facility and threatens how tenants and occupants view their surroundings as a place they wish to occupy.

Accordingly, any facility should have direction within its published emergency response policies for employees and occupants in reporting incidents as they are occurring. In the case of police incidents, consistent and rapid response from police will have a deterrent effect on criminals and people of ill intent, while conversely giving occupants confidence that their safety is important to building management. If police response is quick, the risk level of being caught goes up significantly and makes for an uncomfortable time. This risk may be enough to make persons of ill intent move on elsewhere to locations where police response is slower and they will have time to effect their shady business and escape. The police response also depends to some degree upon the rapidity upon which the facility manager or a tenant places an emergency call. To ensure effective response based on the needs of the building and its occupants, managers need to establish good relations in advance with the emergency responders so that it is clear to responders how procedures will unfold and what the first-line responder can expect when arriving at the front door.

This philosophy of response leads into the *Broken Windows Theory*, described in the *Crime Prevention Through Environmental Design* (CPTED) portion of the book in Chapter 5. If repairs are not quickly made to vandalism and wear and tear, the facility will begin to look worn down. Couple that with slow or nonexistent police response, and people of ill intent will view the area as attractive for their purposes and a general deterioration will occur as crime increases. The facility and area will quickly gain a reputation for not being cared for by the community and the persons of ill intent will view the area as a safer place for them to exploit people and resources.

Some may say, "Why bother?" and argue that the police response is always slow, particularly in some municipal locations that are subjected to ongoing crime, night after night. There may also be facilities in areas considered to be risky at best that wish to improve their situation and reputations. These situations may be a result of stretched emergency services budgets where resources are simply not readily available or prioritized for the most serious incidents, which some will argue has contributed to a decline of quality surroundings and a sense of safety. This urban reality does not eliminate the responsibility of the owner/operator and facility manager to make their facility as safe as possible. Owners/operators and facility managers must work together and with police authorities in assessing security and safety needs in and around their facilities and to provide the measures to make it safer by installing proper and accountable access controls, alarms (including panic alert stations), closed circuit television, fire extinguishers, automated external defibrillators, and perhaps even security officers. The key to a successful guard program is ensuring the officers are well trained and practiced (and recertified annually) in responding to situations based on their legal status and powers in regard to citizen's arrest and local trespass laws. Security guard failure is typically a result of poor hiring practices, insufficient training, and weak policy—issues over which the facility owner/operator and facility manager have considerable control and influence. Budgetary constraints are no excuse and are simply a matter of priorities. Owners/operators and facility managers must look past initial cost to see the value in proper security as an investment in making the property safer and more desirable for tenants and occupants. A return on security investment can be noted in crime and damage prevention, lower liability, and perhaps savings in insurance premiums as risk is reduced through demonstrated action by management and statistical success. These measures will also improve the caliber of tenant and help with the overall reputation of the facility and area.

Incident Response: Emergency Codes

Emergency Codes and the Fire Annunciation Panel

Emergency codes are a great way of communicating information quickly through the fire annunciation system of an emergency situation. The codes are generally designed to inform the people that should be informed in the facility such as first-responders and decision makers that may be spread throughout the buildings in a facility. The codes are also meant to hide the meaning from an attacker or the general public, who do not require the information at that time.

Codes, such as those illustrated in Figure 7.1, should be simple and refer directly to a type of incident allowing people in the facility to react as they have been directed or trained in advance. The codes should be published only in nonpublic spaces so that visitors and the public cannot see the codes and figure out what they mean. The figure shows a code list that was posted in a public area, which defeats the purpose of having a code system.

As emergency codes are generally announced through the fire annunciation system, it must be a topic of conversation with the local fire department officials to ensure that they agree with the interpretation of the fire code that allows the fire annunciation panel to be used in this manner. If the fire code prohibits it or the fire chief and/or one of his or her officials does not agree and fails to endorse the use of the fire annunciation system in that manner, then it is imperative that the facility manager comply with

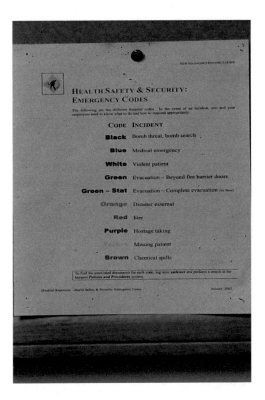

Figure 7.1 This placard was located in a hospital waiting area at a large hospital in a large municipality. The codes look to be well planned and installed formally in policy but, oddly, have been placed in a public area. What should be an internal organizational system of paging and identifying volatile incidents that require certain specific responses has become a system where the people that have entered the facility to conduct illegal activity now will know exactly what the authorities are paging about and what response might be coming. This information should be published internally and circulated via e-mail and placed on boards in employee areas only, where the public has no access. Facility managers must consider carefully what information is being placed where and who might access critical internal response and policy information. (Photo by J. Henderson.)

the direction provided by the fire department, regardless of the pressure from others in the building, including executives. As has been indicated previously but is worth repeating, many occupants of buildings equipped with fire annunciation systems view the building-wide communications system as a public announcement facility that they can use freely to announce general items and publicize events such as fund-raisers or blood-donor clinics, among many other announcements. This must not be allowed to happen as the occupants of the building will become very used to hearing the fire annunciation system and begin to tune it out, reducing the system's effectiveness when an emergency actually does occur. When pressure is applied to facility managers to use the fire annunciation system for nonemergency announcements, the facility managers must argue the problem to the executives accountable for the building. The facility manager may even require the assistance of a fire department official to get the message across, as formal charges laid against the facility manager may be possible when this strict rule is violated.

CHANGING THE SECURITY CULTURE

In facilities where security culture is weak, a change must be introduced to the population and buy-in achieved by facility and security managers. A typical office building with a weak security culture will contain doubting people that complain about slow police response and do not take fire drills seriously by either not having drills at all or by staying in their offices when they are required to exit. Some of the employees will take shortcuts and store equipment and shipments of material in hallways or stairwells, and others will circumvent security measures such as access controls for convenience, despite the fact that they are working in a high-security area and will jeopardize their own safety as well as the security of proprietary information and assets. Such locations suffer from low morale and generally will resist any program that is viewed as emanating from the parent organization.

Changing this kind of a culture is a daunting process but not impossible. It takes a manager with patience and a good plan, with the support of local emergency services and time. The first thing to try to tackle is awareness. People that do not participate or have negative feelings about building security and fire evacuation procedures generally lack awareness and will express aversion by saying things like, "This is a waste of time" or asking, "Why bother?" citing that the building is fairly new and nothing will happen. These are the people that a facility manager must reach and they may even include executives. Communication is the key in this instance, and a great way to start getting buy-in from the executive level is to establish an emergency planning committee that meets monthly or by requirement if a large event is planned. This is done by engaging local emergency services such as police, the fire department and ambulance service, facility maintenance management, a representative of the owner/operator, the security manager, and managers from other stakeholder entities in the facility. Using existing policies and procedures should be enough to get some topics of conversation rolling with the intention of improving how situations unfold. To get all of the stakeholders in one room to discuss events and building-wide problems such as crime, fire evacuation, or trespass can be very effective as these incidents most often involve more than one entity in a response and peak interest as people begin to see value in working together to solve a problem. Planning events also becomes much easier with all of the consults sitting at the same table for discussion. If a particular stakeholder for an event is not part of the committee, he or she can certainly be invited to attend as a guest to work through issues.

An established emergency planning committee will eventually have the credibility to examine facility policy and procedures and begin to propose improvements or new policies to the executive level, representatives of whom can also sit on the committee or attend as periodic guests. If the organizer of such a committee feels that it may be difficult to get executive approval for an ongoing committee, then perhaps it is better to start with a meeting and then report the results to executive leadership so that they can see the benefits. Once there is executive support, then it gets easier to achieve buy-in from the rest of the facility population.

With the emergency planning committee organized, a campaign of general awareness must begin. One could begin with the existing fire wardens and exit supervisors, and if there is no such program, it is time to establish one with executive support and the assistance of a fellow committee member, the fire chief. A new presentation should be created for this group that details not only their mandated responsibilities, but also the reasons for their tasking, including actual statistics and media reports of incidents occurring in similar facilities to drive the point home. This begins to get the word out to the different entities in the facility. Next could be organization-wide presentations where committee members attend meetings with each entity in the facility to deliver the message of facility security and safety and that each person in the facility has a responsibility toward making the facility a good place to be. Including the fire wardens and exit supervisors in this communication event is critical as it helps spread responsibility from the committee to the end user and it implies that everyone is important is making the facility safer by stopping security breaches, participating in fire evacuation drills, and reporting incidents as they occur in order to develop a proper facility profile of what is really going on in the building and surrounding grounds. An educated facility population is aware of issues and will participate in improving their own security and safety as they realize it is their responsibility and not that of someone in some other obscure work unit on another floor.

Getting buy-in can still be a difficult prospect even when executive management gets behind it and the emergency management committee is working efficiently. Where there are still employees deliberately making it difficult and refusing to do their part, it may become necessary to hold people accountable if, after being gently reminded of the policies and procedures, they continue to not leave the building during fire drills and commit security breaches, such as taping locks open or placing bricks on secured doors to prevent them from closing so that they can sneak a smoke break. When evidence of such activity appears, with the support of the emergency management committee and executives, discipline may be in order to get the last holdouts to comply. It will not take long when that happens for the other people to fall into place once they realize that the organization is serious and will not tolerate such behavior. Consistency and direction are important in changing an organizational culture into one that actively participates in safety and security practices; once converted, employees can be the best part of the system as they view such activity as violating their workplace and their safety.

ELEVATORS

Elevators are an essential mechanical system in multistory buildings for the purpose of efficiently moving persons and assets between floors. As such, they are regulated by government and maintained strictly by specially trained and certified technicians. Each elevator is required by regulation to have a log book and an approved maintenance schedule tended to by certified technicians, usually through a maintenance contract. This is serious business in ensuring that this work is performed as contracted and that the elevators are always in working condition. High-traffic elevators in large facilities are constantly running and require regular maintenance and emergency calls to ensure they continue functioning safely and effectively (Figure 7.2).

There are two main types of elevators in most multifloor facilities. Passenger elevators are designed to carry people between floors quickly, efficiently, and safely. Generally, the capacity of passenger elevators will

Figure 7.2 A high-traffic bank of elevators in a hospital that requires constant maintenance to ensure safety and mechanical reliability. (Photo by J. Henderson.)

vary most often up to twelve people; however, to get twelve people into a passenger elevator would be a very crowded experience.

The second type of elevator is the freight elevator, often with front and back doors and designed for the movement of maintenance and cleaning workers and their supplies from floor to floor. Freight elevators also are meant for moving furniture and deliveries and are built to take damage from the constant activity of maintenance in a building. Freight elevators should be the cars used to remove garbage from the facility as well to avoid contaminating the passengers in the main passenger elevator cars (Figure 7.3).

All elevators can be controlled by card access to isolate areas from the public or to have authorized access only to certain areas. They will also have recall switches that are most often key operated so that maintenance technicians and the fire department can ground elevators during emergencies and control the cars to their advantage.

For safety reasons, any malfunctioning elevator should be put out of service as soon as any problem is noted. To properly put an elevator out of service is to lock it down in order to prevent any person from accessing the elevator and potentially operating it. It is preferable to have the elevator doors locked shut with clear signage advising of the closure for maintenance. There are many examples in buildings where elevator doors have been left open and a chair with signage indicating that some maintenance

Figure 7.3   A typical singular freight elevator designed to carry workers, freight, garbage, and supplies between floors in a building. Passengers should not be using the same elevators to avoid the possibility of contamination from chemicals or garbage. (Photo by J. Henderson.)

is being performed was placed in front of the door—only to have someone move the chair and get into the elevator car anyway and attempt to operate it. Different people will do strange things, such as move whatever is blocking their way without reading or heeding the message on the chair not to use the elevator. It is just safer to lock the elevator car to prevent anyone from getting inside and attempting to use it.

Elevator maintenance can never be compromised, nor should it ever fall victim to budget constraints because the results can be very costly through civil action, formal charges, and a public investigation process. Elevator servicing must be regular and controlled by contract with the elevator maintenance company. Facility managers must take great care in ensuring they know the contents of the elevator maintenance contract, and they must hold the maintenance company accountable for doing the maintenance as scheduled and for abiding by the contract.

One experience with making a building safer was born from a series of elevator mechanical malfunctions in a major office facility where incidents of mechanical failure had been accelerating over a period of months, as well as in the face of numerous complaints to Maintenance specifically about elevator issues. Elevators in this facility were constantly moving volumes of people in three separate elevator banks among five floors in three different towers, and each elevator was having stranding issues with people getting stuck between floors, sometimes for hours at a time. The standing operating procedure at the time required the security unit to call into the elevator car through the installed emergency telephone line to find out how many people were in the car and how they were handling the stress, and to advise them to wait for the elevator technician to come. The security officers were required to maintain communication with the stranded passengers and maintain awareness of how everyone was doing. This was deemed reasonable and safe when the elevator car was stationary; it was considered to be locked in place by the braking system, which had to be mechanically released in order for the car to move. Then a call would be placed by Security to the facility manager, who would summon the elevator maintenance company to come and repair the issues and free the passengers. The physical response of the elevator technician to these calls generally took at least three to four hours, as the technician usually had to travel at least seventy-five miles as an emergency call. They were almost always working in another facility and would have to disengage one task to attend our emergency. The poor people stranded in the elevator car were locked inside for that amount of time until the certified elevator mechanic arrived to open the doors. It was usually an uncomfortable, hot, claustrophobic, and frightening experience for those stranded inside the elevator car.

If response of the elevator technician was too slow and any of the passengers were to suffer a medical emergency while stranded inside the elevator car, the only other option would be to call the fire department, which would come as an emergency call, rescue the passengers, and provide emergency medical care to the ailing passenger(s) as necessary. The upside of this response is quick medical care for a passenger in distress.

The downside is possible and likely expensive damage to the elevator doors as the fire department will open the doors with their equipment and tools in the quickest manner possible to ensure the safety of the passengers. This would probably entail the use of a large axe by a firefighter, which could cause serious damage. The fire department would never be held responsible for damaging the elevator doors in a rescue and the facility would have to absorb the cost. The following anecdote illustrates the complexities of what can happen during an elevator malfunction and the stranding of passengers.

During one particular stranding incident, a high-volume passenger elevator stopped between floors due to what was later known to be an ongoing maintenance issue. When the elevator stopped, a security officer spoke to the passengers through the emergency phone and another went to the closest floor. All seemed well for the first moments and security called the maintenance contractor, who paged the elevator technician. The estimated time of arrival was 1 to 1.5 hours. The passengers would have to be patient and wait, while security continued to reassure them that they were safe and the elevator car would not fall with the braking system engaged. After the elevator had been stranded for some time, a medical emergency began to occur to one of the passengers; luckily, the elevator technician arrived soon after and freed the person before anything serious happened.

However, there was a debrief that produced discussions of what to do to fix these issues and mitigate potential medical emergencies. The dialogue then continued over time between Facilities Management, Security, and the company through whom the elevator maintenance was contracted. To inspect, overhaul, and improve the system would take time, so, to effect immediate change, the group developed an interim plan to train the security staff with an official government-sanctioned elevator rescue course to allow accredited security personnel the ability to lock down the elevator cars and extricate any passengers safely and quickly. This was in lieu of using the busy local fire department and risking damage to the expensive elevator doors with their firefighting equipment. Also coming out of this discussion was the idea and proposal to install automatic external defibrillators throughout the facility as it was a high-stress location full of middle aged to advanced age workers and management.

As discussed earlier, elevator maintenance is a critical, ongoing process that must be considered as an integral part of any building facility program. Regular maintenance keeps the equipment working in a safe manner and the resulting documentation protects the facility and the facility manager from possible complaints. Failure to keep the maintenance at a high level leaves the equipment more unpredictable and prone to malfunction or even failure, which in turn puts people in danger. As mechanical systems, the timing of motion and lubrication of moving parts are critical elements of the machinery. Although contracts for elevator maintenance are likely in place, it is necessary for facility and or security managers to periodically look at the elevator maintenance program for consistency and to even periodically inspect the maintenance log books, which are required to be kept in the elevator mechanical rooms to ensure that they are being completed in a timely manner and on a regular basis. Observing the habits of the elevator technicians is also important to ensure they are using their windows of time for maintenance appropriately. The following anecdote demonstrates what can go wrong over time if the maintenance section gets too familiar with the elevator technician and begins to allow him or her to work without escort and supervision.

Experience had demonstrated actual problems in the area of maintenance and log book compliance as a building of critical importance reached about ten years of age. The aging process of the facility produced a period of ever-increasing mechanical failures in a bank of elevators, to which security staff were always the first-responders. Determined to mitigate the increasing problems, the security manager had the security staff examine the elevator maintenance log books, which were found to be very inconsistent; some entries were completed on time while other entries were left undone, only to be filled in later during different visits by the elevator technician. After comparing the findings with access data and sign-in sheets, it was found that the technician had been sacrificing time, either by not being there at all as the regular visits began to reduce or by the technician's own personal habits that developed over time. The investigation revealed that the technician, with a contracted window of four hours to service eleven elevators, was signing in at the security desk, then going for breakfast at the cafeteria and starting his scheduled tasks over an hour later. This reduced his maintenance time for eleven elevators from four hours to three hours, resulting in the actual servicing time per elevator dropping from 21.8 minutes per elevator to 16.4 minutes per elevator, including walking time and breaks. Conversations with the Technical Standards Safety Authority (TSSA) officials revealed this practice to be unacceptable and insufficient to keep that number of elevators functioning in a safe manner. It produced a situation where shortcuts were being taken to make up for the lost time; instead of replacing parts or properly diagnosing mechanical issues, the technician appeared to be constantly adjusting timings, which directly led to some of the mechanical failures and passenger stranding incidents.

This information was put together following an investigation conducted with the cooperation of the contracted maintenance provider and the TSSA. Armed with a report on the state of the elevators determined by the TSSA officials and the evidence in the log books, including access data from the facility, the facility representatives approached the elevator contractor, who also conducted its own inquiry into the matters. The situation was eventually rectified amicably with the repair of the elevators and eventual reassignment of the elevator technician.

This anecdote is just one type of problem with which facility and security managers need to be aware, that although rare, can actually happen in a large facility that is being maintained through contracts. Most service contracts should and will be honored appropriately; however, as the technicians are human beings, there is always the possibility of error, lack of accountability, and/or bad personal habits of the employees affecting the maintenance of the facility and assets. The awareness for facility management to keep abreast of the technical contracts and the service provision in their facility is critical in ensuring that building mechanical systems remain in good repair and safe for the use of people in their care. Failure to be vigilant eventually becomes the problem and liability of the owner/operator, as well as a potential conflict with the service provider.

The regulating body discussed in the anecdote is TSSA, which, backed with legislated authority, establishes and enforces technical safety standards in the province of Ontario, Canada. The story is a prime example of how a facility manager can effect change when regulated systems are not being maintained properly. It is always best to try to mitigate these issues by communicating with the contracted service provider and getting that company to investigate first. In most cases, the contracted agencies involved will react to an issue and try to rectify it to the standard of the contract in a cooperative manner, as occurred in this scenario. It is only when you have exhausted your options that something more dramatic needs to be done to ensure that the population under your care is as safe as possible when using mechanical systems such as elevators.

PARKING IN FACILITY LOTS

Parking is something that all people seem to need or want at different times during the day and it can be a sought-after privilege in many buildings. Designated parking is a privilege often given to important or high-ranking people as a perk to allow them easy access to the ingress/egress points of the facility (Figure 7.4). In most facilities, there is a lineup of reserved parking spots by the main entrance to the building, often with each space sporting a sign with the title or even name of the special person for whom the spot has been set aside. Although wonderfully convenient for those of enough importance to get one, having designated parking is

Figure 7.4 Designated parking. (Photo by J. Henderson.)

also a direct indication of which vehicle carries someone of importance, making that person an easy target for people of ill intent. The signs will inevitably contain either the title of the person—for example, president or chief executive officer—or the person's name, or even both. Although personally reassuring and satisfying for the spot owner, it gives criminals and even terrorists the opportunity to garner a lot of information about the person of importance. All a person of ill intent has to do is sit and watch, and as soon as the person returns to his or her vehicle, the person of ill intent can discover what the important person looks like or who is connected to an executive parking spot, what vehicle he or she drives. Then, the person decides to follow the vehicle, he or she can even determine where the target and his or her family reside. This is not deliberate information sharing by organizations, but when it is analyzed, it actually has the same impact as a security breach or an internal violation of information privacy by someone in the organization.

Having designated parking may be a perk to which people aspire, but it is poor security practice and can lead to trouble when certain parking spots are celebrated with personal signage. It can be done in other ways, such as disguising the parking spots in the general employee parking area, and communicating numbered parking to employees, with the first row reserved for visitors and the physically challenged.

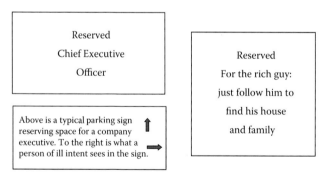

The best advice for facility managers and building occupants is to not inadvertently give personal information away through conveniences such as reserved parking spots. It is not worth putting anyone's family and personal assets at risk simply to have an identified or reserved parking spot that does little more than save a corporate officer fifty steps to the front door.

91

Parking Garages and Underground Lots

Parking garages and underground parking lots can be intimidating and very daunting but necessary places for average citizens to use as they go about their daily lives in urban settings. They are usually dark, dank places uncomfortably full of other cars and strange people walking about going to and from their vehicles in very close quarters. Appointments with doctors at hospitals or lawyers in office buildings and even shopping excursions, among other activities, will put solitary and very vulnerable people in the uncomfortable position of having to walk some distance in a potentially dangerous environment over which they have little control. Of further discomfort and perhaps a very dangerous moment for most people occurs when they reach into their pockets or purses to retrieve a wallet full of money, credit cards, and vital personal information to pay for renting the parking spot.

This vulnerability never eases in places like parking garages and lots, but property managers can make the experience safer and more secure, thereby increasing users' sense of safety and security. They can take measures such as maintaining excellent lighting and removing obstructions as much as possible so that there are few isolated spots and that sight lines make it uncomfortable for persons of ill intent to gain their advantage over solitary garage users. The installation of panic alarm stations in strategic locations will also add to the comfort of patrons and discomfort of criminals by giving the users a very loud method of calling for help that will increase the criminal's stress level and discomfort over being caught. As with other facilities, however, layering the security measures is critical in ensuring safety and security because nothing is as effective as hitting persons of ill intent with one measure after another, each of which must be defeated in order to achieve success in attacking a user. Add into the mix a closed circuit television system with monitors at a security station or in the payment booth or having patrolling security staff walk throughout the parking facility to reduce reaction times to alarm signals. These layered strategies will assist a parking facility in gaining a reputation for persons of ill intent as a risky place to rob patrons or steal items and vehicles. Persons of ill intent will simply move on to find less risky targets to ply their illicit trades.

Enhanced security measures do not, however, release the parking facility users from responsibility for their own safety. Publishing and distributing policies and security suggestions will also produce a more educated clientele and can serve to reduce liability if the user failed to heed the recommendations and policies of the garage. Advising users to think about and know where they are going before exiting the vehicle, rather than spending too much time exposed in the uncontrolled space of a parking garage is excellent advice, along with advising the driver to park in a location so that there is as little distance as possible between the car and the entrance to the destination. Advising users to have their belongings organized before they open the car door so that they are not leaning inside the car fumbling around distracted and unable to see who is coming is sound advice. Such activity not only blinds users to dangers and other people lurking in the area but also lengthens the amount of time that people will be exposed to that unpredictable environment and prolongs their exposure to potential danger. Other good policy suggestions are to advise occupants that, before they exit the vehicle, they should look for people, other vehicles, and anything that looks odd or out of place. The vehicle occupants actually remain in control of their own safety until they open the door and leave that vehicle. If occupants of vehicles do not like what they see, they do not have to get out of the car and abandon their security. This written policy suggestion could be an item that becomes very important in a lawsuit brought forward by an attack victim who did not pay attention to the surroundings and walked right into trouble with persons of ill intent. If people do not like what they are seeing, they should stay in the vehicle and/or leave the area. Although it may be inconvenient, it is better to remain in control of the situation by being *inside* a locked, moving car instead of isolated on foot in an unfamiliar place, locked *out* of a parked car.

Having such an organized security program in a parking facility is not only prudent in preventing crime and chaos, but also a very professional approach that will attract paying clients as they will feel they are being looked after by the business owner/operator. It is one strategy among many that can help change the perceptions of an area and perhaps begin to reverse the effects of the Broken Windows Theory if it has been relevant to a particular area.

DRONES

News organizations are increasingly bringing stories to their audiences about powered drones and their use for electronic eavesdropping or delivery of goods in a commercial application. Unfortunately, there is a group of people that use drones for bad or illegal purposes and the laws in place either have not been tested in particular jurisdictions or have been found lacking in dealing with drones and the inevitable clash with privacy. As we are in such a developing situation in regard to drones, there are some factors to consider before making decisions about what to do if a drone flies over your property. People assume that it is automatically considered to be trespassing if a drone passes over private property. It may not be in certain jurisdictions and before assuming that it is trespassing, it is highly advisable to check local laws and ask local law enforcement how they view drones and what considerations they use to interpret an incident.

For example, if a property owner sees a drone equipped with a camera over his or her private property, whether just passing through or otherwise, some people will try to knock the drone out of the sky or even shoot at it. Initially, many people might think that to be a reasonable course of action to end the breach of privacy. However, if the drone is knocked out of the sky, one must consider how a court will view this action when the drone owner sues the property owner for damaging or destroying a drone that was simply flying from point A to point B. If the property owner uses a firearm to disrupt or shoot the drone down, there are similar issues of whether the court will consider that action as reasonable or necessary. Further, the property owner that fired a gun at the drone could also be facing criminal charges of negligent use of a firearm by endangering other people. The fact that bullets have been fired into the air makes the shooter responsible for where the bullets eventually land and it is a good bet that not all the fired rounds are going to strike the drone. What a difficult predicament to be in if the property owner was held responsible by authorities for killing or injuring an innocent person by firearm because he or she was shooting at a drone! If the property owner is sued for damaging or destroying the drone and has to pay several thousand dollars to the drone owner in a settlement or award would be adding insult to injury. The point is for property owners not to over-react to the advent of drones flying about, which is only going to increase in the future. It is highly recommended for all people to keep an eye on this emerging issue and to find out how drones are viewed by local government and law enforcement before taking any kind of action against them. It is simply not worth it to either react or over-react to the inevitable presence of drones in the sky above us and take unilateral action against these crafts and their owners without having some kind of knowledge of how that action will be interpreted by local law enforcement and the courts. A court may take the view that the drone controller's intent was not to spy on the person that destroyed it but rather to fly on its way for another specific purpose.

In that case, the person that took action against a drone could be held culpable and face penalty, although, for many people, that opinion defies logic as they struggle to view it in the context of trespassing and privacy. These are the issues that must be worked through before the drone industry gets its much-needed regulation.

Although at the time of publication of this book there is no drone management in regulation or legislation in Western governments, there is better news on the horizon for the drone industry as the National Aeronautics and Space Administration (NASA) continues to research the technology of low-altitude traffic management for drone flights. Technology is being developed commercially to achieve low-altitude air traffic control in an effort to control this unmanaged but burgeoning industry that will revolutionize the direct delivery of goods to clients by commercial drone.

8

Contracting/Subcontracting Work and Services

Contracting and subcontracting are a way for facility managers to get the work done when they do not have the available staff, equipment, or expertise to perform particular tasks. Having in-house staff performing tasks gives a facility manager more control over how things are done and better accountability. Most often, the in-house staff take pride in their work and realize they have a daily stake in the quality of work they perform as it will affect every aspect of their work in that facility.

Contracted and subcontracted staff on the other hand, are mandated and legally obligated to do everything stipulated in a contract. If a task was not included in the contract, the task is not the responsibility of the contractor. Omissions from contracts happen and they can cause problems for facility managers if they are not careful about ensuring the contracts are complete with tasks, instructions, deadlines, and anything relevant to getting the job done efficiently. Facility managers should always check previous contracts and seek advice on designing contracts before they engage a contractor and sign the contract to avoid missing something important that could wind up costing the budget extra money for something that should have been included. An example would be for a facility manager contracting out snow plowing in the facility's large outdoor parking lot. Not only should the contract stipulate completion of the plowing of the lot by a particular time before business hours begin, but it should also stipulate any requirements to use sand and/or salt products to reduce the slippery surfaces, as well as snow removal to avoid losing a percentage of parking spaces with piled snow. Failing to include these items could result in problems such as the snow plowing interfering with the morning rush hour as vehicles come into the lot with drivers looking for parking spaces that are either still covered in snow or are blocked by ongoing snow removal activity. One can see how obvious it is to have it included in the contract that the snow clearing activity be completed by the time rush hour starts; otherwise, a major traffic jam will ensue in the parking area, which has the potential to affect business inside the building.

Other contract considerations include having window washing and hot welding work contracted to be performed outside building business hours to avoid potential alarms and strong toxic odors from affecting workers. Contracts can be designed to require contract workers to use particular entrances or to use particular materials among many options, which should be discussed in advance with the contract manager as it is best to cooperate rather than squabble over contracts. A well-designed contract will include everything the client requires under the conditions for which the client requires them, and the contractor, knowing what is expected up front, will be easier to work with as nothing should be a surprise that will cost additional money.

Subcontracts are simply other work parceled out by the contractor to do some of the work in the contract. Recognition of whether use of subcontractors is acceptable or not to the client should be included in the contracts. Of course, any contractors and subcontractors should be subject to security clearance procedures to avoid having criminals and persons of ill intent performing work in a facility or putting employees, assets, and information at risk. An example of subcontracting in the case of the aforementioned example of a snow removal contract would be for the contracted company to subcontract another company to send a dump truck and remove the snow.

Other situations that may require sudden engagement of contractors often involve sudden mishaps or weather-caused damage where the facility is required in short order to be functioning normally. Facility managers must then engage professional repair and cleanup services that will come in and clean and/or repair serious damage. The following anecdote illustrates the rapidity of need to stem the outflow of money when disaster strikes.

In one example used elsewhere in the book, one day the sprinkler heads popped off in the basement of a dormitory due to spiking temperatures after steam pipe insulation had been removed for replacement. This required very quick cleanup and repair to reduce the costs of having to put students in a hotel until the dormitory was functional again according to fire department expectations. The contractor employed to do the original work had to pay for the service company to repair the damage, which still took about a week to rectify, so that several hundred people could return to the facility.

Facility managers must have these types of companies listed for such quick service with preestablished relationships to try to get priority service when it is needed. Being organized can save money and time for facility and security managers, as well as having thorough contracts in place that cover every task conceivable before the signatures are added.

9

Inclusiveness and Accessibility

ACCESSIBILITY

As the developed world moves toward inclusiveness, it just makes complete sense for facility owners/operators to incorporate accessibility into renovation and building plans, even before legislation requires them to do so. Many jurisdictions have already moved toward accessibility legislation and many more are looking at the issue to begin the process.

Accessibility is about removing barriers to services or facilities so that all persons have equal access, freedom of movement, and the dignity of being able to perform basic functions without having to seek assistance. Many jurisdictions are already legislating compliance to have barrier-free retail, restaurants, and workplaces to allow persons with physical challenges to participate fully in what society has to offer. To the building owner/operator, this means keeping the issue of accessibility in mind at all times to ensure that barriers are not inadvertently installed as they are repairing or solving a different issue. Accessibility also means the consideration of effective design in the first place or retrofitting older buildings with accessibility-friendly equipment.

For example, in an office building, steps going in the main ingress point should always be built with a ramp and railing for use by persons in a wheelchair as well as persons still able to walk but that cannot ascend the stairs. Once at the front door, there should always be functioning handicapped access buttons that open the doors when depressed (Figure 9.1). One problem that facility managers will face with the handicapped access buttons is the constant use by nonhandicapped persons who use them as a convenience to power-open the doors for them. This increases wear and tear and requires more expenditures on maintenance. Another problem for wear and tear occurs when the building is locked and someone pushes the handicapped button. The system will continually try to electronically open the door while it is locked, thereby possibly burning out the electronics or at least using up the life expectancy of the unit and using power continually until it is shut off. Facility managers must keep an eye on these factors and try to communicate with building occupants to reduce this annoying but widespread problem.

Once inside the building and past the handicapped button, many reception areas are constructed for persons of average height, to allow them to approach, sign in, and produce their identification while standing up. When a person in a wheelchair rolls up to the same kiosk for the same service, he or she may not be able to reach the sign-in sheet or pass an identification

Figure 9.1 A typical handicapped entry button. Nonhandicapped people often use these buttons, which have been installed for the convenience of the physically challenged, and contribute unnecessarily to the wear and tear of the devices. (Photo by J. Henderson.)

card to a receptionist behind the glass because the distance from a seated position in the wheelchair may not allow the dignity of this simple action. Designers with forethought will build this into the design of the reception station by having two levels of desktop or by allowing the wheelchair to move directly up to the service window without being blocked by a protruding section of desk. Other systems to add to designs or retrofitting older buildings include specially designed elevators that will accommodate wheelchairs for moving between floors that it would otherwise be impossible for a physically challenged person to access (Figure 9.2).

In buildings with secure access through turnstiles, there must be an alternate method to allow physically challenged persons the dignity of entering the facility without asking for help. When an employee uses a wheelchair or walks with crutches or a walker, using another set of doors as an exception with a secure access card reader controlling it would be preferable so that the employees can access the doors without having to compromise their dignity by having to request assistance every time they enter the building. This may also factor into a disabled person's ability to leave the facility during an evacuation event. Management and security might have to build a special access level for the employee's access card that allows him or her special access to the door, without allowing the able-bodied employee to take advantage. This is a very reasonable solution for an older building without such considerations and, from experience, it is certain that the affected employees will be very supportive and quite pleased that they were considered important enough to get special consideration of their situations that allowed them to enter the workplace

Figure 9.2   Retrofitting of a three-floor building built in the last century with the installation of an elevator specifically designed for the physically challenged to move walkers and wheelchairs between floors. The system was placed in a stairwell long after the building was built and provides equal access to those who need it, with the dignity of being able to operate it without assistance. (Photo by J. Henderson.)

103

and maintain their sense of dignity, without having to request assistance every time they approached the front door. Newer buildings should have these issues anticipated and worked out in advance by being incorporated into the design.

PUBLIC RESTROOMS

Public restrooms or washrooms are as much a security issue as they are an accessibility challenge. Restroom or bathroom facilities with public accessibility (not including outdoor facilities that have different challenges) should always be designed without doors for two reasons:

1. The first reason is basic security. Similarly to any application, doors located on public washroom facilities serve to keep people in or to prevent entry. Installed doors with latches will keep some people out as they will not be able to physically grasp the latch and open the closed door. The doors may also keep people in as they can serve as a trap where a person of ill intent can stop a victim from leaving, providing a closed, sheltered spot where violent crimes may occur. Washroom facilities in public areas should have a walk-through design, where the walls provide privacy but will also allow voices to sound alarm and where the winding passage will direct the person in easily. Washroom facilities should also be equipped with panic devices so that someone in trouble can easily summon assistance. Facility owners/operators should be always aware of the safety and security of their building occupants and visitors; likewise, washroom facilities must be kept as clean as possible and in operating condition. The owner's/operator's reputation is at stake as well as maintaining liability protection from litigation resulting from mishaps or crimes. Owners/operators, as always, must be able to testify that they did everything they could reasonably do to make that space as safe as possible.

2. From an accessibility perspective, the washroom must be easily accessed by persons using wheelchairs, canes, and walkers. Putting doors in front of these people will only serve as a barrier to access, and if a person of ill intent locks or bars the door behind them, they will be trapped and can easily fall victim to violent crime. There must also be larger stalls, at least one or two that are equipped with not only extra space for manipulation of wheelchairs and walkers,

but also metal grab-bars that people can grasp to help themselves maneuver onto the toilet. The sinks must be low enough and far enough from the wall, with plumbing underneath tucked away, so that someone sitting in a wheelchair can still operate the faucets. Paper towels or hand dryers must be low enough and easily operated by physically challenged people. A professional designer can be consulted for an excellent design that incorporates the desire to be accessible, as well as remaining safe and secure.

The examples of an inclusive restroom in Figures 9.3 and 9.4 allow flexibility for pregnant women, physically challenged people with walkers

Figure 9.3   A restroom door in a retail box store. It is highly dysfunctional for a handicapped person, who would have to somehow open the door and push a wheelchair through, but avoid the wall in the interior. The handicapped person would then have to exit by pulling the door toward him or her and then pulling the wheelchair through. The door also provides criminals with opportunity to confine a victim inside and commit a violent crime. (Photo by J. Henderson.)

105

Figure 9.4 An inclusive restroom facility located in the automotive section of a major box store. There is room for a wheelchair, handles to pull oneself about, and hidden plumbing allowing a chair to move up close; everything can be reached from a wheelchair. (Photos by J. Henderson.)

or wheelchairs, or even a parent with a small child to use the facility comfortably. The cleanliness is also apparent and it all goes a long way to making a wide variety of people feel comfortable in this retail store. Facility managers must think of how this particular situation can impact whether a family will decide to use this store as opposed to stores that have filthy, noninclusive restrooms where no thought was put into the needs of a variety of clients.

10

Reviews and Proposals

BEYOND CPTED: USING IT AS A TOOL

Crime Prevention Through Environmental Design (CPTED) is most often used by itself as a tool for police services to reduce the risk of crime in targeted neighborhoods or simply provided as a service to businesses that have suffered from criminal acts. As a CPTED-trained member of such a police force, the author saw value in using CPTED principles during security audits as an information collection vehicle by utilizing CPTED-trained employees and assigning them specific information-gathering tasks based on their training and experience. As a business continuity planning consultant faced with a series of security reviews on government facilities with a very tight timeline, the author selected a team of individuals consisting of a security technology specialist/locksmith, and four to six CPTED-trained employees. The idea was to set up a central point where the author was deploying reviewers with specific tasks, who would then report back with information to be entered into the main project document. To achieve an effective flow and capture of information, the author gave specific training to each of the reviewers so they would know what their specific tasks and methodologies were before they even visited the site. Once on site, the author requested a briefing from the site owner/manager to ensure that the purpose and scope were clear. The review team also participated in this briefing for clarity of mission and to give each reviewer an opportunity to ask specific questions before the project was to begin.

The author then had some preparation work to perform in order to organize the task assignments, compartmentalize tasks, and estimate time of completion to establish an active and flexible timeline. Some of the background work included checking facility occurrence reports, alarm responses, and local police records of incidents reported or where a police response occurred. The first general task for the participation of all reviewers was the *interview stage*. This was simply an effort to find out what was really going on in the facility, for comparison with what the owner/manager had told the review team during the briefing. The purpose was not to expose the owner/manager for using incorrect information but to find any gaps between what the owner/manager thought was going on versus what was actually happening in the facility. The results were always surprising as reporting mechanisms were traditionally weak where they even existed at all and a lot of routine incidents were never recorded or reported. A lack of reporting might translate into a lack of incident volume in the eyes of building management for the simple reason that management just was not hearing about things being looked after by employees or occupants. Without a centralized information-capturing mechanism—or, where there was one, undisciplined use of it by unmotivated staff—a lot of information could be lost and never come to light unless something dramatic happened and either ambulance, fire, or police showed up and actually created an official report.

Information collection is a process either missing from or is highly inconsistent in most facilities, particularly when there is no security service providing incident response services. In facilities lacking dedicated security services, the maintenance manager or building superintendent becomes the individual toward whom the building population will look for reporting incidents, simply because the maintenance person/building superintendent is the most visible representative of the property management and will be the only person most occupants think can do something about an incident. In most cases, an incident will be solved without any record being made of it unless the police become involved. Even then, the facility likely will not retain any record of the incident—with the written report being prepared by the police and remaining police property, combined with the fact that the facility lacked its own system of information collection.

What building owners/operators need is for the building population to adopt a sense or culture of security awareness, where they are educated to realize that they are part of their own safety and security environment and have to actively participate in maintaining the general security of their building—for example, ensuring the door closed properly, and not buzzing people in through the front doors unless they know them, removing bricks placed to hold a door open, reporting even the smallest incident through an established incident reporting system, and advising the building's appointed security person that suspicious people are hanging around the basement doors, among other issues. This kind of security awareness can really improve a facility to the point where participating occupants begin to feel that sense of belonging to something bigger than themselves and begin to take ownership of and responsibility toward the facility. It also gradually affects persons of ill intent because they begin feeling paranoid enough that someone is going to turn them in, so they will take their business elsewhere. As the occupant's sense of safety and security grows, the sense of security and comfort previously enjoyed by the person of ill intent declines in direct proportion. This is the point where the Broken Windows Theory experiences a reversal in prospects and municipal revitalization can take hold.

REVIEWING A LARGE FACILITY

Large facilities and complexes with multiple buildings, outbuildings, paved lots, and grass yards are a major project within which to conduct a safety and security audit/review. As previously discussed, as large a task as it may seem on the surface, a major security review can still be accomplished by a skilled security review leader in a reasonable amount of time with good organization and a trained and experienced team. The review team leader can make a huge difference by setting up the parameters of the audit/review in prereview briefings with the client. These meetings are discovery sessions to find out what the purpose of the safety and security audit review is, what the eventual goals are, and what the information will be used to accomplish. The team leader must be direct in collecting information from the client to be able to then assign tasks in an efficient manner to keep the amount of time spent on the review at a minimum. The most important question to ask the client is, "Why are you having this review done?" There is always something at the root of the exercise that has caused the client to spend a considerable amount of money bringing in outside professionals to potentially uncover some embarrassing information. The client also knows that recommendations can cost money and that there will likely be recommendations at the end of this exercise. Once an organization has been alerted to security gaps and the need for security upgrades, failure to act can place the organization and decision makers in jeopardy of accountability and lawsuits when crimes occur within their midst.

111

NOT MUCH HAPPENS AROUND HERE…

One of the gaps that reviewers must find and for which to specifically look is what the operator/owner thinks is happening versus what is really happening within the facility, as discussed previously in the book. As a corporate entity with multiple entrances, working machinery, numbers of people coming and going, and often vehicles stored or coming and going at all hours, facilities can be very active places with accidents and unexpected incidents occurring with regularity. The potential for accidents or incidents of any type presents a substantial level of risk and liability that any responsible owner/operator would want to minimize, not only from an ethical standpoint but also to reduce the risk of actual liability from a financial perspective resulting from property damage, injury, or death. The author's experience, many owners/operators think they know what is going on inside their facilities but in reality have not spent any time to purposely investigate what goes on because many activities and issues occur without being noticed, and typical silo structures within many organizations make it impossible for information to move efficiently from the incident to upper levels of management. As the author tasked his reviewers with interviewing receptionists and maintenance personnel, it became very clear, very quickly that the perspective of the owner/operator can be very different from the perspective of the people present in the facilities on a daily basis, who deal with basic building functions and who see and interact with who is coming and going. For example, an owner's perspective can be such that he or she has spent a hypothetical $100,000 upgrading the building locking system and key control in a facility, with a firm belief that a security issue has been addressed and liability reduced significantly. However, a simple conversation with the basement janitor could reveal that building employees, seeking convenience for reaching the smoking area or for unloading items from a vehicle, among other reasons, have been propping the back door open with a brick, and then not bothering or forgetting to remove it after they are done.

This type of activity goes on all the time in facilities around the world, where an employee can easily defeat an expensive security measure, leaving all of the employees and assets within the facility exposed to potential harm, loss, and unauthorized intrusion. In this case, and despite the big money thrown at an identified issue, it would seem that owner/operator liability has actually not been reduced, as the policies in the building may not have been strengthened and employees not managed properly and continued to be allowed to violate access policy without penalty. This is a perfect example of the complexity of upgrading security through a planned and layered approach that includes not only security hardware, but also policy development/revision and most important of all, safety and security awareness and the compliance of the building occupants. An owner's/operator's risk level will only reduce when he or she has taken such a comprehensive approach and demonstrated a sincere effort to make the facility a safer and more secure place to be. That will be the question on the mind of an inquest judge or hearing chairperson in determining the level of liability for an owner/operator in an incident: "Did he or she make a sincere effort to improve safety and security in that facility?"

The author experienced this gap in one of his assignments as a facility security manager. When the author first became manager of the unit, the author was advised *by his own security staff* and management that "not much happens" around the building on a daily basis and the unit was simply opening and locking doors for the most part. The security unit personnel also seemed to have absorbed this unfortunate attitude and seemed to reflect it in their actions and how they approached their jobs. Feeling that this reality must be inaccurate, the author started by examining unit structure and reporting/notification requirements. The unit lacked structure, having been formed relatively recently and undergone the unstable experience of being moved from one department to the next as it did not seem to fit anywhere properly. As the section was now placed under the Facilities umbrella, the author began strengthening roles and reporting relationships and the tight relationship of Security and Facilities began to take hold. The old paper reporting system for incidents was analyzed to determine what was being reported and what was actually happening on a daily basis. This was accomplished by examining the radio log activity through which incidents were being dispatched and what was actually winding up as written incidents in the occurrence book. A large gap was discovered whereby, at year's end, the security unit was only reporting on average 350–375 incidents per year, or just about one incident per day, which suggested that not much was going on in security. An incident analysis and research was then initiated over several weeks to determine what constituted an incident in the minds of the employees, how they were submitting reports, and what type of occurrence they felt required management or executive notification. From this effort, the author was able to redefine how an incident should be defined and new incident types were listed using categories such as mechanical failure, fire alarms, medical incidents, theft, and trespassing among many others. Many of these actual incident types were not previously considered to be incidents for reporting or notification purposes, although security officers were consistently providing first-response services. Along with the nonreporting of incidents went a lack of executive notification, as there appeared to be little of interest deemed important enough by the employees and first-level supervision to send up the chain of command. Therefore, the inevitable development over time throughout the organization was a highly inaccurate reputation of "not much happens in Security" and that the building and grounds were very quiet.

Unfortunately the security operations budget also reflected the reputation of nothing happening in security, as did the attention given to the unit's needs and importance. The ongoing result had been fewer resources, no operating budget for security, and poor unit morale, reflecting the organization's disinterest in an entity that appeared to provide little service and even less value.

The author was quite dismayed by his own realization over his first several weeks on the job that his security unit was actually far more active than believed by the organization, and that personnel suffered from poor morale as a result. The author also was cognizant that the future of his unit depended on changing this attitude, not only from within his group of security officers, but through the rest of the organization in order to successfully compete with every other business unit for increasingly scarce financial resources. It was also a serious matter of unit morale and pride to reflect the range of tasks that the security officers were actually performing and identifying the value of services being provided to the organization and then to be able to identify training and budgetary needs based on actual incident response and service provision. To effect those changes, the author had to examine the dispatch log records to see how, why, and to what incidents the officers were responding. It was discovered that many of the dispatched incidents and calls for service were not being recorded as incidents when the information most certainly should have been captured for accountability reasons and to protect against complaint and liability. The author then retrained his security supervisors in how they identified incidents, how they categorized them, and how they physically responded to an incident or dispatched other security officers. This included the report writing and notification requirements.

The supervisors were given a list of incident types that more accurately reflected what they were doing and contained the following:

- Alarms: by type (fire, intrusion, deployed intrusion, smoke, heat, appliance or mechanical). Were they actual alarms causing response or false signals that could represent a different problem from a system perspective?

- Protests: any persons appearing at the facility with a reason and/ or intent to protest, including those that actually performed an act of protest. This included labor disruptions from the unions as well as individual protesters.
- Trespass: any person or incident where an unauthorized person has accessed or attempted to access a secure (nonpublic) area in the complex or appeared imminently about to attempt a trespass. There were numerous trespass incidents over the years with intoxicated people attempting entry past the secure gates or being found inside the secured compound.
- Liquor License Act: any offense pertaining to the liquor possession laws of the province such as having an open container in public.
- Motor vehicle collision: where vehicles have collided in the parking lots with other vehicles, assets, or physical sedentary features. This information had never been captured before but with over 1600 parking spaces in three separate vehicle lots, collisions were routinely happening, and security officers were responding.
- Suspicious person/vehicle: any person or vehicle on or near the properties that appeared not to have specific purpose connected to the facility and/or simply appeared to be behaving beyond being a passer-by. The nature of the building attracted this sort of activity from criminals and the potential for terrorists was there.
- Suspicious packages: as a routine, suspicious packages were being identified in the public areas and specifically in the mail room/ loading dock coming as deliveries, but a specific handling procedure was lacking and there was no consistency in how these incidents were being addressed. These incidents were usually being handled by local work units and frighteningly mishandled as potential explosive or chemical compounds. None of these were being reported and they were simply unknown to upper executive elements.
- Major events: anytime that a business unit or individual sponsored outside events with large attendance and an influx of vehicles that required advanced planning. These events required operational plans to ensure that the massed movement of people and vehicles was not causing the blockage of operational vehicles coming and going or established fire routes, or violating fire code occupancy requirements inside the buildings. Also critical was the effort to work out extraordinary incident response protocols, not only with the security officers but also with local law enforcement, the fire department, and health responders/hospitals.

Planning for what could happen became a necessity as public use of the facility increased.

- Medical response: in a building holding close to 2000 people per business day, there were periodic medical distress incidents requiring first aid response from security officers and/or ambulance response. Examples included heart attacks, persons fainting, training injuries, or people slipping on ice in the parking lot, among others. A variety of calls were occurring on a scale of what one might expect in a community approximating the size of a small town.
- Security breach: any incident where a security measure had been defeated either by an employee or a visitor requiring investigation and reparation. These were happening with surprising regularity and could include anything from a trespass incident to a visitor bypassing a reception area and being located inside a secured work area.
- Suspicious vehicles/persons: any incident where the intent of a person becomes unclear and suspicious in nature, or where a vehicle has stopped near or on the grounds, again with either an identified activity that may threaten the facility, assets or persons therein, or a vehicle with no clear agenda. Examples include a vehicle parking in proximity to the facility for unknown reasons and a person appearing with a recording device. In such an instance, given the era of terrorist threats in the post-9/11 era, these types of incidents must be investigated with the capture of descriptions, license numbers, and even the identification of the individuals involved. Often these protocols should involve a multiagency response through established and cooperative procedures where detection has occurred by building security, which would then call police for their investigative ability and to spread the observation through zone broadcasts and, if necessary, to obtain the involvement of federal investigative agencies.
- Security escorts: where a security officer has been asked by a security-cleared employee to escort a visitor into the facility for a specific purpose or meeting or for maintenance repairs and contractor work.
- 911 calls: The author was dismayed to find that, on an ongoing basis, the security staff would watch an ambulance pull up to the front door; the paramedic would ask the security officer, "Where are we going?" only for the security officer to reply, "I don't know what is going on." This was quickly rectified with a new building policy where any call of a 911 nature had to be made to the

security unit main desk, where security would place the 911 call and coordinate response. This policy allowed security officers to make an emergency first aid response to the victim, while other security staff could position themselves to receive an ambulance, fire truck, or police car and efficiently escort the responders to the correct location, saving valuable time and much frustration.

- Diesel transfer tests: monthly testing of the emergency diesel generators that provide backup power to the hydropower grid required the physical assistance of security officers through fire annunciation panel announcements. Previously, the UPS generators and fuel supply had lacked maintenance for years and were found unusable. This was rectified with new fuel, engine maintenance, and monthly testing procedures.
- Noise complaints: with a educational institution on site with a dormitory, all kinds of incidents were occurring requiring dispatch of security officers; however, few of these were being identified through the incident reporting system and they went unreported to the educational managers.
- Many other incident types were included as well, such as thefts, key calls, unsecured premises (being a secured facility), facility damage, elevator failures/strandings, employee escorts, and on and on…

Having identified these categories of incidents that were happening routinely, it was a matter of getting the supervisors to capture the information, assigning an incident number on the incident log register, and then ensuring that security officers compiled their own properly completed notes while completing an incident report at the conclusion of the incident. Both the security officers and supervisors required training to recognize the incident types and to realize that they formed part of the reporting and notification process in order to properly address the issue at hand.

NEW DEFINITION OF REPORTABLE INCIDENT

The main change in **definition** of a reportable incident shifted from unstructured guesswork to

> any action performed by a security employee as a first response, any client originated service requests, or any action performed toward securing the site.

This new definition formalized the collection of information and became an instant risk reducer for the organization, which was now capturing all volatile and site-relevant incidents consistently as a matter of policy; this provides a formal record to examine if a complaint is laid or an action at the premises has been challenged. Parallel to this increased incident awareness for security personnel was to communicate the same issue to the general population of the facility to encourage people to report what they should be reporting for proper response, such as suspicious packages, trespass incidents, or even medical assists. As an example of how the population was hindering the ability of the security unit to perform its core duties, there were many security breaches occurring within the facility, perpetrated by the employees themselves either for convenience or simply for the challenge and the amusement of employees. This had to stop and be subject to incident response from a security officer. Employees had been caught

- Propping outside doors open for smoke breaks
- Slipping access cards under main doors to allow friends to enter unscreened
- Taping door hardware open and defeating secure locks
- Two people attempting to enter through a pod turnstile at the same time! They managed to jam the door and had to be extricated from the pod by security

It was time for these professional employees to start taking things more seriously.

The interesting part of this paradigm shift of incident recognition and reporting for the security personnel was that the totals of their incidents reported soared from approximately 350 incidents per year, or about one per day, to over 1700 incidents per year, or close to five incidents per day, not including regular patrols and daily locking/unlocking schedules. The surge in recorded business included suspicious person and package incidents, motor vehicle collisions in the parking lots, medical responses in the building, and many more that were happening every week. Anyone challenging this sudden surge in business simply had to look at what was being recorded to be instantly satisfied that, yes, the security unit was actually almost five times busier in a single day than had been previously thought. The author put this information to work through business cases and proposals to improve funding and equipment purchases, as evidently the security unit was doing far more than simply locking and unlocking doors as had been the unit's previous reputation. This simple revelation actually opened many doors with time that led to upgraded closed circuit television, an x-ray machine for the loading dock, and other equipment improvements. Also, executives began to take the security discipline more seriously by investing money into training for the employees, which included basic training of 40 hours that featured legislated arrest powers and how to deal with volatile persons, as well as specialist training such as locksmithing skills and more, including electronic access control, x-ray operations, automatic external defibrillator operations, and others.

HOW TO MAKE AN INCIDENT REPORT

Incident reporting beyond the recognized categories of incidents requires a consistent approach in order to compile critical information that will support further investigation, for complaint and litigation protection, for the storage and future reference of information for audit purposes, and to maintain an accurate history of the property.

A facility manager should either select a preprepared incident reporting form or design a tailored form to his or her specifications. The incident reporting form should contain the following items for consistency and historical reference:

- **Name** or identifier of the facility and/or entity
- **Date and time** of the start of the incident
- **Specific location** of the incident, including physical address (not mailing address), building numbers, and telephone numbers as applicable
- **Identification** of people involved, including victims, suspects, first responders, witnesses, accountable managers and employees, or anyone that has relevance to the incident, including addresses, phone numbers, dates of birth, license plate numbers and vehicle information, insurance company information, company affiliations and anything that might help in the future, as well as the name and contact information of the person completing the report
- **Name of agencies** called for response such as which police service, what fire department and ambulance service among others and their contact names and numbers

- **Description of the incident** as a detailed narrative of what happened in chronological order that contains the five Ws—who, what, when, where, why—also including how; any updates to be included after the incident is concluded, including results of what happened
- **Conditions:** whether the incident happened inside or outside (if outside, include weather conditions and lighting)
- **Injuries:** to whom and where the person was located or was taken for treatment by naming the hospital or clinic, and, if first aid or CPR was performed, by whom
- **Damage** descriptions and cost estimates

The incident report is in addition to any personal notes compiled by a facility manager and/or investigator of an incident. Consistency is important in these reports and they should be compiled on an official form so that the information is taken and referenced in a consistent manner that will become second nature to facility managers, technicians, and any security staff employed at a site. Such incident reporting forms also look professional, greatly assist first-response agencies, and are very useful to insurance companies when claims are being made.

A facility manager implementing an incident reporting form should provide specific instruction to the employees or contracted personnel as to expectations and include reasons for using it as instructed so that they understand what is expected. Otherwise, the facility manager may be shocked and disappointed in the results when the forms are handed in incomplete and poorly written. Incomplete forms will cause more work for the facility manager and the possibility always exists that the information will not be available in time after the incident, which could be a critical point in a prosecution or litigation case.

With a formal reporting form, the facility manager must organize the reports with a legend and a method of storage. If he or she uses a paper file system, each incident in the year 2015 could be numbered, for example, 2015-001, 2015-002, 2015-003, and so on. If it is done on computer, then a file should be named for incidents in the year—for example, 2015, and the incidents numbered as they come in the same manner. Managers can use whatever structure suits their needs but it should be organized in a chronological fashion with the year so that over the years, investigators or researchers can refer back and everything can be stored in an organized manner.

In conclusion, it is important for a facility manager to remain organized and to maintain formal filing of work and incidents. Anything can be part of the file system—for example, not only incidents but also mechanical calls, projects, business cases, employee attendance, and performance management and evaluations. A little organization in the facility manager's office provides reliability, historical context, and protection against complaints and litigation; it provides the data from which analysis can be performed to determine what is going on and what types of measures should be taken in the facility.

MAKING PROPOSALS TO UPGRADE FACILITIES AND SECURITY

In the world of maintenance and security, most often the only way to effect change is to propose it through a business case to the executive level. Being in constant competition with other higher profile entities of course means that the business case had better be very good, well timed, supported by at least one executive sponsor, and thoroughly researched and developed. It is very easy for executives sitting around a meeting table to dismiss a proposal as too costly or unnecessary or even of less priority than something from the core business of the entity. That makes it essential to point out what is going wrong as being critical or embarrassing to the entity and as something that needs immediate attention to address by approving the resources being sought.

To start, the proposal must have the support of the immediate manager and executive to even enter into using the time and local resources to formulate a proposal. Secondly, the problem must be outlined in detail and explanations provided as to what went right and what went wrong that requires change and new resources. The example to be used in this case will be the post-9/11 acquisition of an x-ray machine for the loading dock of a facility of critical importance.

For five years since the facility of critical importance had opened, mail had passed freely from delivery services and the post office through the front door and the loading dock of the facility. Once inside the building, unscreened mail was delivered to every floor and every level of employee from reception clerks right up to the executives running the organization. Every now and then, security was being called to investigate what appeared to be or actually was a suspicious package that had already been delivered to its intended recipient. Some deliveries were gibberish sent by various mentally ill and/or disgruntled persons, while others were threatening in tone, which was a little disconcerting as this was the post-9/11 period when envelopes containing white powder that was thought to be anthrax were being delivered to government agencies and politicians as a method of intimidation.

The timing seemed right for a basic screening device that most other similar facilities were using already. The security manager was able to convince the executive through whom he reported to support the project and the research began. The research consisted of compiling statistics from the building of how many suspicious packages were being delivered and the disruption they were causing when the packages could conceivably be stopped right at the back door with screening equipment and some policies. Comparable facilities were then described and how they were dealing with suspicious package deliveries and the equipment being used to screen them. Support was sought from the maintenance department, local police, and fire services and a potential policy was developed and vetted through these same groups. Research was done on potential technology and specific items that could be used, including the cost and whether clerk-level employees and maintenance and security personnel could be trained to effectively use the equipment with the support of maintenance and security. Facilities management was consulted, as was business and financial services, to determine the procurement rules to follow in preparing a request for purchase and getting a competitive procurement prepared to follow rules about using fair, competitive procurement processes to acquire new purchases of big-ticket items. The price of the x-ray machine was over $100,000 plus ongoing maintenance and service costs.

The proposal was completed by compiling the research and building a highly descriptive rationale for the facility in catching up to other similar facilities. Also of importance was improving the relationship with other first-response agencies as the ongoing costly and time-consuming response efforts of these various agencies could be reduced in frequency with the use of an x-ray machine to identify the suspicious nature of a package as it entered the loading dock. When a package could still not be cleared for delivery, it was contained right there on the loading dock, disrupting no one else and allowing first-responders easy and quick access for investigation. The proposal made complete sense and was tied in contextually with a current facility trend and potential saving of money and time. The proposal was approved at the executive level, an x-ray machine was acquired and installed, employees were trained in operation and basic maintenance, and the technology was put into service about three months later. New procedures were developed for screeners to recognize what would be deemed suspicious under the policy; then security was called as the first responder and a supervisor was to come to the loading dock. The security officer would then examine the image as a second set of eyes to help determine the next steps.

Many items were screened out in this manner, including electronic devices sent in for replacement or repair but improperly packaged and addressed, a *soiled diaper* addressed to an executive, and many other threatening pieces of mail. Such items were now being isolated in the loading dock for investigation without disrupting work areas throughout the building. One could imagine the disruption of an executive office if a soiled diaper sent by a disgruntled person was delivered to the desk of an executive. Such is the skill level that employees pick up as they gain experience and are able to distinguish biological from nonbiological material and to ascertain what an item with wires protruding actually was, knowing it was correctly destined for repair in the building as opposed to being a potentially explosive device.

Not every business case needs to be as detailed and time consuming as the acquisition of an x-ray machine—particularly lower priced equipment and supplies that have a lower level approval requirement, where a simple written business case could be approved by a unit level manager with a budget code. The main components of success in writing a business case are

- Identification of the issue and need for change
- Timeliness and context
- Timelines
- Comparables
- Support from within
- The experience of comparable facilities
- Good logic backed by solid research
- Showing the benefits and saving of money
- Acquisition strategy
- Implementation strategy
- Policy implications/new policy required

If the business case author can achieve these components, the business case has a good chance of success in any organization.

THE PROPOSAL: GETTING BUY-IN FROM THE OWNER

Preparing a proposal to purchase security hardware and equipment is not only the actual request for the financial resources to purchase expensive items and the selling of a security philosophy to executives, but it is also often an employee's shot at gaining recognition for administrative skill sets, teamwork, leadership, and budgeting. At stake as well is the reputation of the proposer, who had better have done a lot of research and answered as many questions as possible before the questions are asked by executives. Such questions from an audience can actually derail a proposal if the author did not use due diligence in researching and preparing his or her topic. This discussion of creating a proposal is made under the assumption that the reader does not have access to corporate resources such as a project management team to put together these types of proposals. It is meant as a guide for those facility managers that have to do the work themselves, without the experience of having done it before.

Research and knowledge of the topic are therefore the first item that a project proposer must take on with passion and enthusiasm—knowing what options are available, the different companies that make similar equipment, what the costs are, and why you have decided to recommend a certain direction using certain suppliers. Putting together a *pros and cons* list is a good way to examine options so that the best option can be selected and the less desirable options eliminated. Using such an exercise will force the proposer to look at details and compare the equipment and computer applications to the situation at hand, including existing systems and computer applications.

A point should be made clear about using money and cost as a decision point in selecting security hardware, software, and equipment. Any final decision should never be made based on cost alone as there are many times where it may be better to choose a more expensive option to get better equipment that will last longer. Cost over time should be considered, of course, as entities have budgets within which to fit their purchases; however, project managers must bear in mind that a more expensive system up front might actually save considerable money down the road and last longer than a "budget" system. Project managers can never lose sight of what they are trying to achieve, even with small budgets and costs factored in. It is essential to reach the goal of increased security at the end of the day. If budgets are being stretched, then perhaps a phased-in approach over time might achieve the goal of using better equipment while fitting in with scarce budget money.

Every piece of new equipment, hardware, or software must be compatible for a new installation to work smoothly and it is incumbent upon the proposer to ensure that all questions of compatibility have been put to rest before the questions are asked and, in particular, before the formal proposal is made. Compatibility should be one of the first questions asked of vendors that are seeking your contract. Beware of a salesperson that says, "but we will make it work." New equipment must be proven up front to be compatible with existing security equipment and computers, and to work without becoming a Band-Aid solution, as patchwork with security systems usually does not solve the problem and can result in malfunctions and higher costs over time. Always consider as well that as fast as technology is manufactured and then quickly installed, it is already outdated by the time it starts being used. Technological advancements continue to accelerate and it is never a good idea to purchase an older or dated system simply to save money. The system selected should be easily updated or upgradable as new technology becomes available. Good suppliers will often write into the contract that they will supply updates and upgrades either free of charge or under an agreed schedule and appropriate costs.

An example of what can go wrong occurred about ten years ago in a large facility security unit that was using an older fire annunciation panel that had been altered to combine the facility electronic security requirements. It was essentially patched together as security/fire panel and run through an old 486 personal computer that was programmed through floppy discs from the mid-1990s. As this system eventually began deteriorating and malfunctioning with increased regularity, there was one final episode where the 486 computer (not of Pentium technology) had ceased to work. When the alarm technicians arrived to reprogram the system, the technician reached behind the computer and set the building off in a full evacuation signal, requiring the evacuation of two thousand people midmorning of a business day. It was later determined that they could not reload the programming as one of the twelve floppy discs used to reprogram the computer was evidently corrupted. Finally, Facilities and Maintenance were required to install a new Pentium computer to operate the system. Over time, this new computer functioned much better and with much improved reliability so that building-wide evacuation alarms trickled down in regularity to almost none and to the point where the building population could return to using annual evacuation drills, since there no longer were false alarms causing evacuation of the building.

Along with the new Pentium computer, a new panel was installed with up-to-date technology, but the whole experience resulted in a week

125

of extra cost and some disrupted operations in the building as fire watches had to be initiated for twelve subpanels, 24/7, to keep the building operating while repairs were made. One silver lining to the deteriorating 486 computer-driven system was that security staff in the building had become very skilled at leading evacuations and the building population had become accustomed to the procedures, while the local fire department became quite familiar with the building in a positive manner for future evacuation requirements. These experiences in system deterioration and regular evacuation signals demonstrated that practice really does increase skill level in your security and facilities staff, as well as within the building population. If it is not in law in some jurisdictions, facility managers should adopt evacuation drills anyway as an annual or semi-annual function because, in the security world, *weird things happen when you least expect them* and it is always preferable to be ready.

WEIRD THINGS HAPPEN WHEN YOU LEAST EXPECT THEM...

To back up the statement that *weird things happen when you least expect them*, the following example serves as a reminder of the various kinds of unexpected incidents that can occur just when one thinks everything is quiet and *nothing is going to happen*.

Following a busy week and a routine Friday on a beautiful summer evening, everyone had gone home for the weekend at a large facility of critical importance. At this time, even the maintenance personnel were going home on weekends, with no staff on hand as a money-saving effort in times of tough budgets. The only people on hand were a skeleton staff of security officers, one sitting in the control room handling the access control system, alarms, closed circuit television, and dispatch of the lone security patrol officer who did the rounds checking doors and visiting the outbuildings, including a dormitory, a heliport that was used by police and air ambulance, and other facilities. The security manager had gone home feeling good that at last the weekend had come and things should be quiet now at the facility. As dinnertime rolled around, the security manager received a frantic call from the security control room advising that *the heliport fire-dousing foam retardant had dumped in the heliport and there was a helicopter inside the building; also, foam was running down the ditch along the main road.*

This was a unique problem that no one had ever thought possible or a scenario that anyone had even imagined could occur at all. Suddenly there was a multimillion dollar machine inside a garage being dumped upon by chemical retardant and all of the maintenance and most of the security employees had gone home for the weekend. The security manager had to think quickly of what to do with no resources on hand. The order to call a helicopter pilot and get maintenance on the scene as soon as possible was given, but as maintenance personnel were not on call, there was a 1-800 number to a central dispatch center 400 miles away in another jurisdiction that would call someone in good time, as was the past experience. The security manager then opened his book of emergency numbers and directly called the maintenance manager, with whom he had developed a good relationship. The maintenance manager advised that he was on his way and would get more help, but that it was essential to get the helicopter out of the bay immediately.

As good fortune would have it, the pilot was miraculously still in the heliport in the office and once he realized what was going on, he opened the bay doors and pulled the helicopter out of the garage and away from the foam. It was done before security and, later, maintenance arrived on the scene. It was determined by the maintenance manager that the foam was not poisonous and would disintegrate quickly but that the helicopter would likely need a thorough cleaning and mechanical checks to ensure no damage had occurred to the engine or any moving parts. The investigation continued the next day and it was determined that a malfunctioning switch caused the foam to dump without fault to anyone. It was going to cost over $100,000 to refill the foam tanks and maintenance was going to have to repair the malfunction.

Lessons learned from this incident were that staffing of security was too low, that another patrol officer, as a minimum, needed to be added, and that having a maintenance employee on site, or at least on call, was necessary in the future. Informal arrangements were confirmed between the security manager and maintenance manager to ensure that the slow paging system of the parent maintenance company could be bypassed and someone put on site quickly if not there to begin with already. This was one incident requiring a combined effort of security and maintenance and it was apparent that there were systems and potential problems that the units were not even contemplating. This was part of a rationale to have the fire evacuation system revisited and to ensure procedures were in place for unexpected incidents.

IMPLEMENTATION OF THE SUCCESSFUL PROPOSAL

The implementation of the proposal will have been organized and approved by executives as part of the proposal plan. Implementation most often costs money and time that should already have been earmarked and become part of both the financial and time budgets. Implementation requires the cooperation and participation of any person or business unit that is impacted by the proposed hardware or the new policies designed to make it work.

The proposer must be diplomatic in approach and be sensitive to the chain of command before engaging workers in another work unit. To begin working with these people, the proposer should have cleared it with his or her management first, which most often will produce a high level of cooperation and participation. That makes the task much easier when the dots connect outside the proposer's work unit.

When implementing successful proposals, previous equipment or policies or whatever the nature of the proposal must be kept operational until the new equipment, policies, or procedures are ready to go live and have been tested for operational reliability. Shutting down old equipment or changing policies and procedures before the proposed changes are ready or have been tested can cause gaps in production or operations that can be both embarrassing and costly to the organization. The proposer will likely be held accountable for any gaps in service provision and it is just not worth it not to be well organized with good planning.

11

Maintenance

FACILITY MAINTENANCE

Looking after facilities and the grounds connected to them is big business and a large part of managing facilities. Whether maintenance employees are directly employed by the owner/operator or maintenance is conducted by contractors and subcontractors, maintenance is a balancing act between the ongoing but essential cost of doing business and expenditure decisions to replace worn-out fixtures and equipment or simply to improve efficiencies in the effort to reduce the ongoing cost of doing business.

By the time a building project is completed and occupants begin using the facilities, most often the technologies inside are already obsolete and less than efficient. As soon as the buildings open, they begin to age and require ongoing maintenance and care to lengthen the service life of most equipment and fixtures. Failure to keep up with these requirements often leads to unexpected equipment malfunctions and structural problems that can multiply the ongoing costs. Cutting budgets and trying to save money in maintenance is never a good idea as cuts to budgets most often lead to service cuts and maintenance Band-Aid solutions, rather than making long-lasting repairs or replacing fixtures and equipment that really should be replaced. Real cost can also accumulate through extending the life of aging hardware rather than spending more money up front and purchasing new hardware that would actually function more efficiently. The balancing act is in finding the right time to replace hardware efficiently to reduce overall and ongoing costs, despite the up-front cost of the replacement item. Missing that optimal replacement time will lead to overall higher costs in keeping obsolete equipment functioning past its point of efficiency. It can also lead to structural failure when hardware and structural surfaces are pushed past their point of integrity in an effort to save up front on budgets. The facility manager must become proficient at producing solid and well written business cases to convince those executives holding the purse strings to make the hardware purchases at the right time. Maintaining the structural integrity of a building is critical in maintaining security and safety, as water always finds the path of least resistance and leakage will cause havoc in your facility by short circuiting electronics and causing structures to shift, mold to grow, and wood to change shape or disintegrate.

Experience shows that the smallest leak can cause major expenditures and disruption of a major facility containing several thousand people.

In the middle of a summer rainstorm, an evacuation tone sounded in a facility of critical importance and forced the shutdown of operations as all employees were required to evacuate. Not only did several thousand employees, including executives, get wet in a sudden downpour, but business was also disrupted for a period of two hours until the alarm was checked by the fire department and alarm company, and traced to a fire pull station on the main floor of the four-story building. It turned out that a trickle of water had come through the roof, four stories up and found its way down through the floors along a steel support beam that continued on into the basement. The trickle of water encountered the fire pull station on the main floor, shorting out the electrical supply and causing the alarm system to believe the fire pull had been activated, throwing the two-stage alarm system into instant full evacuation. Following the two-hour disruption to the work day, maintenance employees then had to find the source of the leak on the roof and have the section retarred to close the leak.

This was an easily avoidable maintenance issue that wound up costing over two hours of productivity and engaged emergency services (police and fire department) unnecessarily; it also forced costly emergency repairs when simple low-cost regular maintenance might have avoided the situation altogether. More importantly, full evacuations that are not drills cause unnecessary risk to building populations where injury and perhaps death are possible during actual evacuation events.

Mobility-challenged people are particularly at risk as other occupants try to help them escape and where many facilities just have not practiced evacuations enough or planned for special-needs employees. Was the maintenance contractor trying to shave money off the ongoing budget by either skipping or prolonging a maintenance schedule, and is that why the roof was suddenly springing leaks? These are the questions that building management would be asking after a costly event such as an unplanned evacuation. This example demonstrates how a little prevention through strict maintenance schedules and avoidance of the temptation to find savings by perhaps altering a maintenance procedure can save money in the long run. Spending money at the right time achieves the balance of efficient maintenance and avoidance of structural failure, saving money in the long run.

MECHANICAL MAINTENANCE

According to RECO: Principles of Property Management [1], mechanical maintenance involves the following:

- **Heating systems** consisting of boilers, vacuum and circulating pumps, hot water heaters, sump pumps, compressors, heat exchangers, and water softeners
- **Cooling systems** consisting of water chillers, cooling towers, fans, and refrigeration units
- **Electrical and electronic systems** consisting of breaker panels, transformers, lighting systems, emergency lighting systems, energy conservation systems, thermostats, aquastats, and other gauges and controls
- **Mechanical systems** mainly consisting of elevators/escalators, uninterrupted power supply generators, garbage compacters
- **Fire detection and evacuation systems**, starting with the fire annunciation panel, subfire panels, smoke and heat detectors, pull stations, alarm units, pressurized water sprinkler systems and foam systems, halon and other extinguishing systems, and magnetic locks
- **Security systems** consisting of electronic access control, closed circuit television cameras, monitors and recording devices, motion detectors, infrared and vibration detection, communication systems

Heating, ventilation, and air conditioning (HVAC) and the equipment required to keep it in optimal working order comprise the first two categories of heating and cooling systems. HVAC in a large facility is a complicated system of boilers, fuel supplies, water pipes and drainage pipes, industrial chillers, and the ventilation system that connects every space in the facility to the source of service coming into the building and to exhaust vents going out of the building. Timely and scheduled maintenance of HVAC is a critical component of the responsibilities of the maintenance manager. Failure to maintain any of these systems can cause failure and loss of service and equipment or hardware failure that may force a facility evacuation or failure to maintain cleanliness that can cause the spread of illness through unclean ventilation hardware throughout the facility. Properly maintained HVAC contributes to a positive and healthy environment in facilities; this is a major responsibility of a maintenance manager.

Relating to HVAC, most large facilities contain CO_2 refrigerants for the industrial chillers; they also have detectors but, according to Jason D. Reid of Life Safety Systems, only about 5% of facilities have emergency procedures to deal with issues. This could result in significant problems in a facility when leaks occur and no one knows what to do as facilities management did not ensure that all safety systems had correlating emergency procedures or that employees were trained in how to use existing emergency procedures (Figure 11.1).

Too Hot or Too Cold?

Another aspect of HVAC and mechanical maintenance in a large facility is the phenomenon of growth in a corporate entity. When companies or government experience growth and begin expanding departments, they inevitably experience personnel crowding and lack of space as corporate planning often complicates office space issues. This impacts the workplace as corporate or government managers begin inserting workstations into common areas and atriums, and they start subdividing larger offices and boardrooms to accommodate more staff, which is cheaper and more convenient than acquiring another floor in an office tower or another building. These renovations often occur without the consultation or inclusion of the maintenance department in the planning stages, preventing the important input of the maintenance engineers and experienced HVAC technicians. A frustrating and long-lasting result of this dysfunction occurs after the money has been spent and renovations completed, when employees begin complaining about being too cold or too hot, depending on where they

Figure 11.1 The CO_2 refrigerant detector to the left will detect leaks and send out both audible and visual alarms. Emergency planning must correlate directly to the equipment at hand so that people know what to do and who to call when alarms sound and lights go off such as the one in the photo. (Used with the permission of Jason D. Reid.)

are located in the section. This extremely common complaint is a result of the renovations, where planners failed to take into account the setup of the HVAC above their heads in the ceiling tiles, or they simply sacrificed the task to save money. Regardless, as the planners do not see the HVAC, they may not think to include it in the renovation planning.

The HVAC vents in the ceilings of most buildings have been designed to the specifications of the original office setup. To be specific, air intakes and heating vents have been set during the construction phase to access and feed the office spaces specified in the blueprint drawings. This allows for a consistent environment controlled from one point in the area according to the square footage, among other considerations.

When managers begin renovating and subdividing spaces, if they have not planned to move or install additional air intakes and air conditioning and heating vents into the new spaces, the result is that smaller subdivided spaces still serviced by the same HVAC vents and intakes that were designed for the larger original spaces get a very cold effect in the summer, as air conditioning is piped in, and a warm effect in the winter, as heat is vented in; other offices become either cold or warm and stale because there is no HVAC service at all anymore as the vents and intakes are on the other side of the newly installed wall. People assigned to these uncomfortable spaces begin complaining to the maintenance department about being too cold or too warm and ask them to adjust the thermostat, which in turn has the workers circulating through the building adjusting thermostats with poor results because the HVAC system is now out of whack and not functioning efficiently as designed. Soon enough, workers begin taking matters into their own hands by purchasing personal fans and heaters that they plug into local power outlets, thus increasing the use of power, which so often is paid for with the business unit's budget. Walking through a large, open work area can be hazardous, with fans and heaters plugged in at every workstation. In some locations, this may also raise the risk of fire as workers begin using power bars and other items to extend the accessibility of hydropower at their workstations. The following anecdote actually happened in a large facility but in a reverse fashion to subdividing rooms.

As a security department expanded to include a new processing counter and an extra employee for the processing of access control cards and clearances, the only solution to accommodate both was to create a larger common space by removing a wall to make a larger space and sacrificing a hallway that led to three supervisor/manager offices. At the rear of the space, a new small boardroom was created where there had been none and generally made the office setup more efficient. Soon after operations resumed following the renovations, employees began to complain of being too cold or too hot. It was comical in the fact that one employee sitting by a desk on the south side was too cold, while another employee on the north side of the same space was too hot. It was all a result of the fact that no one had investigated the placement of the HVAC feeds and vents before the renovation started. Also not taken into account was how often the front door to the main hallway was open for business, creating even more pressure on the underserviced HVAC supply to that office. Complaints about the situation to Facilities Management were answered with, "It should have been done before the renovation started as part of the engineering stage." The project manager replied that it was not in the contract. The lesson learned here is for the managers involved and particularly the facility manager to anticipate this issue and address it before it becomes a problem.

Too hot or too cold is a complex situation that is too late to fix in a cost-effective manner once the renovations have already been completed, and it would be exorbitantly expensive to go back and redesign the HVAC feeds and venting after the walls have been physically changed. The lesson learned in this example is to always check behind the ceiling tiles for HVAC when considering any kinds of renovations and to include an HVAC consultation in the planning stage before it is too late.

FENCING

Fencing is commonly used for large stand-alone facilities to announce the facility boundaries and to keep unauthorized people away from workers and assets. There is usually a mistaken belief that fencing will keep undesirable people out of an area, so it must always be explained that fencing really is a visual deterrent that reinforces a claim over space for trespass purposes. *Fencing does not stop people.* It may slow them down, but even the taller fences with barbed wire can be scaled or cut through very quickly by a determined trespasser. Fencing must be used as part of a layered security system for maximum effectiveness. These layers can include motion detection, closed circuit television, vibration detection on the fences, and infrared sensors to sound an alarm when people climb the fence, as well as having responding security staff provide the protection being sought when people consider fencing as a protection. Fencing on its own is simply a visual statement of claim on the space that most people will respect, but persons of ill intent will not. A fence with *No Trespassing* signage prominently displayed will, in most jurisdictions, be sufficient in the courts for the conviction of people under trespass to property legislation.

MAINTENANCE STAFF: CERTIFICATION AND TRAINING

Maintenance workers have become a critical part of the facility management effort in large buildings, and advances in technology and complications in design require professional maintenance staff. Accordingly, maintenance personnel require extensive training and should have recognized certifications to do the tasks assigned in running a building. It is no longer acceptable to hire a "jack of all trades" who can muddle through with Band-Aid solutions. Maintenance staff must be certified and large facilities require professional and certified plumbers, electricians, HVAC specialists, fire system technicians, security system specialists, trained locksmiths, hazardous goods specialists trained to handle chemicals, and others, depending on the functions and requirements of specialized facilities.

Operating specialized equipment should only be done by persons certified in that particular field or function. It is not acceptable, for example, to ask the night shift security guard to close a gas valve or deactivate an electrical panel in the effort to avoid overtime costs for the callout of a system specialist. If an incident were to occur where a person was injured or killed as a result of a gas explosion or electrical fire and it was discovered that a security guard, rather than a certified technician, operated the gas valve or electrical panel, there would be significant accountability assigned to those involved—especially to the manager that allowed or ordered it to occur.

Certification and training produce a professional and skilled workforce that have pride in what they do, as well as accountability. Such staff are highly valued and there is less turnover in hiring professionals, and the payoff is immediate in the higher quality of work in a facility. Successful facility managers will also use certification and training as part of a reward system and as motivation for employees. Offering training and certification demonstrates to employees that the manager has trust and confidence in them, which will be repaid down the road with increased loyalty and less turnover—not to mention that more highly skilled technicians will be saving money by doing the work themselves rather than management hiring subcontractors.

REFERENCE

1. RECO: Principles of Property Management. August 2014. Real Estate Council of Ontario, Media Linx Printing Group, pp. 180–181; 455.

12

The "Gap"

LIABILITY

Liability is a much discussed situation that can be the end of an organization if the corporation itself or individuals within it have been found significantly liable for an incident or accident causing loss, death, or injury. Victims of crime and accidents are increasingly seeking monetary damages from owners and managers of properties, as courts are being used to parcel out percentages of blame to account for what happened in a tragedy.

Any organization that has not done a threat and risk assessment can be held liable following a tragic incident for not following due diligence, just as an organization that has completed a review but failed to implement reasonable recommendations within a reasonable timeline can be held liable for knowing about problems and weaknesses and failing to act reasonably to repair or mitigate the issues. Following an accident or a criminal incident where injuries or death has occurred, a victim might allege that a property owner did not make the area safe enough with the implementation of adequate security measures, which in turn contributed to or facilitated the criminal incident, resulting in loss, injury, or death. The absence of reasonable security can actually be used by the victim to suggest that a crime was predictable in the absence of security measures and that the owner had an obligation to make the space safer and more secure [1].

The notion of a premises owner being responsible for the safety and security of clients or visitors, or even renters and any occupier, comes from early American case law, where there exists an assumed duty by the owner or operator to take measures to ensure the safety and security of someone in the owner's care, who otherwise cannot control his or her own safety and security by reason of being in that location. This relationship has evolved over time from no duty of a proprietor to protect to a significant duty for those inviting persons on the property, to providing for their protection. An obvious example of this notion can be seen in any hospital where the relationship between hospital staff and the patient is one of caretaker and patient. The patient is incapable of looking after himself or herself and relies on the hospital staff for safety as well as treatment. In an apartment building, persons pay the building owner rent to reside in a safe and secure place and expect safety and security to be reasonably provided. A common-law version of this explanation is provided by Gordon and Brill as a special relationship where one is taking on responsibility for the safety and security of another: "Two of the earliest special relationships were that of an innkeeper and a guest and a common carrier and its passengers" [2].

The expansion of the proprietor–client relationship from everyone being responsible for himself or herself to an expectation of the owner to provide safety and security to an occupier is a twentieth-century manifestation achieved through court decisions. This reality has created a situation ripe for the advent of physically designed spaces that can manipulate behavior and reduce the likelihood of crime. Adding this simple step into the design of a facility before it is even constructed can affordably change the safety and security of future patrons as well as protect the owner/ operator from liability.

The concept of *Crime Prevention Through Environmental Design*, described in detail elsewhere in the book, is to manipulate the surrounding area such that authorized people will feel welcomed and secure in the space, while unauthorized people or those looking for trouble will feel uncomfortable and be more likely to move on to another target from which it might be easier to profit without getting caught.

THE "GAP"

The gap is an excellent descriptor in the business of threat and risk assessment to describe the state of safety and security that the facility is in currently to where it needs to be from a practical standpoint. Safety measures generally consist of life safety systems in a building that are required by the local fire code in a municipality. These will be the fire alarm system and smoke and carbon monoxide detectors, as well as the published emergency evacuation procedures; it could also include additional systems not required by the fire code such as placement of external defibrillators and other first aid equipment. Security measures will consist of access control (electronic and manual), key control and physical locks, incident response procedures, lighting, alarms and panic devices, security procedures, closed circuit television, or even security guards if they are in place.

In the author's experience and as previously discussed, the gap is usually a major surprise for the client who often believes he or she has intimate knowledge of the building and has a firm grasp on what is happening. Managing buildings and facilities has become a necessity, growing along with the size and complexity of buildings everywhere. Historically, smaller buildings could often be run by one individual maintenance person, and most of them often were. As facilities have grown over the decades in size and variety of use, the need to revisit how facilities are managed has grown as well, along with responsibilities of owners/operators and the liabilities involved in what goes on in large facilities.

Threat and risk assessments generally became more mainstream and deemed much more important following the 9/11 terrorist attacks in New York City and Pennsylvania in September of 2001. As governments and private corporations became aware of their vulnerabilities post-9/11, the threat and risk assessment (TRA) suddenly became a very important necessity in the lives of government, facility management, and security personnel everywhere. Even the terminology can vary from location to location and corporation to government. Other terms include security review and security audit, but they generally mean the same thing. It is an effort to review the state of safety and security in a facility, gauge risk factors, and discover the gap in order to prepare recommendations to close the gap.

Defining the gap requires the establishment of a baseline of current safety and security in a facility by assessing what is going on, what measures are in place currently, what procedures are in use currently, and how incidents are handled and recorded and by whom. This is where most of the surprises for building owners/operators occur. Most facilities have some security and safety procedures in place but they have never been revised; in particular with older buildings, existing procedures are usually inadequate or outdated. This is where the first gap becomes important.

The first gap is a measurement of what a building operator/owner thinks is going on versus what is actually going on. The analysis begins with local police and fire department records of statistics from the area, actual incident or complaint reports that are on file in the building (if there are any), and interviews with building staff and occupants. Interviewees should be a cross section of occupants including maintenance personnel, receptionists, building users, and even frequent visitors if possible. What begins to emerge is a picture of what is *actually* occurring on a daily basis in and around the facility. This picture is then compared to the description given by building management to the reviewers before the process started. The gap is often found to be quite startling in scope and very different from what management thought was going on in the facility. Suddenly, the safety and security measures in place look extremely inadequate and, further, the existing measures often do not mesh with local fire code requirements. From this collection of information we can establish the main gap: where the facility is currently in terms of measures versus where it needs to be to improve safety and security, to ensure compliance with the fire code, and to reduce the risk and liability of the owner/operator.

FIRE CODE COMPLIANCE

Not being in compliance with the local fire code is an unintended but all too frequent finding during safety and security reviews, and can lead to huge liability if something were to happen and someone died as a result of a practice violating the fire code. One example of this is a well-intended security measure protecting against break and enters that actually puts lives in jeopardy.

More than once in downtown locations, the review teams discovered multiunit apartment buildings with ground-level or below ground-level living spaces that had security bars installed to keep bad people out and to protect the good people inside. The intent is obvious and generally could be deemed to be a positive measure; however, in most cases the local fire code strictly forbade this measure as it actually provided a dangerous barrier for people trying to escape the space through the window or door if a fire were to occur in the facility and egress points were blocked.

In unimproved or older buildings, this kind of measure might only be discovered after a tragic fire where the hallway or only stairwell was blocked and someone was unable to escape through the window because of a deliberately installed security system of a locked set of steel bars on the window.

Safety and security measures as a result must be installed in layers together as part of an overall safety and security plan. Police and fire department officials should be included in this planning to ensure compliance with the law and correct interpretation of fire code regulations.

The gap assessment may uncover the following issues, among others:

- **Loss of key control**: master keys have been circulated widely, lost, copied, or allowed access to by general employees. Missing keys generally means that the facility manager has lost key control, requiring an entire and expensive rekeying of the facility.
- **Unpracticed or inadequate evacuation procedures**: old procedures failed to grow in proportion to building population increases and renovations to the structural interior of the building. Failure to practice procedures would allow these changes to occur without anyone noticing; the building population may become unskilled at evacuation just when it might be needed in a real incident that occurs suddenly. The result during a real evacuation alarm is chaos and increased danger of injury and death.
- **Unauthorized access and misuse of the facility (sex and drug use in basement areas)**: security breaches of doors lead to unauthorized entry by people using the facility for their own purposes, often performing illegal activity without the knowledge of building management.
- **Ongoing thefts**: loss of control of what is occurring in the facility and failing to record and investigate theft incidents and missing equipment incidents ensures that budgets will be negatively impacted as employees will continue taking items for their own use, either within the building or in their own homes, constituting theft.
- **Unknown volume of incidents occurring**: this is as opposed to what was thought to be happening (the gap). Incorrect analysis occurs and the unit and facility gain an incorrect reputation as being a place where nothing happens, usually reflected in the resources and budget provided to security.
- **Fire code violations**: as security reviews often find, one problem has been solved at the expense of safety. The previous example of security bars securing the room, but violating the fire code and potentially trapping people attempting to evacuate during a fire event, is a perfect example of outdated measures not in compliance with current legislation. Not knowing about a fire code violation simply is no excuse when death or injury has occurred.

141

As previously explained, these gap items usually are happening without the knowledge or awareness of building owners/operators and constitute tragedy and liability just waiting to happen if something goes wrong in the facility. Any building owner/operator does not want to have the local fire chief testifying against him or her in a court case about a fire code violation that directly or even indirectly resulted in the death of an occupant. The owner/occupant will be held accountable in court if someone dies or is injured as a result of a safety or security omission.

RENOVATIONS CAN CREATE A GAP

It is critical to note that ongoing building renovations can inadvertently create gaps very easily if proper planning and consultation do not occur. As corporations grow, it is extremely expensive and time consuming to build or purchase new facilities to accommodate increased production, work, and the workforce population that goes with it. What tends to happen in corporations and, in particular, government is the attempt to use existing facilities to accommodate growth, which requires renovation of existing buildings.

When renovations begin occurring slowly at first, people do not take notice and the work is done in isolation, resulting in a bigger office area or, for example, now six offices where there used to be three. In a contained area, this may not matter much other than the previously mentioned discomfort of HVAC servicing one office but not another as a wall was put up in the middle of a previously bigger office without adjusting the HVAC.

The other issue with renovation planning projects is to update the fire evacuation planning, which must be included front and center with any major renovation project. If evacuation planning is not included and updated, the building population winds up with evacuation plans that do not match the current building plans. The result can be disastrous during an evacuation alarm, where evacuating employees turn left down a hallway because the evacuation plan directs them to access a stairwell, and they suddenly find a new wall blocking their normal exit point that another work unit had installed for its own purposes. There have also been instances where this occurred because the exit signage, mandated in the jurisdictional fire code, was still in place according to the old plan and directing the evacuating group toward a sealed wall. In a real evacuation alarm, this now panicking group of evacuees would have to retrace their steps without getting lost and caught up in an advancing fire to find another, less familiar route to exit the building. This could have a tragic ending if an actual fire event has filled the building with smoke and the evacuees get lost looking for another exit that lacks signage. **For this specific reason, facilities management of the building must be in centralized control of construction activity and be an approving body for any renovations in a facility.** Uncontrolled renovations can have disastrous if unintended consequences without facility-level consultations and analysis of fire planning, security services planning, HVAC repositioning, and policy revision to capture any differences from previous fire and security plans. The time to realize that someone forgot to update the plans to include new walls and changed exit signage is not in the middle of a serious, life-threatening incident.

Security Layers

"It is like peeling back an onion...." Building security should be planned and implemented in overlapping layers. The simple reason for this is that any single security measure can be easily defeated on its own, and once it is defeated by a person of ill intent, that person has won. The effective way to secure a facility is to strategically layer a number of security measures and/or assets so that once one measure is defeated, the person of ill intent will be thrust into another one if the activity of dealing with the first one did not activate the next one automatically. An example of layering is as follows:

A large corporate headquarters with valuable proprietary information is going to want to protect people, assets, and information, while remaining accessible to customers and business. In this scenario, while protecting itself and its interests, the corporation still must move people and their vehicles into and out of the facility without compromising security. The layering of security can begin with the prescreening of individuals so it is known who is arriving and how far into the facility he or she should be allowed, based on the results of the screening. Next would be the actual gate entry where a security guard checks identification and records the license plate, while video is taken on the closed circuit television (CCTV) system. Once visitors are parked where they have been told to park,

143

again, video would be taken of the individuals as they approach the front door. Once inside, the visitors are greeted by a reception-ist or security guard who would check photo identification again and have the visitors sign in and receive a visitor pass. The visitors would then wait until their building sponsor arrives before they are escorted inside past the building access control and alarm sys-tem. At no time should these visitors be allowed to walk about on their own. Even restroom visits should be subject to escort, leaving no opportunity for the visitors to access anything without being detected.

This strategy is effective for two reasons. The first is that all activity has been recorded several times in writing and by closed circuit televi-sion images while, during his or her time in the facility, the visitor has been escorted by a building sponsor, removing opportunity for misdeed. The second reason is that once a visitor with ill intent realizes that there is a highly organized and layered security system, he or she will seek an easier target where it is much less likely they will be detected doing anything wrong. The departed visitors will also talk about their secu-rity experience widely, improving the reputation of the organization as one that takes security seriously and has a formidable, layered system in place. Layering is as much about deterrence as it is about actual physical security, but it should be strategized so that even an insider person of ill intent will know it is likely that he or she will be detected if a misdeed is attempted.

For layering to be effective, the organizational security culture must be as strong as the policies, as it requires the dedication of each employee to take action if he or she sees something wrong, such as a person wan-dering in a secure area without authorization. It also takes employees who will not prop doors open for convenience and, if they do, are held accountable for the breach of security in a way that will encourage future compliance with the security policies. In the end the security program is only as strong as the policies, the strategy, and the employees who oper-ate within the program. This is where and how the first risk for any cor-poration or entity comes from. The easiest way to defeat security is from within, and managers need to incorporate this reality into their security planning so that they can cope if an employee violates security from within the system.

CLOSED CIRCUIT TELEVISION: STRENGTHS, WEAKNESSES, AND ADVICE

In response to security and access control issues at facilities, people often blurt out the advice, "Just get some cameras!" without realizing the full implications of what they are saying. Facility and/or security managers must therefore make educated and considered decisions in the application of CCTV. It is a wonderful technology that records moving images when activated and comes in either black and white or color options, with static (nonmoving) cameras, as well as pan–tilt–zoom, and motion or heat detection options for even more flexibility. The technological options are as wide as the potential applications and CCTV can be a great addition to the layering of security at a facility.

Experience demonstrates, however, that managers must be very careful in the selection of CCTV as part of the security layering and they must never use is it as an isolated measure, lest it actually cause more problems than it solves. The example of this issue came from general discussions in the ASIS International course, "Managing Your Physical Security Program":

CCTV has been installed on a swimming pool deck at a hotel, for example, to record pool activity and because no lifeguards are present. One must consider what the hotel manager intended with the installation versus what pool users may think upon seeing the camera when they use the pool. The manager considered damage issues from users and investigative potential in managing the pool area without the presence of employees. The manager knows that a camera that is not monitored live is of no use in supervising the pool area. However, the manager may be using the camera as a deterrent to crime and bad behavior, as well as an investigative tool.

The user, on the other hand, sees the camera and decides to use the pool thinking that *someone at the front desk* is watching and will come if there is trouble. In the unfortunate circumstance where a weak swimmer gets into physical difficulty or a violent crime occurs and the victim expects someone to come and assist, that victim may have tragically mistaken expectations as no one is likely monitoring the CCTV system that was set up for the manager's purposes mentioned earlier. Even CCTV feeds that go to a hotel lobby desk where staff are present

145

do not meet the definition of monitoring. These desk employees are busy with the administration of the hotel, booking people in and out, assisting guests, running errands, and all sorts of ongoing activities and they are not able to pay attention to a CCTV image. If that is what the manager wants, then he or she must hire employees and task them solely with watching that CCTV screen when people are present.

It is similar to false advertising as a concept where the hotel management has elected to protect themselves by installing CCTV, when in fact they have placed themselves at greater risk of liability because, as an example, someone saw the camera and went swimming, expecting help if it were needed and then tragically drowned when no one came. The court will look at such a situation and consider that the tools were present to potentially make a difference but were not being used by management when they allowed a person to use the pool. The unspoken intention may matter little. To mitigate this issue, often signage will accompany the CCTV camera that advises no lifeguards are present, there is no live monitoring of the CCTV system, and swimming is at the sole risk of the swimmer, which becomes part of the legal agreement for the pool user to access the facility, especially when published as a policy. Of course, in any application of CCTV, **legal advice must be sought** by management in consideration of the intended applications to protect against misuse and/or liability if a complaint arises or something unexpected occurs.

Facility and security managers should always be in a frame of mind where they consider not only what their needs and the needs of the facility might be, but also how the action may be viewed by building occupants, users, and guests alike and that there may be a gap between what the manager intended and what users are in essence getting as a result. The main advice is to consider seriously all points of view and get appropriate advice from suppliers/manufacturers, certified security consultants, and the legal community to ensure the right solution has been applied and that it does not cause problems or even litigation.

Closed circuit television is an amazing tool for many applications but it has to be chosen correctly and managed consistently to make it work for you and not against you.

REFERENCES

1. Gordon, Corey L. and William Brill. 1996. "The Expanding Role of Crime Prevention through Environmental Design in Premises Liability." Washington, DC: US Dept. of Justice, Office of Justice Programs, National Institute of Justice.
2. Gordon, Corey L. and William Brill. 1996. "The Expanding Role of Crime Prevention through Environmental Design in Premises Liability." Washington, DC: US Dept. of Justice, Office of Justice Programs, National Institute of Justice, p. 2.

13

Parking Issues

PARKING AT LARGE FACILITIES

Facility managers in developed nations face unique situations when it comes to the parking of vehicles around the facility. For the purpose of this chapter, we will use the example of a 1000-space parking lot to make the points.

Some parking lots at facilities are wide open, allowing anyone to park whenever they feel and wherever they wish. Without controls such as gated access, little can be done to control who parks in the lot and for how long. It also makes accountability and enforcement much more difficult without controls and having staff assigned to control the parking lot and who comes and goes. All facilities have established fire routes with signage around the facility designed to give fire trucks and other responders the ability to access the facility from any angle and to use previously installed equipment such as fire hydrants, hose attachments, and water sources installed in the walls of the facility.

Gated access is a good method of controlling who enters the parking lot (Figure 13.1). This requires a card swipe with a programmed access card authorized by a database of specific users. Those without the authorization cannot get in, which keeps the integrity of users intact and allows the facility manager peace of mind in knowing only those with an access card can get a vehicle into the lot. It also records the identity of the person entering through the gate. Combined with closed circuit television, there might also be a record of the vehicle for investigative purposes, as well as behavioral evidence.

149

Figure 13.1 A typical electronic gate with both ingress and egress lanes. This particular model has higher accountability, with aluminum arms and transponder readers instead of access card readers. This setup will record entry and exit activity for high accountability at a hospital. This is beyond what one would find for public parking or regular employee parking. (Photo by J. Henderson.)

The gates themselves are fairly simple, requiring an underground power source that usually feeds through a cement island to the gate controller. The gate controller is an electronically run mechanical device that lifts and drops the gate arms as programmed through the access control computer. The gate arms are generally made of light wood and are more of a visual deterrent than a method of keeping vehicles out. For that purpose, a wired gate made of steel or a ground-based tire shredding system that works when a driver fails to swipe an authorized access card would be required. Most facilities use light wood gates as they are much less likely to cause injury and will break off if someone inadvertently drives through one, even if on a motorcycle. When damaged, the wooden arms can be replaced easily by facilities maintenance employees. Any person damaging the wooden arms on a gate should be contacted immediately to see why they drove through and ensure they are permitted to be in the lot or, if it is a prepaid parking facility, to ensure the fee is retained and gate repaired. Facilities managers should also consider the possibility that a medical incident may be occurring and that the driver should be spoken with just to make sure that everything is fine.

What is most important for facility and security managers (where there is a security unit) is that fluid movement in the parking lot must be maintained at all times because business inside the building can be dramatically affected by what happens in the parking lot. If disruption occurs for one reason or another in the parking lot, people will not be at their desks performing their work tasks, potentially costing the entity money and new business.

To maintain fluid movement, the parking lots must be clean and parking spots well marked so people know where the parking spots are; fire route areas must be clearly marked and enforced. Many people will deliberately park in fire route areas to avoid walking for a distance, which happens when all the spaces near the entry doors are filled or when the entire lot is filled to capacity. These improper parkers must be dealt with quickly and forced to move to a proper parking space, and if they fail to do so, the security or facility manager should not waste any more time and simply have their vehicles towed, as there will be official support from the local fire code. Failure to deal with these fire route parkers will erode the rules and cause chaos as other people will begin to think it is acceptable to park wherever they think is necessary when the lot starts filling up (Figure 13.2).

In parking lots that usually tend to fill up to capacity, there **must** be other options, such as an overflow parking lot that is closed until it is needed or at least instructions on where to go and what to do. A predetermined overflow lot gives the facility flexibility for visitors and event parking. One note of caution is that leaving the overflow lot open all

Figure 13.2 A typical fire department hose connection that the pumper trucks will use during a fire event. If a vehicle is parked in front of one, fire officials will push the car out of the way with their push bars, or smash right through a car window to get the hoses connected properly. Do not allow people to park in fire routes! (Photo by J. Henderson.)

151

Figure 13.3 The bush line between the two facilities was to be fenced, much to the chagrin of the employees that wanted to cross uninhibited to access the gym at the college. See text for details. (Photo by J. Henderson.)

the time must be avoided as employees will start using it, particularly if the overflow lot is closer to the doors than some of the furthest spots in the general lot. Some people will do anything to avoid walking an extra fifty feet!! The following anecdote illustrates this point very well.

There is a large facility with a 1000-space parking lot that borders immediately with a community college (Figure 13.3). As the college contained a full-service gymnasium, employees would cross directly in a straight line from the facility doors, through the parking lot and the tree line, to enter the college lot and access the door leading to the college gym. As the larger facility was of critical importance, plans were being discussed to fence the perimeter, including the parking lot, as part of security upgrades and layering. During these discussions, a segment of the building community was up in arms about the fencing idea as it *would disrupt the path to the college and access to the gym*. In effect, it would force them to walk an extra 500 feet around the fence to enter through the gates. The outcry was quite forceful and these people were trying to propose tens of thousands of dollars of extra expenditures to install a gate so they could still walk straight through to their destination. The ironic point is that these were fitness enthusiasts going to a gym—complaining about having to walk a few hundred extra feet to go around the gates.

Such is the mentality of a minority of people in the general population of a building. Like water, they want to find the path of least resistance to get to their destination. They are willing to violate access control and security policies to do it or, as in this case, spend extra taxpayer money to put a gate in a remote spot covered by brush and trees just to avoid walking for an extra minute and a half so that they can get to the gym to exercise! These tend to be the same people that violate security policy inside the building as it disrupts their personal sense of convenience, while they either fail to see or purposely do not care about the security concerns of the facility.

In these situations, the requirements of the facility come first and must not be derailed by the distractions of a minority of building occupants with a narrow self-serving point of view. When proposing these kinds of projects, facility managers must have as much researched information as possible to deflect distractive points of view from impacting the ultimate goal of the proposal, which in this case was to complete the security layering of a facility of critical importance with the installation of a perimeter fence. The fitness enthusiasts would have to simply add a 500-foot walk into their workouts to compensate for the security fence.

PARKING WHEN THE SNOW FLIES

An issue with snow fall in parking lots for facility managers to consider is that when the lines of a parking lot are covered, people begin parking too far away from each other when they cannot see the lines. In these conditions, the facility parking lot will lose 30% to 40% of its parking capacity, which can seriously disrupt a lot that is near or at capacity on a daily basis. In other words, if a parking lot has capacity of 1000 spaces, on a snowy day only about 600 cars will be able to park in the lot, forcing 400 cars to go elsewhere or violate parking rules by parking wherever drivers think they might get away with it. This causes major congestion problems in the parking lot as individuals begin parking their cars in fire routes, creating their own spots by extending the normal width of each section and partially blocking the roadway around the parking sections.

153

Other cars begin circling around to find a spot, hoping that someone will leave, and actually cause congestion for others trying to access the lot, as vehicles will seem to be everywhere with poor visual conditions from the weather. It becomes a nightmare of activity and also quite dangerous for people walking to and from their vehicles. This situation also affects the workplace as people are not at their desks on time. For these reasons, it is critical to have snow plowing done as soon as possible, before business hours, and to try to avoid accumulations of snow in the lot. When congestion begins under these conditions, the only people that can generally do something about it will be the facility manager or a security employee if there is a security entity.

Excess snow must not be piled in the parking lot, but rather trucked elsewhere or thrown over the fence line, lest significant capacity for parking at the facility begins to be lost. Compounding the problem is that the number of people trying to access the lot remains the same. Care must be taken by the facility manager to not allow snow removal services to pile snow against the fence line, whether it is inside or outside the fence because this will inevitably cause damage to the fence as holding clips will snap under the pressure of the snow and the snow removal service might even inadvertently create a snow bridge, making it even easier for a person of ill intent to get over the fence.

In the spring when the snows have melted, maintenance personnel should inspect the entire fence line for damaged fencing and clips and have them immediately repaired. Otherwise, persons of ill intent will be able to lift entire sections of the fence from the bottom and squeeze through without anyone noticing that the fence has been compromised.

Snowstorms can also cause significant traffic delays in entering facilities, particularly when electronic access gates are involved. People seem to instinctively drive more slowly as the snow begins to fall, which is not a bad thing on the roadways; however, it tends to clog up entry points to facilities as electronic gates open and close with a card swipe. This can cause unacceptable delays that also result in traffic backups onto the actual roadway as employees line up to get in. Facility and/or security managers must keep an eye on this situation to prevent dangerous backups from occurring. Bad weather and lineups on a highway are recipes for a serious motor vehicle collision, which is not something the facility and/or security manager wants to have to explain. In these situations, the facility or security manager should consider opening the electronic gate to speed up the process and posting an employee at the gate to visually screen the accesses. As security was hopefully layered in the first place as recommended, images will still be taken and identity screening will occur at other doors. The traffic backlog must be avoided as much as possible and facilities management and/or security should manage the situation before it becomes an emergency.

VISITOR PARKING

Most large facilities and major box stores have visitor parking areas, which for large box stores would comprise most of their parking areas. These parking areas lead right to the front access door to the facility, where visitors and/or customers are supposed to get inside the building. There is one problem, however, that facility managers must manage and enforce: the tendency for some employees to use the visitor parking spaces for their own convenience, to avoid walking a few extra feet from the employee parking areas. When employees park in visitor parking areas, they are actually blocking the visitors from using the space, which in the case of a facility often may be an executive from another entity or someone appearing at the facility to give a presentation, benefitting the inviting entity. This makes the visitor's experience diminish at the expense of the operator/owner and perhaps may even force the visitor to park off-site and walk a considerable distance or pay for parking at a city pay lot. In the case of a box store, employees should be parking at the rear of the lot and leaving the closer spots for customers, many of whom may be mobility challenged (such as the elderly, persons with arthritic issues, and pregnant women), but do not qualify for handicapped parking. Employees that take parking away from visitors and customers should be dealt with quickly as they are affecting the customer experience and damaging the reputation of the employer.

LONG-TERM PARKING

Long-term parking in facility lots must be tightly controlled, again since any extra vehicles reduce the percentage of available space for daily traffic and may contribute to congestion in the lot. Employees that have a vehicle and wish to park long term when they go on vacation or for storage purposes must be subject to a request procedure that enables facilities management to consider the request and keep track of how many employees have done this and how it is affecting the parking lot. Violations should result in the towing of the offending vehicle. Facilities management and/

or security must always remain in control of the parking lots or chaos will take over, eventually leading to a crisis that will attract the attention of executives. It is not a good situation for facilities managers to be answering questions from building executives about why the parking lot has gotten out of control, particularly during an event when executives from other entities are present.

14

Facility Wellness

ENERGY AND ENVIRONMENT

Energy consumption and the environmental footprint are aspects of facility management that are rapidly gaining in importance as the impacts of global climate change have become a daily issue in the news. Facility managers have unique opportunities to improve the carbon footprint of their facilities by replacing old, inefficient technology with newer, more energy-efficient and self-sustaining technologies that meet government standards and use best practices. This process can actually be self-funding simply by the fact that new technologies are so much more efficient than old equipment that it more than offsets any up-front extra costs for installation. Switching to energy-efficient and environmentally sound technology may require good planning, research, and a solid proposal to get buy-in from the executive level both for the premise of using green technology and for predicting accurately that there will be efficiencies and cost savings by going in that direction.

The United States Environmental Protection Agency has the Energy Star program that will guide homeowners and facility managers/owners/operators through establishing an energy-efficient program for managing energy and waste (http://www/energystar.gov/buildings/index.cfm).

To proceed with this program, the organization is required to

- Make a commitment (an organizational commitment)
- Assess performance and set goals (with executive support)
- Create an action plan
- Implement the action plan

- Evaluate progress
- Recognize achievements
- Reassess and set new goals in a continuing cycle

Operational examples of efficiencies and saving potential for facility managers include the following:

- Identify electrical waste by performing an audit, similar to and perhaps part of the security audits discussed elsewhere in the book. The purpose of the audit is to discover equipment and lighting that is powered up when no one is present to use it. Particularly at night, if no one is working in an area, the lights and equipment should be powered down to save on hydropower (hydro) costs.
- All maintenance equipment and systems should be examined regularly for efficiencies and state of repair. Well-maintained systems and equipment cost less to run.
- Many facilities are equipped with exterior handicapped entry buttons. If these buttons are depressed after hours and whenever the doors are locked, the device will still activate to open the door and will also stay on all night if not shut off, devouring electricity. Having security or maintenance check these devices several times each night will ensure they are not costing money unnecessarily.
- Regular maintenance of heating and cooling systems will result in efficient functioning and cost savings.
- All plumbing, vents, ducts, and HVAC components should be inspected and maintained/cleaned, while thermostats can be lowered when the building is not staffed. Air filters should be regularly replaced as recommended by the manufacturer to avoid clogging of filters and inefficient/poor function. These small measures will produce efficiency and cost saving.
- Office equipment such as computers, fax machines, printers, and copiers left running will bleed power 24/7. Shutting them off when not in use can save considerable money over time.

Lighting practices can be examined for efficiencies and savings:

- Lights not being used should be shut off manually or be programmed to shut down automatically after a few minutes without activity. Using daylight where possible can combine with these practices to reduce costs by 10% to 40%.
- Using sunlight where possible to illuminate common spaces can significantly reduce costs. The installation of skylights can reduce

internal lighting requirements during the day, resulting in the removal of overlighting.

- Using desk lamps for individual lighting of work stations can reduce the common-area lighting requirements significantly, resulting in savings.
- Regular maintenance of lighting systems can identify problems and inefficiencies before they cost money.
- Closing blinds in summer daylight can help keep the cooling costs lower, while opening blinds in winter daylight may encourage heating with sunlight.
- Ensuring vents and air intakes are not blocked can reduce the power needed to move air in the system.
- HVAC chillers, heat pumps, and air conditioners require cleaning and maintenance of evaporator and condenser coils. Clean equipment facilitates heat transfer and saves money through efficiency.
- Ensuring that building occupants keep exterior doors closed will prevent the situation where an entire section must be reheated in the winter as, for example, someone left a door open for convenient unloading of a vehicle, but emptied out the warm air in the section to the outside. This requires the heating system to work overtime for a long period just to replace the warm air in that section. The same concept applies in summer for cooled air in the building if someone allows it to escape into a hot and humid afternoon. It will take time for the air conditioner to run fully to replace that section of cooled air. These costs add up over the seasons.
- Repairing leaks in steam traps and compressed air systems will save money.
- Making good use of insulation is important for heating and cooling efficiency, as well as replacing it where it is damaged or wet or has been removed.
- Rainwater can be collected for use in irrigating lawns/gardens.
- Solar panels can be installed for electricity generation.

Programs such as Energy Star can assist facility managers with planning efficiencies, tracking projects, and realizing real operational cost savings. Other countries will have similar agencies and opportunities for efficiencies to reduce operating costs and maximize profits (http://www.energystar.gov/buildings/about-us/how-can-we-help-you/improve-building-and-plant-performance/improve-energy-use-commercial).

ENVIRONMENT

The environment in a facility is another important element in ensuring that people are not only comfortable but also safe. It is one of the elements in facilities that commonly can creep up on an owner/operator and cause significant damage to the facility, injury or illness to occupants, and unnecessary litigation from occupants either through actual illness or upon discovery by an occupant that has recognized an unsafe environment.

Environmental problems can be many, particularly as buildings age, regardless of how modern they look.

One particular experience in a modern-looking building was quite surprising as it had opened in 1996, but was experiencing some shifting. By 2004, the shifting appeared to have caused a large interior atrium window to pop out of its mooring and shatter into thousands of small shards of glass, although they were still held in place by the safety glass laminate. The pane of shattered glass bowed out into the space, wavering precipitously over the heads of the people assigned to the work stations below in the atrium. It posed a significant safety hazard if it were to suddenly give way, collapse, and fall, whereupon the compromised coating would likely split, spraying the shards of glass in all directions. This would cause serious injury or even death in what was supposed to be a safe and highly secured environment. The pane of glass had to be removed immediately and replaced by a similarly sized sheet of plywood to prevent anyone from falling through the gap into the space below and to await repair and keep the business units below functioning, which were actually processing pay for the employees, to be issued the following day. That was added pressure for the maintenance department to get the window pane gap closed quickly in order to get payroll back to work so employees would get paid on time. Facilities maintenance in this case acted quickly and were able to clean up the mess and replace the pane with a sheet of plywood, enabling the workforce to get back to work with only an hour of wasted time.

The window pane was replaced properly and safely after business hours and all appeared normal when employees reported to work the next morning.

Other problems that begin to surface in large facilities can be air quality and dust accumulation, with miles of duct work and air intakes in a large facility and mold resulting from accumulated moisture and roof leaks. The air intakes should always be in a protected area and sealed off from tampering or the introduction of noxious substances by persons of ill intent. Exhaust vents also should be examined periodically as employees that smoke will congregate at exhaust vents in cold weather because of the warm air exiting the facility. These employees appear to forget or are oblivious to the fact that this is exhaust air and probably not all that healthy to have blowing on them. Maintenance employees may also experience the appearance of wild animals seeking the warmth of the exhaust vents. These animals will be carriers of disease and insects, which can cross contaminate the persons warming themselves by the exhaust vents, some of whom are also attracted to the cute small mammals and will even begin feeding them. This can lead to the introduction of insects to the building as they come in on the clothing of employees and fly away inside the building environment. Although rare, the possibility also exists for animal bites to employees in these locations requiring a medical response.

Other environmental issues that can occur but are entirely preventable are atmospheric in nature. Carbon monoxide is an odorless gas and a silent killer that is in the news more and more often as poisoning accidents and suicides occur. This gas should not be a problem in most large facilities with central heating systems and venting kept in good repair; however, smaller air conditioners/heaters in rooms such as hotel rooms or apartments can become dangerous if not regularly maintained and tested for efficiency. To have an occupant be injured or even die from a poorly maintained room heater would not only be a tragedy but also a very expensive lawsuit for a landlord to defend. Any rooms with separate heating and ventilation should be equipped with carbon monoxide detectors, as well as smoke and fire detectors, whether the local fire code requires it or not. Not only is it ethical to install such devices but it can also protect against litigation. It is recommended to have the devices hard wired into the existing building electrical wiring by a certified electrician to eliminate the problem of having to replace batteries on an ongoing basis, but also have battery backup. All such devices should also be subject to a scheduled maintenance/testing regime based on the manufacturer's instructions for those particular devices. This is not something to ignore, to take lightly, or not to use the specific instructions from the company of manufacture for maintenance. Lives can be at stake when these devices fail and equipment begins to malfunction due to age or lack

161

of maintenance. The owner/operator will be held accountable if these devices fail and something tragic occurs as a result.

Other atmospheric problems can occur when exterior air intakes for the building take in poisoned air from car and/or truck exhaust or smoke from grass fires, among other unpredictable problems. Car exhaust is actually predictable and it is a design flaw and oversight to install parking lots by the air intakes of a facility, simply because many vehicles are always moving about, or inconsiderate drivers stop near the intake vents and allow their vehicles to idle for long periods of time while they load, unload, or simply wish to warm their vehicle up on a cold winter morning. Complaints from building occupants about the smell of car exhaust from inside the building should be taken seriously and investigated immediately with the potential of temporarily shutting down that particular air intake until the problem clears. It does not take long for fumes to fill a space and for people to begin feeling ill. Facilities with security personnel can always send a security officer out to investigate what is occurring and to educate people about the impact of idling their vehicles for a long period of time. When there is no security presence, the maintenance staff or a designated person in the building will have to shoulder this responsibility. Direction about not idling vehicles should also appear in the facility directory as a policy to support any attempt to stop a person from unnecessarily causing an atmospheric problem in the building from an idling engine.

Buildings with diesel generators installed as backup sources of power for hydro outages will also have these issues to consider when decisions are made as to where to securely store and operate these engines during a power disruption. As the diesel engines might be operating continuously for hours or even days on end, consideration of disposal of that distinct-smelling exhaust must be made by business continuity planners to avoid poisoning the people inside the facility for which the engines are providing power. Placement must not be in a location where fumes can enter the facility through either entry points or air intake grills. Likewise, owners/operators of apartment complexes should also have prewritten and published facility rules about the use of grills and barbeque units on balconies and the use certainly should be prohibited inside the building due to fire and carbon monoxide hazards. Having such rules published in the occupancy contracts and facility directories will make enforcement much easier to effect and it may reduce the pressure of litigation if an occupant disobeyed an already published building policy and used a grill indoors, causing a fire or carbon monoxide poisoning.

A terrific example of an unexpected carbon monoxide poisoning incident in 2015 comes from Fire Chief Trent Elyea, Chief in 2015 of Collingwood and Blue Mountain Fire Department in the province of Ontario, Canada. The author often worked operationally with Chief Elyea in Orillia, Ontario, when he was fire chief there and the author was the security manager at a major facility of critical importance. His example came as new carbon monoxide regulations were being developed by the provincial government in Ontario and it actually served to develop more regulations based on what could happen and how dangerous carbon monoxide is when it comes in contact with people in building situations. Chief Elyea's example has been used with his permission.

We had a large six-story hotel being built recently, prior to the new (carbon monoxide) legislation being adopted or even in for reading (at the Ontario Provincial Parliament). Our fire prevention staff convinced the owners that rather than just installing smoke alarms, they should put in combination units—smoke/carbon monoxide—and all through the building. They agreed.

Well, about a month after they opened, we got a call there for an alarm and we found that a rooftop unit had misfired and was pumping high volumes of carbon monoxide into the hallways of the hotel. We evacuated and eventually found the problem, but not before we measured about 80 parts per million in the halls. It was at night and if they had not had the smoke/carbon monoxide combination units, the potential for fatalities was great. We ended up determining that a couple of the people had exited their room and, when they did, the carbon monoxide had entered their rooms as well. We evacuated 160 people out of the building and had to send them to a different hotel. It took all night to get the rooms and halls ventilated so they could get back in.

This is a perfect example of where the owners wisely paid the small amount more for the protection that at that time was not yet required, and it made all the difference in the world.

This story of an actual incident came from a forward-thinking fire department led by a dynamic and forward-thinking fire chief, who suggested that facility owners install equipment not yet required by law. Good ethics were in use here by both the fire department and the hotel owners, who were under no legal obligation to make the more expensive purchase of combination carbon monoxide/smoke detectors. In this case, thankfully no one was injured or killed; however, if someone had been, the owners of the property would have been on solid ground during any subsequent investigation or inquest, given their extra expenditures for sophisticated equipment that was not yet required by law. The owners would have been deemed to have made reasonable and even extraordinary efforts to ensure the safety of the clientele of the hotel by installing equipment that was still in the regulation development phase in government.

IN SICKNESS AND IN HEALTH

The subject of illness is an important factor in the daily function of facilities, from isolated employee illness due to bacterial or viral infection to viral epidemics that spread from one person to the next, often within the confines of facilities. Disease is something that facility and security managers must be educated for and contend with as they engage in their daily work. Outbreaks of influenza, the common cold, and bacterial infections such as salmonella poisoning can spread quickly through the population of a facility as people carrying disease touch common surfaces such as doorknobs and latches, water faucets, and coffee makers, for example, or they sit down at a desk or meeting table and leave viral or bacterial infection in their wake for an unwitting victim. These illnesses occur every year in every facility and cause impactful absences in the eyes of any organization that must either contend with a loss of productivity from the missing employees or bear the high cost of replacing them with temporary workers.

Most employees are caught in the conundrum of "I am sick but have to go to work." They feel this way for a number of reasons as follows:

- They may feel their tasks are generally too important for them to miss a day or two due to illness. This happens to supervisors and managers.
- They have an important meeting that morning and feel that they must attend.
- They are competing for promotion and do not want their competitors to gain an edge.
- They take pride in never missing a day and work hard to win those perfect attendance awards each year.
- They are not full-time employees and, due to their contracts of employment, will lose salary for missing a day.

There may be even more reasons, but the reasons for not staying at home while ill matter little. The effect is the same on the workplace and workforce. Sick people that come to work bring the illness with them and will spread it to other workers. As some short-sighted managers encourage people to come to work and pressure employees to not miss a day due to illness, these managers are only damaging their own productivity in the long run as well as making their employees feel less valued.

The negative effects of encouraging or even forcing employees to come to work when they are ill include the following:

- The ill person will lack productivity and energy. He or she may as well be home recuperating for a better day to come.
- The ill person will be resentful toward the employer and management for being subtly forced to come to work.
- Non-full-time employees may conclude that this is the wrong employer for them, encouraging turnover.
- People coming to work ill will spread the illness to others, creating dissension as people who are not ill know they are at risk, and it will impact office productivity as other employees will become ill and many of them will stay at home for several days.

Employers that encourage full-time employees or force contract people to come to work when sick through a lack of sick day provisions are actually damaging their own efforts toward productivity and keeping a healthy workforce. There are times in any office "when people start to drop like flies." Managers must ask themselves why this happens and how their work policies and performance management policies and procedures are actually treating the employees that come down with the inevitable illnesses that sweep through populations every year. One person coming to work ill can wipe out or seriously affect an entire work unit for weeks to come as, for example, the year's strain of influenza that was brought to work by one over-enthusiastic employee spreads throughout the entire section and beyond.

The risk does not stop there either. The sick employees that willfully attend or feel forced by the lack of sick day provisions in their contracts to come to work may be putting pregnant women and employees with immune-compromised chronic conditions at serious risk. These are the unseen impacts for managers that ignore sickness or treat it as something they will not accept as a reason to not attend work. The impacts can be enormous on the budget of a company that suddenly must replace the pregnant employee months ahead of a scheduled maternity absence because another employee brought influenza to work and the pregnant person was forced to attend the hospital and leave her position early. The manager then must spend extra nonbudgeted money replacing that person with a contract employee.

Facility managers must stay on top of illness trends as summer turns to winter and the flu season begins. Facility managers may have to contend with having a daycare center in the building, where sickness can spread quite easily into the building population. In these instances, it is critical for the facility and/or security manager to establish and maintain excellent relations with the daycare manager to ensure communication of influenza and other outbreaks at the daycare. In those cases, signage should go up isolating the daycare and preventing people from attending that do not have to go in until the outbreak concludes.

Figure 14.1 is an example of an *enteric outbreak tracking* form that was used in a facility of critical importance that also contained a privately run daycare facility open to the public but mainly for the convenience of the building occupants. The outbreak form contained a checklist of actions that the daycare staff were to follow during outbreaks. The completed form was shared with facilities management and security as a cooperative gesture for the protection of building occupants and an effort to contain the outbreak by limiting attendance of building occupants and rescheduling various maintenance procedures until the space was cleaned and declared disease free. This type of cooperation comes as a result of relationship building between the facility manager, maintenance manager, security manager, and the various tenant representatives in a facility.

Workplaces can be collection depots for bacteria and viruses just from the sheer volume of people coming in and out of the facilities. At particular risk are 24/7 operations where two to three or even more shifts are rotating in and out. This maximizes the people coming and going while the constant activity often makes it difficult to clean the work areas effectively. Daniel J. Denoon of WebMD Health News looked at this problem and found that testing swabs revealed high contamination on the following surfaces:

- Break room sink faucets
- Microwave door handles
- Computer keyboards and mouse
- Refrigerator door handles
- Water fountain buttons
- Vending machine buttons
- Desk phones
- Coffee pots and dispensers

These surfaces are common places that all people will touch at some point during the workday but most people will not think twice about it. Without even realizing, they may have contaminated themselves with an illness if someone with an illness has come to work as previously

Day Nursery Enteric Outbreaks

Enteric Outbreak Management Checklist	Date Initiated yy:mm/dd
1. Health Unit notification – CD team, Barrie	06/11/15
2. Enteric precautions:	
a) Hand-washing – staff/volunteers and children ✓	06/11/16
- review use of hand sanitizers ✓	06/11/16
b) Review diapering procedures ✓ *prep.*	
c) Review staff assignments (staff providing care should not handle food)	
3. Identify cases and staff. Start Enteric Line List (separate lists for children/staff cases).	06/11/15.
4. Isolate any symptomatic children until alternate daycare arrangements are made *info office*	06/11/15.
5. Cohort care of children, as able.	06/11/16
6. Exclude ill children & staff. Exclusionary period to be reviewed with health unit. Have supervisor discuss with symptomatic employee the issue of exclusion from working in other centres. *48 hrs symptom free.*	06/11/16
7. Discuss deferring admissions until outbreak under control.	06/11/16.
8. Notify parents. Educate visitors/parents/volunteers re precautions. Post signage indicating outbreak.	06/11/16
9. Cancel social activities, field trips and community functions. *next wed PGM park meeting - re-assess monday!*	
10. Review activities and sensory play. Water play should be discontinued for duration of the outbreak.	06/11/16
11. All bedding, dress up clothes. plush toys laundered on high heat.	06/11/16 - all week.
12. Thorough cleaning/sanitizing of equipment. toys etc. with high level disinfectant. *JAVEX*	06/11/16
13. Specimen collection: Number of kits on site _____ Expired? ☐ Yes ☐ No Call CD Team for arrangement of pick-up of specimens.	
14. Complete documentation – i.e. Line Listing. Daily update of new and resolved cases to be faxed to health unit – CD Team.	06/11/15.

Reviewed with : ▇▇▇▇▇▇▇▇▇▇▇▇▇▇

Date: _____ 06/11/15. _____   Copy faxed to facility ☑ Yes ☐ No

Revised November 4, 2005

CS-CD
Revised Oct'05

Figure 14.1   Enteric outbreak management checklist.

discussed. The following quote in an article from Charles Gerba, PhD, from the University of Arizona, sums it up well:

> People are aware of the risk of germs in the restroom but areas like break rooms have not received the same degree of attention. This study demonstrates that contamination can be spread throughout the workplace when workers heat up lunch, make coffee, or simply type on keyboards. (Denoon and Gerba 2012)

Considering that shift workers often use the same work equipment or desks, computers, and phones as the shift before them makes it critical that these areas be cleaned before the next employee uses them. A quick wipe-down with sanitary wipes supplied by the organization may help reduce the spread of illness through a workplace and it can be the employee's responsibility to do that with the organization's participation through written policy and the supply of sanitary wipes and hand cleaners (Denoon and Gerba 2012).

Irritants and allergic reactions also permeate the modern workplace. Many people are either sensitive to or downright allergic to chemicals, foods, perfumes, molds, and anything one can think of in a facility. Organizations are now beginning to recognize this issue by establishing scent-free zones in the effort to prevent perfumes and odors from causing illness and absence in the workplace (Figure 14.2).

Rather than trying to address the products themselves, the policy raises the issue of victim symptoms and the prevention of exacerbating the symptoms as being the reason for banning scented products. Publishing the policy forces accountability on all employees to maintain the standard of not using scented products in the workplace.

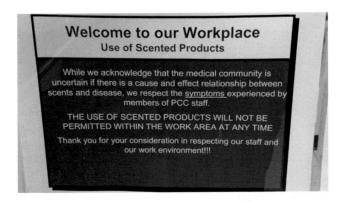

Figure 14.2 Posting of a policy on use of scented products in a 24/7 workplace.

Many organizations allow their employees to manage lunchrooms and kitchen facilities, including refrigerators and ovens among other kitchen appliances. The cleanliness of these areas must be enforced daily and in 24/7 facilities, at least once per shift as discussed earlier. Used dishes must be cleaned and refrigerators must be emptied of leftover food before they become science experiments sitting beside the edible food of other people. It is a good idea to appoint someone in the group of employees to act as a kitchen manager to ensure these tasks are done by the people that use the facilities. A once-a-week cleaning out of the refrigerator should become an official task with alternating people taking the responsibility. These are important considerations in order to reduce the spread of both viral and bacterial illness in the buildings and avoiding the habits of employees creating problems in the workplace.

Other potential measures include the following:

- Inviting health agencies into the facility to hold sickness awareness seminars for employees
- Inviting the same health agencies to hold influenza vaccine clinics for employees
- Encouraging employees that are obviously ill to stay home and get better, including observing them coming to work and telling them to go home until symptoms are gone
- Putting some kind of sickness provisions in the contracts of temporary and part-time workers so they do not feel compelled to attend work when they are ill
- Strategizing with the daycare manager about posting illness outbreaks at the daycare and monitoring what happens
- Supervising the cleaning staff to ensure they are properly sanitizing bathrooms and common areas, including doorknobs and latches
- Providing handwash stations and keeping them full of sanitizer for the use of employees and visitors
- Educating and providing cleaning wipes for employees to wipe down their own workstation items, such as the desktop, keyboards, telephones, and computer mouses, before beginning work

These and other measures can contribute highly to containing the spread of illness throughout a workforce and a facility. It is a better way of thinking for any manager, let alone a facility or security manager, although the facility/security managers may be in a good position to get programs rolling in a facility.

WATER QUALITY

All facilities have water sources and plumbing bringing water into the facility for both human consumption and industrial applications. Facility managers must be cognizant of the human consumption aspect of the water supply and ensure the water supply is clean to a standard where it can be consumed by humans. It is best to be proactive with water quality as neglecting it will eventually be brought to the attention of executives in the form of a complaint from a building occupant. Facility managers can examine pipes to see if they are corroding or are so old they need to be replaced. They can also examine the general state of the delivery and drainage systems as well as testing the water coming out of the taps and drinking fountains at the user end. Where there is any question about the safety or quality of the water supply, certified experts should immediately be brought in to test the water and examine the delivery and drainage systems. It is simply not acceptable to have water problems in a functioning facility. If the water quality is allowed to deteriorate to a point where people are at risk of serious illness, a facility manager can lose the confidence of executives and the building population. The facility manager could be facing serious questions if someone actually did fall ill due to water problems within the facility.

CLEANLINESS AND JANITORIAL SERVICES

Part of a facility manager's portfolio inevitably includes directing in-house cleaners or those hired by contract to fulfill an essential service. The essential service is ensuring the ongoing cleanliness of a populated facility. This is a service that every facility requires but one that is not supposed to be seen during the workday. Most offices and boardroom areas will be cleaned after hours simply because the spaces are being used during business hours; this presents a security issue that is rarely thought about in most corporations and government.

The Cleaners

The ironic part of every facility requiring cleaners is that these hard-working but lower level employees have access to the highest security areas in the facility just to get their basic tasks of cleaning floors, windows, and fixtures done. The cleaners in essence have access to top-secret proprietary information on a daily basis, but most clients do not consider this issue or take it seriously. How were the cleaners hired? To whom do the cleaners report and what are their accountabilities?

In-house cleaners are not a problem as the entity has complete control over the hiring and background clearances. If the group chooses carefully, an excellent and fully accountable employee will be cleaning office space with loyalty and integrity. However, many entities will hire contract cleaners that do not have the same level of accountability and where someone else did the hiring. If a facility manager is seeking a contract cleaning company, he or she had better have a look at the company's hiring processes, and whichever candidates are presented to work in the facility should be subject to background investigation to ensure reliability and reputation.

Just Ask the Cleaner...

It is well known that if you want to know what is going on, just talk to the cleaner or the mail clerk because these two lower level positions access every work unit and level of a facility to do their jobs. They often talk and gossip to people all over the building and generally have a good sense of what is going on, even to the point of having relationships with the executive level. They are also in a position to see classified documents and to hear high-level conversations as they go about their daily duties. This is how rumors start to fly, and at times people find out through gossip that they have been laid off or promoted before an announcement has been made. Facility managers must be cognizant of this reality and care must be taken about who is being cleared to work in the facility. When something unacceptable happens concerning the cleaning staff, executives will come looking for the facility manager for answers.

THE GARBAGE

It is a critical aspect of a successful workplace to maintain general cleanliness on a daily basis and to ensure **all** garbage containers are emptied and processed for removal by waste services in the municipality. The simple reason for this is that there can be biological waste in any container (including recycle bins) on the property that, if not removed on a daily basis, will begin to decompose, smell, and perhaps attract or release insects into the environment. Biological waste may consist of part of someone's uneaten lunch; a dead animal, bat, or bird found either inside or outside the building; human excrement and diapers or specimens of human illness that may by dropped in the waste container rather than disposed of in a proper receptacle; or even live plants that a building occupant no longer wanted to keep. Left to rot, these examples of biological waste will cause problems in the building environment and will either just start to smell badly or will contaminate a space, requiring decontamination services.

Recycling

Most facilities recycle nonbiological waste to be part of the green movement in reducing waste. This is a very practical exercise for a facility in reducing the amount of landfill garbage leaving the site. Recycling containers are generally located beside garbage receptacles in common areas and hallways, and they usually accept containers made from metal/aluminum, plastic, and other materials. Separate containers should be available for paper and cardboard waste. Many organizations also have desktop recycling containers that should be checked. One important aspect to note is that there still may be biological waste among the recycling waste and therefore recycling waste must be removed or checked as often as the biological waste.

Because shredded paper waste is often proprietary information or secret documents, it is included in recycled waste if there is not a contracted company removing shredding bins directly from the workstations. Shredded waste is usually removed in clear plastic bags. Shredding bins should *always be locked* until the contents are to be disposed of either in the shredding room or by the contracted shredder.

Processing/Storing Waste

Facility managers must always keep an eye on the lower level area of the building where the waste is brought, processed, and stored prior to removal from the site. This central area must be kept sealed to the outside, clean, and free of rodents and insects that are attracted to waste and that will infest the area if allowed. In-house employees and, in particular, personnel placed by contractors to handle waste must be supervised closely by facility managers to ensure that shortcuts do not develop and the integrity of the building's "outer skin" is not compromised to avoid the infestations of rodents, bats, birds, and insects that will naturally occur. Any infestations that do occur must be mitigated as soon as possible by the

Figure 14.3 This is a well planned garbage enclosure that keeps everything in one place and allows garbage collection vehicles to pull up directly and empty the container. The bollard serves two purposes: It protects the wall from someone backing into it trying to park and also indirectly forces vehicles away from the enclosure from the left. The enclosure is also far enough away from the main building to avoid insects and animals affecting the building. The one issue standing out is that the container is full and there is no way to lock it. It is from a government facility. (Photo by J. Henderson.)

appropriate experts in the removal of insects, animals, birds, and whatever else might appear.

After being brought to the central point in the lower level of the building, the waste should be stored outside the building in secure garbage containers to ensure animals cannot get in and the waste is ready for the municipal garbage collection to pick up. These containers will also be subject to insect infestations and intrusions by animals/birds and should be cleaned as often as possible to maintain a hygienic area in the facility compound. Corporate or government garbage and recycling storage may also attract human interest and the storage facilities must remain within the security perimeter and doors should be locked at all times (Figure 14.3).

WEATHER AND FACILITIES MANAGEMENT

Weather is one aspect of facilities management that is inescapable because, regardless of where facilities are located, weather will impact them in one way or another. In North America and Europe, there are varying zones of subtropical to temperate forest and in the far north, tundra and the inevitable Arctic temperatures. Facility managers across the spectrum must prepare their facilities for violent and severe weather events to minimize damage by preparing beforehand or by repairing damage after a storm and getting the facility back to normal as quickly as possible. A good reference for weather preparedness and recovery is with FEMA, the Federal Emergency Management Agency, in the United States. FEMA produces a document called "The Emergency Management Guide for Business and Industry, 1993," which is a guide for preparing and coping with severe weather events. The website to access this manual is http://www.fema.gov/library/viewRecord.do?id=1689.

The following are typical weather situations that facility managers will face, depending on their locations. Included are what the facility manager will be looking at in terms of what might happen to the building and some considerations that will disrupt operations with the employer's workplace. It is the facility manager's job to mitigate these disruptions as quickly as possible and get people back to work to avoid loss of business and productivity.

- **Hurricanes/cyclones**: in the southern United States and Pacific Coast, during every year in the summer, residents and facility managers must prepare for the hurricane/cyclone season. Hurricanes and cyclones, which are basically the same thing, develop in the southern Atlantic Ocean and the Pacific Ocean, respectively, as the water surface temperature heats up, evaporates, and winds start to swirl. Hurricanes and cyclones are well known for extremely high wind speeds, hard driving rains, storm surge as the ocean moves in shore, and the inevitable damage to facilities and infrastructure left in the wake of the storm. Facility managers usually have several days of notice to prepare the facility for the high winds and heavy rains. This is the time to tour the facility and look for potential problems, such as insecure external items that need to be secured inside a building or tied down to prevent them from becoming airborne during the storm. Boarding up windows is an activity often seen before storms when it is possible. Also of concern is the possibility of the windows blowing out where they cannot be or are not boarded up, so items of value, paperwork, and other office equipment should be protected and secured against water and wind, while electronic devices should be unplugged and covered tightly. With the possibility of flooding, basement and first-floor items should be kept above the flood level for the area. FEMA also recommends that important records be stored both on computer and in hard copy, with copies stored off-site in secure locations not susceptible to storm damage, perhaps as planned in a well-selected business continuity plan location. Computers should be above the flood level and hard copy stored in watertight containers so that the business can get back to work as soon as possible after the storm. Other items must be secured in case the building's outer skin is compromised and heavy rains and wind enter the building through windows, doors, or even the roof. Uninterrupted power supply (UPS) in the form of a generator and fuel might enable the facility to get back to work before hydro service returns.

In buildings where people are present, food and water for several days will support people until help arrives, while UPS in the forms of a generator and fuel are good items to have on hand after a serious hurricane or cyclone. Candles, flashlights with batteries, radios, matches, and firewood are always good to have on hand. These should be checked throughout the year and maintained or replaced as needed to ensure they work when needed.

- **Earthquakes**: although small bumps can periodically be felt on the eastern side of North America, the serious earthquakes tend to occur on the West Coast where most public buildings have been retrofitted to earthquake standards to resist the violent shaking associated with a nearby earthquake. There is not a lot people can do to prepare for an earthquake other than preparedness before one strikes, as they can occur at any time. Loose objects that might fall must be removed from shelves while items hung from walls should use interlocking connections that give a little during a building's swaying during an earthquake. Ensuring that fire protection measures are constantly ready and well practiced is advisable as fire often accompanies heavy earthquakes as infrastructure is damaged. Consultations with experts are necessary for earthquake preparation and planning.
- **Winter**: there are varying degrees of winter—where there is very little snow in the south to heavy snows around the Great Lakes region, where the great snow squalls can spring up as the temperature drops while open water is present on the lakes. The North Atlantic coast also gets major storms from the ocean as the warm and moist air currents move north and collide with Arctic air masses. These great snowstorms cause traffic nightmares and

people are sometimes best just staying at home rather than trying to get to work. What the snows do to facilities, however, is that they require the parking lots to be continually cleared by snow-plows as explained in detail in Chapter 13. This creates issues of where to put volumes of snow—piling it, having it trucked away, or dumping it over fences. Inevitably, each spring requires a tour of the fence line to find and repair all of the damaged fencing caused by the pressure of snow being pushed against it as snow plows clear the lots. As discussed in Chapter 13, it is critical to clear snow from parking lots to avoid loss of capacity and traffic congestion in the lots and to free up the entry points. Other facility issues include roof pressure from accumulated snow, requiring facility managers to clear snow from roof tops to lessen the weight and avoid roof cave-ins.

- **Severe cold**: severe cold can also cause issues in facilities where flash freezing can cause slip hazards in the parking lots, resulting in serious injury to employees and clients. A serious fall in an iced lot can break bones and require emergency response. Facility managers must always have a supply of sand and/or road salt to put on the walkways and pavement for employees. This will add traction for vehicles and people alike. One caution is that road salt stops working at about –11°C, so there must always be sand present as a backup. Combination sand and salt should be kept for parking lots and sidewalks to try to mitigate slipping, even when the temperature drops to extremely low levels (Figure 14.4).
- **Tornadoes**: tornadoes occur out of massive thunderstorms as cold and warm air masses start spinning together. There is not much one can do about tornadoes, as they develop quickly and are completely unpredictable as to where they are headed when they form. Tornadoes then disappear just as quickly as they appeared, sometimes leaving destruction in their wake. Facility managers in tornado-prone areas should ensure the exterior of the facility is free of detritus and items that could become potential projectiles when a tornado strikes. Emergency evacuation planning should also include a section on what to do and where to go during an imminent tornado, including post-tornado instructions.
- **Summer severe heat:** heat in the summer causes hydro usage spikes as air conditioners are turned on across the continent, threatening facilities with hydro blackouts. Facilities with UPS will not even notice the difference while generators fire up to supply

Figure 14.4 A sand/salt box inside a fenced and paved perimeter at a public school. It is highly recommended to keep boxes like this during winter weather to spread sand and/or salt on the pavement when ice accumulates. Many people have slipped on untreated ice and broken limbs and hips on lots like this. Litigation can result from a lack of preparation for poor weather resulting in injury. (Photo by J. Henderson.)

power to keep the facilities running. Those without UPS may be out of business until hydro comes back on line. Facility managers must ensure that UPS fuel supplies are full and that the system is tested monthly with diesel transfer tests so that it will function reliably when required. Otherwise, thunderstorms and lightning strikes can cause localized flooding problems or other damage and often disrupt alarm systems, causing trouble alarms that will send maintenance and security running around checking areas for fire and resetting alarms.

IT TAKES A VILLAGE ... WHOSE PROBLEM IS IT?

Security is often thought by most people to be someone else's issue, problem, or responsibility. How often do people enter facilities and say to themselves, "Do they know what is going on here? Why isn't Security or someone doing something about it?" The person, however, usually moves beyond or just forgets that thought as quickly as it formed in his or her mind as he or she turns the corner and walks toward a destination. A successful security program is inclusive and requires the awareness and participation of everyone in the facility, including visitors. The answer to the preceding question could be that, since no one bothered to advise the building management, maintenance personnel, or security, no one connected to the facility is yet aware of an issue, which could be the reason nothing has been done. Security awareness in the post 9/11 era is an increasingly critical component of any facility and its occupants and legitimate visitors, and certainly everyone has a responsibility to help secure facilities by realizing that it is not someone else's problem and for all to be engaged in closing insecure doors, reporting broken locks, and telling a building official about suspicious activity going on.

Conversely, building owners/operators also have to make it easy for people to be engaged by introducing safety and security programs and making it obvious, even to a visitor, how to get in contact with building management or maintenance or, if there is an on-site physical security entity, to contact a security officer. Unfortunately security can be a distraction to many building occupants and might even become a spectacle when something happens; however, strangely, people do not want to be involved:

About nine years ago, a trespasser was arrested in front of a major facility with a population of about 2000 people. As the trespasser was approached by security, building occupants could be seen gathering at the windows in the three interconnected towers as the arrest had become somewhat of a workday distraction. In fact, an official later joked that one could feel the building tip as so many people came to the windows on one side of the building to watch. No one, however, came out to assist with the arrest, with the exception of a another security officer who was already outside exiting a vehicle. When the call went out for some witnesses for the pending court case, not one person stepped forward to assist.

Security does not work in isolation and must become everyone's business for it to thrive, particularly in a high-security environment. For security to thrive, there must be an active security culture fostered through communication and education. Building occupants must be educated about threats to their facility and how they fit into the security measures, policies, and procedures. They must be included as part of the detection system where, if they see something, they will report it quickly rather than turn a blind eye and not get involved. This is even more critical in buildings and facilities that do not have security personnel assigned. In those cases, occupants must know when and to whom they should report any security breaches or criminal activity, and they must become part of the deterrence and detection system of the facility to have any positive effect on the safety and security of their own environment.

RISK FROM WITHIN...

After having conducted many physical reviews of large facilities and taken security courses, as well as utilizing threat and risk matrixes calculated mathematically such as the Texas A&M Engineering Extension Service (TEEX) threat and risk matrix, it has become a matter of demonstrated fact to the author that facility owners/operators must come to the realization that the highest threat to daily activity *starts from within* an organization. On various levels, the threat from within comes simply from the regular use of a building where people are coming and going with various levels of caring about or even ownership of what happens in the building. When people live in a building, human nature ensures that they will take more care about what happens in and around it because they want to live in a pleasant, secure place. However, when people are simply visiting, they are less likely to notice or care about things that they see or damage that occurs because it does not affect them directly and they do not want to become involved. Likewise, some lower paid employees (but more likely those that feel poorly treated) are also less likely to care and perhaps more likely to cause damage without conscience in a facility. To qualify that statement, a majority of people that are paid a lower wage will still have some caring about the building and will even have a degree of loyalty to the organization from which they receive their paycheck. But there almost always is someone in the group that lacks that loyalty for one reason or another, be it from having been disciplined or simply from the fact that the person lacks the integrity or honesty traits inherent in most people. It was found that a majority of facilities, buildings, and, in particular, government buildings, businesses, retail stores, and others suffer from theft and misuse by some of the very people employed to look after assets. So, often many work units and employees and managers are faced with missing equipment purchased through the unit budget ranging from low-cost items such as pens and paper to very expensive equipment such as projectors and computers. Often, employees cannot seem to find a power cord or some other item placed on a desk or one hears a manager down the hall suddenly yelling, "Where is that Lite Pro?" just before his or her presentation. Many of these situations are the result of employee theft, where someone has taken the item home thinking, "They won't miss it," when in actual fact there is a hidden cost as the item must be replaced through the unit budget, which affects the manager's ability to purchase new items of importance because of the need to repurchase items that had already been acquired through unit funding. This also occurs between business units, where one unit has purchased an expensive item and another unit acquires that piece of equipment without anyone realizing from whence it came. This activity has an impact on budgets as well, as the unit that lost the item may have to purchase another one. Some employees are able to disassociate themselves from the concept that they are actually stealing these items when they take them home for personal use or stealthily move them from one unit to another. These employees have convinced themselves that they are not doing something unethical or dishonest and feel for one reason or another that they are owed by the company or, in the case of the movement of equipment, that the company still owns it and nothing is wrong. This is an ongoing hidden cost to employers and facility operators/owners and often does not get counted because items are replaced as a normal course of administrative business. Identifying these issues as an actual loss or cost can make a huge difference to companies of all sizes, as the larger the company is, the bigger the potential for loss from within can be.

With a revelation such as *loss from within*, what can operators/owners possibly do to reduce the impact of the threat from their own employees or building occupants? Always investigate the circumstances and hold people accountable. A good strategy may be to publish the cost of theft at the end of the year and let employees know in a general manner how it is affecting the employer and decisions made that may affect employees.

ACCOUNTABILITY

All too often, when equipment goes missing in a facility, nothing much is done about it beyond a quick search and local inquiry of staff. Many employees and managers do not know what to do, feel they are too busy to do anything, or simply lack the interest to try to do something more about missing items. They will simply purchase a replacement and carry on; this impacts the budgets year after year with unnecessary expenses that can actually amount to thousands of dollars as these behaviors become accepted and the normal practice is to simply buy to replace what is missing.

Managers must take responsibility for their assets and begin to take the time to investigate instances of missing equipment. To be able to do that, the business unit must keep track of equipment, lock assets away, and itemize them—particularly the more expensive ones. In many instances, the simple realization of staff that investigations occur when items go missing is enough to stop most pilfering from within because most employees do not want to risk the embarrassment of being caught with items they should not have and having to explain themselves. Simple sign-out procedures for expensive assets can protect them from theft and someone is then always responsible for the whereabouts of the assets. Having one employee responsible for the distribution of office stationery and low-cost items such as staplers, pens, and other office necessities will remove the open concept of going to a cabinet and helping oneself to whatever is needed or wanted.

Another important scenario to point out is the organization that supports a fleet of motor vehicles and/or marine vessels. These organizations often have large numbers of expensive tools and supply rooms containing costly engine parts, tires, and just about anything required to keep vehicles on the road and boats in the water. They simply must have control over their supplies through inventory management, where a person is designated to maintain the inventory through secure lockup and is accountable for use of the items. In other words, each item must be counted and signed out when used, with a name attached to the time of signing the item out and back in. These companies cannot afford to be the suppliers of parts for the recreational vehicles of their workers simply because of an open-door policy in regard to use of parts and supplies.

There are too many people in our society that rarely pay for school supplies or other supplies at home, since they can just simply remove them from the workplace in anonymity, without accountability and without cost to themselves. Such are the hidden corporate costs of internal theft. It may seem to some people to be an excessive or harsh term in calling it theft, but that is exactly what it is, and it costs business and government a lot of money over time. In difficult times with shrinking budgets and layoffs, this kind of activity causes unseen damage and can be one of the differences between profit and loss and, ironically, may even cost the jobs of those that are partaking in the practice.

REFERENCE

Denoon, Daniel J., and Charles Gerba. 2012. http://www.webmd.com/news /20120523/the-6-dirtiest-work-places PhD-University of Arizona, p. 345.

15

Employee Management

SELECTION PROCESS SCREENING

Screening is a critical part of any hiring process that selects personnel to work in a facility. Since we have established that the routine daily threats may come from within, it is critical to consider screening as important when selecting people to work in a facility. This is where owners/operators have some control over the level of threat from employees. Properly screening applicants can go a long way toward reducing the risk of internal theft and other problems such as sabotage, drug use, and the resulting misuse of the facility.

Requiring applicants to be screened for drugs and to produce a recent police records check, as well as using a good interview system with background investigations, will reduce the likelihood of hiring people that will cause problems down the road. Knowing applicants' real reputations in the community is critical because they routinely present in their applications what they want hiring managers to know and exclude what they do not want them to know. It is up to the hiring managers to dig deeper and find out if there is something that the applicant was trying to hide and does not want the new employer to know about. This is the threshold of effective hiring: finding out the real reputation of the applicant.

Other facilities such as retail stores, gas stations, banks, and museums, among others have obvious need to be careful who they hire to prevent internal theft and other problems. It is also important to screen for skill level in order to support operations within the facility, but basic safety and security start with the people that the manager employed. Hire a thief and the facility security has already been compromised to a point where no security system can be effective because the insider eventually knows where everything is and how it works. He or she simply has to wait and watch for the gaps in the layered security; once these are found, a thief can function undetected in what he or she believes is a safe environment where he or she is unlikely to be caught. Internal theft immediately starts to increase costs for a business, or the reputation of the organization. It may not be noticed for some time, however, and if not checked early, can become a culture resulting in a slow bleed of costs from inside the organization.

It all comes back to who was hired and how that person was screened, including the vital step of verification of resumes and references. Due diligence requires that hiring employers verify information presented by prospective employees during hiring processes. Any personal references given should be contacted at least by telephone—if not interviewed in person, which is preferable. It can be very surprising what personal referees will disclose about a candidate, particularly if that referee was not even aware that he or she had been listed as a personal reference. Likewise, it is important to know that if the candidate claimed on a resume to have successfully completed a masters degree at a reputable university, that he or she actually did complete the program with official recognition from the institution. The employer will not only be uncovering inaccurate information in a competitive process, but also learning about the real ethics of the candidate before any hiring has taken place. For employers such as government, it is far easier to reject a dishonest candidate before hiring has taken place as opposed to trying to remove someone after he or she has been trained and working for a period of time and established a positive work record before the dishonest traits were uncovered.

SECURITY CLEARANCES

Related closely to the issue of internal risk is requiring security clearances within a facility with access levels based on function and level of required security to protect proprietary information. Through experience it became evident that work units in a major facility were hiring new employees prior to the completion of security clearance processes, or even failing to do them at all. In numerous cases, there were employees already hired that actually failed to pass the security clearance process and could not be issued an access card. This situation creates major problems as employees required for meetings inside the secure area cannot get in without the access card. The result can be friction between work units and managers and subsequent work delays. In one experience, the problem was solved when building-wide hiring packages were designed by Human Resources that included detailed instructions on when and how to seek security clearances to ensure that this critical piece of the hiring process is completed prior to hire. Standardization always helps with these situations, but support must be there from the executive level for it to work.

PERFORMANCE MANAGEMENT

Facilities managers often have mixed results in regard to hiring both full-time and part-time workers and technicians. This is a common problem in all organizations that can be rectified to some degree with either introduction of performance management policy, if none existed before, or making more of an effort to follow performance management policy already in existence. Sometimes, existing policy needs to be examined and improved. Successful organizations tend to be ones that have developed good policy on the standardized and effective selection of employees and then provided the support for developing their careers.

Along with screening candidates properly prior to hiring them is the ability to retain and maintain the employee to standards of performance. It is also critically important to manage performance through a program of performance management and employee development. This gives the owner/operator documented proof of the employee's competence and ability to use equipment to an accepted standard, and it shows ongoing development of the employee that serves also as a retention tool satisfying employee desire to improve himself or herself. These written records serve to help protect the owner/operator against liability if he or she has taken reasonable steps to hire and maintain a quality and skilled workforce. It also gives employees measured satisfaction with their jobs through positive feedback and the ability to improve where necessary to maintain standards of behavior and performance. Employees can build on documented performance to improve their careers and seek challenges, and likewise they can be held accountable for substandard work and behavioral issues. Substandard performance can then be improved through management coordinated work improvement plans, which document the efforts to get the employee back to acceptable performance and/or behaviors.

HIRING FACILITIES MANAGEMENT
TECHNICIANS AND WORKERS

Hiring quality facilities management technicians and workers can be a successful venture if enough time is devoted to the process and quality policies are used. Approaching the hiring process as a waste of time or something Human Resources should be doing demonstrates misunderstanding of the process. Facilities managers should be viewing the screening and hiring process as an opportunity to find a dynamic new member of the team who will contribute in a meaningful way for years to come. Searching for high skill sets begins at the resume stage as a job description designed to attract the right type of employees, complete with a competitive compensation package. These are not minimum-wage workers that are being sought to run facilities, but rather, reliable, skilled and certified professionals that will be trusted with multimillion dollar facilities and the lives of many people. Trying to save money by offering weak compensation is not going to work and the manager doing it will wind up finding mediocre to poor candidates, which will inevitably lead to high turnover and having to resort to the same hiring process very soon after completing the first one.

The competitive candidate is going to have a balance of solid academic and technical training balanced with experience. For example, an electrician's resume will have to show the school to which he or she went, the courses or level taken and any professional certifications or qualifications, and all of the work history. Sometimes, examining a candidate's work history will show very short tenures and ongoing movement from one job to the next. This in itself is not an indication of an unstable and unreliable worker that will not stay long, but it is certainly a situation the hiring manager should question, as the answers will contain the information to verify the work ethic.

It should also be necessary to be officially certified as an electrician before the application is even accepted for screening. The same goes for other technical qualifications such as welding and gas, as well as fire system technicians and a variety of others.

The first thing that the hiring process should do is to develop a skills test based on a reasonable skill within the facility that the successful candidate should be able to complete. Those successful with the technical skill will move to interview. The interview process will draw upon what the candidate presented, along with standardized questions that all candidates are asked for scoring and comparison.

Following the interview, there should always be a background investigation done by the interview team to verify all information and ensure a candidate is not embellishing accomplishments—or flat out inventing them and assuming the employer will not bother checking. The background investigation should be done with written permission, and if the candidate fails to give permission, the process is done and the candidate advised that he or she was unsuccessful due to the manager's inability to confirm information. Background investigations should always be thorough and all persons and telephone numbers checked for accuracy. It can be amazing what some people will tell a background investigator when they show up in person to do an interview. Experience has shown that references selected by candidates can go as far as admitting that they know of drug activity with which the candidate was involved and/or other behavioral problems. These bits of information might not come out during a quick verification phone call, and they certainly will not come out if the background process is ignored altogether.

The results of this kind of a process should be scored by a hiring panel and then presented to management for a final decision on hiring. At this point in the hiring process, management should have a good idea of whom they are hiring with a reasonable expectation of success.

Once hired, the employee should be subject to a probationary period, communicated up front during the process; candidates should be advised that they could be released if they do not succeed during this period. They should also be guided with good performance management, which includes ongoing developmental support and, in particular, regular appraisals during the probationary period to document progress and provide the evidence necessary to release a candidate if performance standards are not being reached. If employees feel that the organization is developing them, they will more likely stay and represent the organization as professionals, while the organization gets a highly qualified workforce in return.

Security Guards

Among some of the lowest paid employees in North America and Europe are security guards, which has always seemed to be somewhat ironic, given the high degree of responsibility often entrusted to these employees. Security guards are hired to provide access control services, which puts them in control of access databases containing the information and whereabouts of every employee and occupant, including chief executive officers and other high-ranking people. It also puts the security guard in control of electronically operated doors as well as the electronic opening and closing schedules, key control systems, records of access, alarms, and delivery schedules. Security guards know just about everything that is going on in a facility, including the comings and goings of high-ranking persons; security guards have knowledge of any personal transgressions going on inside the facility, just by virtue of knowing who entered the facility, at what time, and where they went once inside. This is enough to give any corporate officer pause to think about who he or she is hiring, how the person was screened, and how much compensation he or she receives. Although this is not an advertisement to improve the pay of security guards, it should be considered that a security guard has a lot of proprietary knowledge that may encourage corporate officers to rethink how they are securing the premises or business and how they provide compensation. Have they hired the cheapest contract guards they could find, making $10 an hour—or have they put effort into screening reliable people on a better pay grade that might encourage some loyalty, not to mention attracting a higher caliber applicant? Stories abound on the Internet about armored car guards picking up cash on their regular routes, only to disappear with bags of cash. This is the direct result of hiring risky people and giving them daily access to money and valuable assets that they could never dream of attaining; they see the very people they are serving enjoying the wealth that these guards were paid just peanuts to transport. It is difficult to predict who is going to commit such acts after hire, but companies can certainly reduce the risk of this happening to them by properly screening and compensating the people placed in positions of high responsibility.

An example comes from the Boston CBS affiliate: "Methuen Armored Car Robbery an Inside Job" (September 27, 2011, 5:21 p.m.): Two contract armored car drivers picked up hundreds of thousands of dollars worth of cash from businesses on their route, only to have the bags of cash worth about $380,000 allegedly stolen, before driving to the police station to report that a robber had taken one of the officers' hand guns, taken the bag of money, and run away. The drivers were quickly arrested and admitted their involvement, but blamed each other for the idea (http://boston.cbslocal .com/2011/09/27/3-arrested-in-methuen-armored-car-robbery/).

The point is that paying someone at or near minimum wage produces automatic struggle in the employee's life just to pay basic bills and to put food on the family table. In security, the low-paid employee also is often charged with securing high-value assets and money or providing service to highly compensated people, which creates a level of frustration and even anger in the employee. Paying the employee a higher salary, and/or including benefits not only makes the employee feel more valued but also reduces his or her family's struggle to survive and thereby helps to satisfy the security aspect of Maslow's Hierarchy of Needs. That satisfaction, combined with a more accountable and in-depth hiring process, can reduce the risk of the employee performing internal theft as an answer to low compensation, thereby reducing the costs for the corporate entity in the long run.

Uniformed Security Guards

Uniformed security guards are seen all over the Western world in cities and towns and are given responsibilities that often do not match their often light-screening and low-compensation rates. Traditionally, security guards do not enjoy high regard in society, and often pay structures and compensation match that reputation. Guards are often stereotyped as people with little training, few responsibilities, and not much to do when at work.

The author's own experience as a security guard is typical of what can occur with some lower end contract companies:

As with many security officers, my ultimate goal was to become a police officer. My first job, in the industry, in 1986, was as a security guard, consisting of poor pay of about $4.50 an hour, which was minimum wage at the time and deemed competitive. On my first day, I reported to the company headquarters, received my uniform, signed some administrative papers, and was given my first assignment as overnight security at a construction site. I was somewhat surprised that there was no training but figured I would probably receive some at the site. I went to the site, which was located in a dark, isolated area, and after looking around for about fifteen minutes, finally found the person whom I was relieving in a small, cigarette smoke-filled shack with no windows. He was sitting in front of a makeshift table with his lunchbox open, reading a paperback novel under a single light bulb. Quite happy to see me arrive, he was getting ready to leave until I asked him what I was supposed to do and what my responsibilities were. I advised him that I had no training and no instructions. He replied, "Just walk around the site once every hour and make sure everything

---

is OK." Then he left me there. I sat in the shack and, although there was an old telephone, there was no phone book, no procedures, no phone numbers, or anything alluding to what my role was and what to do if something did happen.

It always bothered me that I was placed in such a dangerous position by a large company with expectations of performance for a client of protecting a site where the assets were worth considerable money and where the site had dangers around every corner. The possibility of liability was huge in that job—not to mention considerable personal danger for the employees earning only minimum wage with no benefits. After the initial shift, I searched for another security job and quickly found one that actually had a 40-hour basic training course that employees needed to attend before they reported to their first assignments. The job was much better organized, with basic training, better instructions and active supervision, and I stayed with this organization and enjoyed some good posts at a high-tech company and later a national museum. These varied experiences stayed with me and I was later able to use them to establish standards of hire, training, and performance management that I believe are for everyone's benefit, from the employee to the supervisor, the client, and, finally, the company.

HIRING/TRAINING IN SECURITY

Experiences in the security industry also brought to attention how poorly many security companies selected employees, how little the new employees were trained, and then how much value was attached to the assets that these new employees were assigned to secure. Security officers had the most basic of interviews (not behaviorally based) and supplied three references, none of whom were ever called for verification. Officers were then quickly signed up to look after expensive assets for unsuspecting clients, who likely did not perform any due diligence themselves in confirming what they were getting under contract. Individual officers were being placed in a position by the hiring company where they might have to perform an arrest using specific legislation such as criminal code or the Trespass to Property Act, do a first aid intervention, or make notifications when they really had no idea what they were doing or what procedures they should be following. This can be contrasted with the author's own experience years later of commanding a group of well-trained, higher end security officers in a critical facility. Based on those earlier experiences as a security guard and later as a security manager, the author developed my own hiring process for security guards to address job skills and potential, physical ability to perform tasks expected of security staff, and potential future liabilities. The process mirrored that of a police force but at a level appropriate to security staff. This included resume screening; behavioral interviews; a physical/judgment test of climbing five floors of stairs and doing a first aid task at the top; a review of references, including interviewing the referenced persons; a background check to verify the resume and reputation; a police records check; and, finally, a probationary period with frequent progress reports—all done with the applicant's agreement. The author's effort to add a physical test as part of the hiring process came as a result of a fire alarm in a multifloor facility:

The floor supervisor sent a runner, as was our policy under a two-stage alarm system, whose job it was to find the source of alarm and visually confirm that it was false or real based on the presence of smoke, fire, or simply an odor. We had five minutes to make this confirmation and stop the alarm from going into full evacuation mode, which would shut down business for at least an hour and require 2000 people to move quickly out of the buildings. Our runner had to take the stairs, as the elevators shut down automatically and grounded, and we knew from the panel signal that the alarm source was on the third floor. As the time ticked away toward the five-minute mark, I was getting more and more concerned because I was not getting any radio traffic from the runner, who also happened to be one of our older, but long-serving employees. He certainly knew what he was doing but, as we discovered, had other health issues. The security supervisor advised me that she was not getting a response to her calls on the radio, so I sent a second runner and began heading upstairs myself.

Feeling that my runner might be experiencing a medical emergency, I called him again and he finally answered. I asked him where he was and he replied, "I don't know"; he sounded confused, which was alarming because he had worked in the building for ten years. I ordered the supervisor to call for an ambulance and found the employee on the second floor. He was out of breath and completely confused. We got him downstairs and paramedics began to treat him. Although he did not have a heart attack or anything serious, he decided not long afterward to retire as he realized that he did not have the physical stamina to continue answering emergency calls.

Although the author knew from case law that they could not retroactively insert a fitness testing component as an employee standard into the hiring process, the author consulted with Human Resources about inserting a physical/skills test into our hiring process as due diligence and a way to let candidates know that they might have to climb five floors of stairs and perform tasks at the end. This simple test actually eliminated some candidates that had not disclosed physical issues that would have impacted their employment but consisted of things for which they could not screen. The author personally watched a candidate climb three of five flights of stairs and become unsteady to the point where one of our test proctors had to grab him, help him to the ground, and perform first aid on him. Another candidate during the same session climbed to the top of the stairs and, due to his advanced state of exhaustion from climbing the stairs, was unable to think through assessing a cut injury to a person's hand, add pressure, and then bandage the wound in accordance with first aid procedures. Without these simple little tests, we might have hired these employees and discovered their physical limitations during a real emergency when they failed to execute their tasks in the middle of a crisis.

This new method of assessment produced a much more thoroughly checked candidate with a demonstrated reputation of reliability and performance that could then be put in a position of trust with expensive assets and proprietary information. Further to the issue of hiring quality employees is the fact that more and more jurisdictions now require security guards to pass minimum screening standards and hold a government-issued security guard license to be able to function as a security guard or private investigator in that jurisdiction. Candidates are required to demonstrate that they do not have a criminal record and have passed a recognized training program on basic skills. In some jurisdictions, employing agencies must be registered with the state or provincial regulating body before they can hire security guards or private investigators. This is a step forward in establishing standards of hiring and training in the security industry [1].

Performing intensive screening is a more lengthy and somewhat more costly process than many security companies wish to invest in, but it produces a superior, more defendable product in the end; in a personal manner it produces an employee who is far more likely to be a good caliber person possessing the loyalty and integrity needed in this line of work and who will also be more likely to develop a degree of loyalty to the company. Speaking of liability, if your entity is challenged as an organization about the quality and reliability of your employees, a well developed and standardized screening process would likely be deemed appropriate and looks very reasonable in the eyes of a court. We are now in the post-9/11 era where security personnel are the ground-level eyes and ears of society and more directly, building owners/operators on not only facility maintenance mishaps and criminal activity but also increasing terrorist activity. It is not only critical to identify and select the correct employees but also to maintain high-caliber employees with proper training, development, support, and compensation to do the job of ensuring that facilities are safe and secure.

SCHEDULING

Any facility manager or security manager with hired employees or on-site contracted employees will likely be faced with scheduling requirements and the resulting issues that can impact morale, the budget, and workforce effectiveness. These impacts include maintaining work–life balance for the employees and effective coverage for the employer, trying to minimize overtime costs while ensuring that adequate services are maintained, such as having a minimum number of employees not only to keep mechanical systems functioning properly, but also to evacuate the building and perform mandated functions if required. These factors must be considered and staffed accordingly to ensure that the organization does not get caught in an emergency with insufficient staffing by design. The cost might be higher to maintain a higher staffing level, but these costs must match mandated tasks in order for the manager not to be held accountable in an emergency for holding back to save money when people were getting injured or killed.

Creating any schedule can be a complex project at the best of times. It requires a work analysis to be completed first to determine how many people are required to perform daily functions and then off-hours functions as well. For twenty-four-hour coverage, shifts can generally be arranged in two twelve-hour shifts, or three eight-hour shifts. These can also be subdivided into other smaller and perhaps overlapping shifts to ensure adequate coverage during peak or high-volume periods depending upon the nature of the business at hand.

The work analysis also must consider how much work that one full-time position can reasonably perform in one year to come up with the full-time equivalent (FTE). This must be done for each separate position type because, for example, a facility technician does vastly different work than a receptionist. From the FTE count, one can determine how many employees are required per shift to reliably and reasonably perform the work. Other factors to consider include staffing to account for employee absences due to sickness, training, vacation, and acting assignments elsewhere. Larger organizations can be required to staff each shift with an extra employee or two to ensure coverage, while smaller entities might get away with employing part-time workers and temporary employees to fill the schedule holes. These numbers should always be considered with the assistance of the entity's human resources managers and perhaps outside employment counselors. It is critical to get the staffing numbers accurate to avoid either overstaffing or understaffing the shifts.

Supervisors must consider overtime costs during operational situations when the unexpected happens. No shift staffing model is perfect and work units will eventually suffer from more than expected absences. In these situations, overtime may be necessary to fill the holes, but it does not stop the responsibility of supervisors from looking at options in an effort to reduce costs. In these moments, it is possible to look at redistribution of work and prioritization of tasks but, most of all, when part-time and temporary employees are on-site, extending their shifts, as long as they have not exceeded any time constraints in terms of their contracts, such as going past forty hours in a week, which would constitute overtime. These small extensions may alleviate the need to pay time and a half to a full-time employee who would have to be called in to cover. Over the period of a year, these strategies can save the corporate entity thousands of staffing dollars. The main desire, however, is to achieve the optimal staffing level for your shifts with the proper analysis and hiring decisions that will keep the overtime budget from affecting the financial health of the organization while getting the work done.

FACILITIES AND SECURITY: CONFLICT?

The relationship between facilities and security can be strained at times but, ideally, one is actually dependent upon the other for success. There has traditionally been competition between work units in larger buildings and complexes; as security is the emerging trend in the world of facilities management, which has been around for many decades, facilities has a tendency to look down upon security as an expensive and unnecessary competition for the budgetary resources required for repairs, renovations, and new purchases. Accordingly, in many locations, security has suffered from being the new kid on the block with few resources and little political support within the larger organization. This lack of support generally means underfunding at budget time and a situation where security managers have to continually propose expenditures and gain support, often on a case-by-case basis. Experience has shown that in situations when security might have once teamed up with facilities, the two disciplines could become quite hostile toward one another and often were duplicating function in competition rather cooperating to mutual benefit. This self-defeating phenomenon can become a three-ringed circus where facilities, often with the ear of corporate executives, was always pushing the maintenance contractor to do more with less and security was looked upon as a necessary evil and competitor by facilities; in the meantime, maintenance and security had learned to work together for efficiencies and for resources in order to survive the hostile atmosphere. Utopia would have been for all three entities to work together, and this is where organizations can experience true savings and efficiencies and be able to achieve fiscally responsible progress in all three areas if those work units can pool resources and work together.

Consider one example of this kind of conflict in the facilities/security world. Always short on personnel and operating capital, the security manager began seeking the cooperation and assistance of the maintenance manager, realizing that both work units had personnel working in the facility in different locations at different times. The rationale was that, if a security patrol could not cover a particular location, it could ask the maintenance manager to have the maintenance workers assist. Likewise, with security officers circulating the facility 24/7, security could also offer the services of observation of equipment or readings of temperature or trouble lights to speed up detection of problems and response before a critical maintenance problem got out of hand. This kind of cooperation can help work units succeed until the political landscape improves, and the facilities, security, and maintenance work units work together to mutual benefit instead of competition. Sometimes it only takes a change at a leadership position, but it is always advantageous and efficient for the three disciplines to pool resources and work toward common goals, rather than functioning in silos of political conflict.

As a final point, although maintenance and security may work together as overlap and in cooperation, it is still critical not to have security personnel touching maintenance equipment or even turning it off—in reference to asking a security guard to turn off HVAC equipment or a gas supply in a cafeteria, for example. Security personnel generally are

195

not hired specifically for that purpose or trained to use maintenance or technical equipment; thus they can be held responsible or even liable if something goes wrong after they touched it. Observation and recording of readings on behalf of the technicians as a part of normal duties may be fine if they were trained to a specific purpose, but touching technical equipment is not recommended and should be avoided in all circumstances by security staff unless directed to do so by a fire department authority during an emergency.

When security staff are intended to operate or touch technical equipment, or the employer wishes security to handle a technical task, it should be done in the following manner with accountability. The technical task should be an item contained in the position description; the employee should be screened for technical skill during hiring and trained to an established standard (documented with annual refresher recertification); finally, any technical procedure should form part of the security post orders and include instructions on note-taking, formal documentation of the incident, and notification procedures to supervisors and persons responsible for the equipment. When an emergency has occurred, the security employee should also formally notify the responding fire/police/ambulance personnel immediately as that information could be relevant to incident response and medical treatment. Assignment of technical tasks to security employees should never be done without the recommendation and consultation of the equipment manufacturer and the union or association representing the employee; to go one step further, it is always recommended to consult with local fire department officials to ensure the task, when assigned to security personnel, is not contravening the fire code or interfering with a fire department response procedure.

REFERENCE

1. Real Estate Council of Ontario. 2014. *Principles of Property Management*. Ontario: Media Linx Printing Group.

16

Policies and Procedures

SAFETY AND SECURITY POLICIES AND PROCEDURES

In any organization or facility where people gather to work, live, or play, policies and procedures are essential to set standards, to let people know how to behave, to keep the peace, to keep everyone safe, and to make order out of chaos when unexpected situations and emergencies occur. These written rules are the basis of keeping people safe and handling emergencies, and they can also be used by the facility manager and owner/operator to defend themselves against litigation when their actions in an emergency are challenged.

Policies and procedures must be written in a very clear and concise manner, and directed to the lowest comprehension level of people expected to be present in the facility. The most well meaning policy will not be understood and will not stand up to scrutiny if it was written above the level of understanding of the people it is aimed at directing. Experience has taught that the key to excellent policy and procedure writing is not only in the composition, but also in the vetting and editing stages of the writing. The more people that read the draft work, the higher is the chance that the author will purge any misunderstanding, lack of clarity, and potential double meaning. This is not to say that a policy and procedure author can grab anyone off the street to help develop the work, but rather that those chosen must be confidential about proprietary information, strong in experience, strong in education, and generally of a level appropriate to be of assistance. However, near the end of the process it is highly recommended to bring in persons from within the organization but at a lower level to read the policy or procedure to ensure that multiple

197

end users will understand the writing clearly and be able to easily apply the meaning.

Safety and security policies and procedures should be written in a standard format using action words so that the reader can quickly understand what the meaning or intention of the policy or procedure is and be able to assimilate the information easily. People entering facilities in particular do not want to stand in one spot and be forced to read a long and convoluted text and will simply take a quick look and say to themselves: "Forget it!" and walk away. The writing must grab the attention of the reader with an action word and be descriptive in as few words as possible. It must be such that the reader can capture it in one glance. If that occurs, the reader will likely be more willing to read several more policies or procedures if they are laid out in the same manner.

Policies and procedures in the security and maintenance worlds *should never be written in isolation.* A building or facility is a place within a community where multiple types of responders will converge during an emergency situation, meaning that each type of response will be a multi-layered response involving a number of responders from police, fire and ambulance to professional cleanup and repair crews, hydro, and municipal response crews such as road and water/sewage workers amongst others. Accordingly, security post orders should be composed in consultation with those aforementioned agencies to ensure that the response of one group does not interfere with, delay, or directly impede the efforts of another group, and that all tiers of response are recognized by each other through common planning. Building maintenance and/or security should be part of a wider plan to ensure fluid, effective response to an emergency. It is unprofessional and dangerous to have, for example, an ambulance crew attending the front entrance of a major facility to treat and transport a heart attack victim, only to find that the security department was not aware of the 911 call, and further to realize that the ambulance had reported to the wrong building. In a well organized response scenario, the people around the victim, who are calling the emergency in, would have had previously published instructions to call the security unit, which would place the 911 call and enable security to immediately dispatch response to provide First Aid/CPR to the victim. In the meantime, another security officer is waiting to direct the ambulance through to the correct location as soon as it arrives at the facility. This fluid response can save valuable minutes in the response to a heart attack victim, for example, and it removes a great deal of chaos from the emergency when everyone knows what to do and both agencies know what to expect as the emergency response unfolds.

Most security and maintenance departments tend to be smaller units whose hard-working members are dispersed throughout the facility during the working day. Having a well developed, multijurisdictional response procedure gives the facility or security manager time to assemble responders before the ambulance or fire crew arrives, rather than having the manager acting out of surprise when responders suddenly appear at the main entrance asking where the emergency is and what is going on. Those critical minutes can mean the difference between life and death to victims.

THE ART OF CREATING POLICIES

Policies can be short, containing nothing more than a sentence explaining what to do. For example, a policy about smoking near a building entrance can read: "No smoking within 20 feet of the building entrance." This contains an action and direction with clarity of delivery. It may have been written in response to a complaint from nonsmoking employees walking through clouds of smoke on their way into the office building during the winter months as cold smokers huddle near the entrance to stay warm while they take a smoking break. Employees caught violating this policy could be held accountable against the policy, and such actions and remedies would be contained in the approved building policy document.

Written Policies

It is normal for policies to abound in organizations and even apartment buildings and other facilities such as retail stores. When policies are being developed and written, it is necessary to have a place to contain them in an organized fashion so that they remain ever present, relevant, and, most importantly, searchable.

Policies are guidelines that form the *how-to* for an organization and present the opportunity for consistency of activity despite the constant turnover of new employees. Written policies are living documents in that they are never complete. There are always new ideas and/or reactions to incidents that will cause policy revision or creation of new policy where none existed before. Best practices are always candidates to become policy if they have not already been included as they are generally tried-and-true methods of getting work completed efficiently.

Completed or revised policy items should always be signed off by the executive level before one can count on the organization's support when a particular policy is challenged or an employee is testifying to his or her actions in court and referring to the company policy as the reason he or she did a job in a particular manner.

Most large organizations will produce a policy book of some kind and, in particular, physical security units will have what is commonly known as "Post Orders." This is best described as a policy and procedure book that contains all of the duties and rules that security employees must follow and be rated against for performance. Post Orders will contain the mission of that particular post, describe the location and patrol routes, detail the routine to follow, list the electronic and manual locking schedules, describe the duties by rank level, and set parameters for shifts and scheduling. Post Orders will also detail incident response protocols, recording of information, notification procedures, key holders and alarm protocols, administration procedures, and just about anything of importance for the security staff. They can also form the basis of a service contract since most of the information needed to form the contract will be found in post orders.

PROCEDURES

The representation of suspicious packages in Figure 16.1 is used courtesy of Homeland Security and serves as a good starting point; however, every facility or building has differences and specific organizational realities that should be covered by a facility-specific suspicious-package handling procedure.

A good example of a facility-specific suspicious-package handling policy/procedure was born out of the post-9/11 era of realization that such procedures were missing from a facility of critical importance and there were insufficient established procedures for consistency and safety in the management of incidents. Following a year-long stint in the corporate policy section and subsequent posting in corporate Human Resources, the author was in place as the facility security manager by the fall of 2001, just before the September 11, 2001, terror attacks in New York City. The author actually watched the second plane hit the World Trade Center on a work television and found himself in charge of physical security in a large facility of critical importance with 2000 people in his facility and no written policies on what to do in such a situation. In

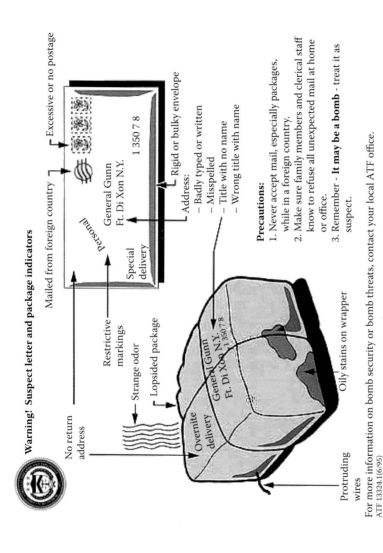

Warning! Suspect letter and package indicators

Excessive or no postage

Mailed from foreign country

Rigid or bulky envelope

General Gunn
Ft. Di Xon N.Y.
1 350 7 8

Personal

Special delivery

Address:
– Badly typed or written
– Misspelled
– Title with no name
– Wrong title with name

Restrictive markings

Strange odor

Lopsided package

No return address

Overnite delivery

General Gunn
Ft. Di Xon N.Y.
1 350 7 8

Oily stains on wrapper

Protruding wires

Precautions:

1. Never accept mail, especially packages, while in a foreign country.
2. Make sure family members and clerical staff know to refuse all unexpected mail at home or office.
3. Remember - **It may be a bomb** - treat it as suspect.

For more information on bomb security or bomb threats, contact your local ATF office.

ATF 13324.1(6/95)

Figure 16.1 What do staff members do when they encounter these suspicious items? (From the Department of Homeland Security: http://www.usps.com/news/2001/press/pr01_1022gsa_print.htm.)

201

those early moments on 9/11, it was being reported live that officials did not know if the attacks were localized or widespread and the author was aware that all aircraft were being grounded and other facilities of critical importance were going into lockdown. The author quickly decided that the author needed executive direction on whether to close the facility to outside traffic and get better information. The author realized that the organization was not prepared because it took some time to get an answer.

Since 9/11, my organization has dramatically improved the corporate policies and procedures in relation to major events in activity, similarly to all large organizations in the post-9/11 era. In my particular situation, the author realized that he needed to lead a major overhaul of written policy and procedures, and develop the existing security post orders to a much more sophisticated and encompassing level that fed into corporate policy seamlessly. One of the missing procedures requiring development was a suspicious-package handling procedure for the building occupants. This procedure has been referred to in particular as an example in this book because every building, facility, or complex in the developed world should have one of these procedures posted for all occupants to use. To develop this procedure, research was conducted with other facilities with a procedure already in place. Direct research and consultation was then made with the mailroom, the loading dock, and an experienced tactical team member who had specific training and experience in response to suspicious items and explosives. The completed procedure was formally submitted for approval several weeks later and quickly attained that approval from executive leaders. The procedure was laminated and posted throughout the building—by elevators, staircases, and entry points, as well as being published in the facility directory. There was also training provided to work units such as receptionists, mailroom workers, and loading dock staff as those employees came into daily contact with incoming packages. Such a procedure for suspicious packages was deemed necessary as the high-profile, large facility had been a target for inappropriate deliveries in the past. Post-9/11, this reality became even more prominent with the deliveries of white powder in envelopes to various government offices around the world.

In the following example, a suspicious package was defined as an unidentified package, misaddressed package, anything looking out of place, packages with oily stains, packages x-rayed and showing batteries and wires, and packages from unexpected senders or no sender listed at all. All of these could consist of written threats from criminals/terrorists or mentally ill persons, explosive devices, biological or chemical agents, or even items sent by angry people consisting of soiled diapers and feces, addressed to executives (which actually happened!). None of these items should make it past the loading dock or mailroom; however, if they did, it was paramount to have them dealt with quickly and safely with a minimal loss of productivity.

Example 16.1: Suspicious Package Procedure

Always treat the threat as real:

1. Contact xxx Security Services Unit at Ext-8721.
2. Notify your supervisor.
3. Do not touch the item further.
4. If you have touched the item, gently place it on the floor in a contained area and stop handling the item.
5. Secure the area to avoid contamination of others and evacuate staff from the immediate area to a safe adjacent location.
6. Wait for security personnel to give further direction.
7. Wash your hands with soap and water to reduce risk of contamination.
8. For your own safety, closely follow directions given by your supervisor and security personnel.
9. Record all names of persons who may have had contact with the suspicious item.

Note: Item 9 was put in place to ensure that cross contamination of biological or chemical agents could be stopped before it became a problem and that any potentially contaminated persons could be located and treated quickly, if necessary.

This procedure was developed, approved, and posted in 2001 and it remains as the standard in that particular facility of critical importance today. It simply instructs the employee to not touch the item further, decontaminate if possible, isolate the area, and call Security. Security's job is to investigate the incident quickly and call in the necessary resources to determine what the package contains and how to dispose of it. What becomes readily evident in the procedure is clarity of message. There is no mistaking the instructions or the seriousness of the procedure. It gives the involved employee a sense of security and safety in knowing what to do, who to call for help, and, if he or she has touched the item, to decontaminate himself or herself.

Further to this procedure, another procedure was developed between Security and Maintenance, who had specific responsibilities. The reason for doing this is, again, clarity of purpose and procedure, and consistency. It is critical to have different work units functioning in cooperation toward the same goal with complementary tasks. Without coordination, chaos ensues as work units working independently will inevitably perform tasks out of order or in direct contravention of each other, often canceling out the efforts of the other. Protocols of response also had to be worked out with the local police responders (including the tactics team) and the ambulance and fire department so that each responder knows how the situation will unfold inside the facility and what to expect when he or she gets inside to deal with the suspicious item. For planning purposes, a protocol provides the leaders of those outside responders enough information to make a reasonable guess on sending numbers and types of resources initially; of course, it is always subject to change once the resources arrive at the scene and an assessment is made by a professional responder.

In the case of the example policy, the security officers responding had to ensure the item was isolated and all persons evacuated from the danger area, including shutting off electronic card readers and magnetic locks and physically locking doors. Simultaneously, the maintenance employees were instructed to shut off heating, ventilation, air conditioning (HVAC) systems to prevent any contaminants from circulating throughout the buildings if they had become airborne. This can be the difference between a localized incident requiring the temporary isolation and decontamination of several rooms or company executives facing a decision to shut down the entire building, which could potentially affect business in a very expensive and time-consuming manner. Such a shutdown after chemical or biological airborne contaminants have circulated through the HVAC system would require decontamination of each space, elevator, hallway, and room in the facility as well as the HVAC pipes, heating and cooling units, and air returns connected to each space, among other problems. In a large facility, this could take an enormous amount of time where costs to clean and make the facility safe could be exorbitant—not to mention the cost of lost business and productivity due to the shutdown. In the case of an apartment building or other living space, occupants would be unable to return to their residences until the facility had been thoroughly decontaminated, resulting in costs of accommodation and food for those displaced. The following anecdote actually occurred in a facility of critical importance.

On one routine morning the security manager was walking through the basement near the loading dock when the door to his right suddenly opened and a clerk thrust a small object into his hand and said "Look what come through the mail!" The security manager looked and was a little startled to realize that the clerk had opened a package, removed a stick of dynamite, and handed it to him. Because it was not known if the stick was inert or live, it had to be treated as live until proven otherwise. The security manager, per policy, walked the few feet to the loading dock and placed the stick of dynamite into a container on the floor, closed the loading dock, and called for police response, which eventually included the explosives disposal unit. The stick of dynamite was disposed later. It turned out that the dynamite was stored for years at a deployed location and a cleaner had found it, addressed it to the corporate headquarters, and sent it, with no ill intent. Amazing what can happen in the world of facilities!

In conclusion, policies and procedures should be a written way of doing things that is designed to detail how work is to unfold and what to do if anything goes wrong. Such efforts can be used to defend against litigation and to demonstrate reasonable efforts to mitigate any resulting incident caused by your or your entity's presence and function. From a facility owner's/operator's perspective, policies and procedures help to make the facility a safer place in a cost-effective manner. It does not cost much to compose a policy and post it on the wall. It also demonstrates to the occupants that the owner/operator actually cares about the people and assets in the facility. The middle of a crisis is much too late to realize that you do not have a policy. Anticipation of potential crises is important, and developing policy to effect an efficient response is going to be viewed in a positive light post-incident and will likely save the organization and employees much difficulty and money in the long run.

17

Occupational Health and Safety

Occupational Health and Safety (OHS) is a topic that often accompanies facilities management no matter where one is in the developed world. It is a method of protecting workers in any potentially hazardous workplace regardless of the type of work with which they are engaged. Although common law applies responsibilities to employers about safety in the workplace in most jurisdictions, common law is based mostly on common sense and past court decisions, without consistent standards or policy and little accountability until the employer is sued following an injury or death. To add standards, policies, procedures, and most importantly of all, protection around such an important subject for workers and their families, governments in the developed world have been enacting OHS legislation for the protection of workers and their families.

Obvious settings for occupational health and safety concerns are workplaces like factories, pipelines, and any work that involves heavy machinery and physical danger on a daily basis; however, hazards actually do exist in every workplace, including offices, schools, and other facilities. Therefore, occupational health and safety remains in a state of growth in workplaces around the world.

Occupational health and safety regulations are enacted within most developed democratic nations as a standardized and legislated method of protecting workers in the workplace and requiring employers to abide by safety regulations in order to protect workers and reduce the risk of death, injury, and sickness caused by the workplace environment. A wonderful example can be found with the government of the province of Ontario, Canada, where legislation exists called the *Occupational Health and Safety Act.* This advanced piece of legislation was enacted for the protection of all workers in the workplace and contains the following sections:

- Part 1—Application: This section legislates exceptions such the Act such as the government or Crown, private residences, teachers, farmers, and self-employed persons as these have their own regulations.
- Part 2—Administration: This section outlines the powers, chain of command, and accountabilities, including appointment of inspectors and directors that make the system work. Also included are the establishment of standardized training, certification of members and local representatives, and the mandatory selection of a representative in workplaces that exceed five persons and provisions for workplaces that do not exceed five persons. Further support for the selected workers comes in the form of a requirement for the employer to pay workers as though they are at work when training or performing other related duties connected to the OHS committee.
- Part 3—Duties of employers and others such as constructors, supervisors, workers, owners, and others of relevance. Also included are policies on violence and harassment and codes of practice.
- Part 4—Toxic substances are covered; this includes the material safety data sheets and hazardous material identification data sheets, as well as assessment protocols.
- Part 5—This section covers the right of a worker to refuse or stop work due to hazards and safety issues in the workplace and where health and safety are in danger due to work conditions.
- Part 6—This section prohibits reprisals in the form of discipline or dismissal by employers against workers that bring forward concerns or stop work due to safety issues in the workplace.
- Part 7—This section contains information about notices for various types of incidents such as death, injury, explosions, accidents, fire, or violence in the workplace causing injury.
- Part 8—This contains enforcement with the powers of the inspectors appointed under the Act, and various powers of entry for the purpose of site inspection and enforcement. Also specified are warrants and powers to seize items, notices of compliance, and obstruction of inspectors.

- Part 9—This section contains the offenses and penalties, trial information, publication of convictions, and limitation on prosecutions.
- Part 10—This section contains various regulations and includes a special section covering the taxi industry.

This legislation works well in Ontario from a worker's perspective, and it does not disrupt business from an employer's perspective but rather becomes a cooperative venture with the OHS committees.

OCCUPATIONAL HEALTH AND SAFETY COMMITTEES

Most large organizations and facilities have OHS committees, often featuring the participation of both management and workers, which is the actual intention and gives the effort a great deal of credibility. The OHS committee must be sponsored by the corporate executives and cannot function without that support. The committee should never be used for any purpose other than ensuring a safe work environment for the building occupants and OHS committees should always be developed *in partnership* with management. For any employer, occupational health and safety is a vital topic in a litigation-driven society such as has developed over the generations in the developed world. Although it is organized protection for the worker, it also provides protection to an employer that pays sufficient attention to it and complies voluntarily with OHS requirements in his or her jurisdiction. Occupational health and safety regulations provide standards of working conditions that are generally accepted as safe for the worker, yet still productive for the employer.

The tasking of these OHS committees is generally to meet as a group, perhaps once a month but as often as deemed necessary by the committee. It brings together people of different levels from across the organization with varying perspectives to ensure that the working environment remains a safe place for all employees from the lowest ranked employee up to the chief executive officer. Items to be discussed generally surround employee safety concerns including, for example, upcoming deliveries of fuel or chemicals as well as possibly complaints about water quality within a building or storage of large items in a hallway that is violating fire code clearance regulations. This is a small sample of items that can be discussed in these meetings, often concluding with management-supported solutions. These committees will openly discuss what is going on in the facility, what potential hazards may be caused by certain activities, and then might plan how to mitigate any potential problems. Following the formal meetings, OHS committees often go on scheduled walking tours of the facility to look for hazards that can be easily corrected, often just by speaking with the manager of a certain work area. Ongoing problems that are not getting fixed can be referred by the committee to a level of management that might hold the local manager accountable and get the hazard corrected. Examples of problems often found during walking tours can include unstable stacking of heavy items in hallways, blocking of emergency exits by furniture or delivered items, propping open of secure doors for convenience, safety issues such as emergency exit doors not functioning properly, or a myriad of other issues that go wrong over time in populated buildings.

Typical recommendations that come out of occupational health and safety committee meetings following debate about specific problems have been known to include things like installing automatic external defibrillators (AEDs) in the facility, or installing handwash stations with antibacterial solution, eyewash stations with water solution, or even just having first aid supply boxes installed in certain strategic locations. These kinds of recommendations are usually well received but can run into the problem of who is going to pay for them and, secondly, who is going to maintain them. Although well intentioned, none of these items will be of value if no one is willing to pick up the responsibility of maintaining them and/ or providing training. Failure to maintain them will result in the rapid collapse of the programs as the building population begins pilfering first aid supplies, just as the batteries run dead in the AEDs, the eyewash stations go dry of water, or the handwash stations simply run out of solution and become useless wall decorations. The supports and money must be in place before such fantastic items are added to the life-safety system of a facility.

Occupational health and safety committees usually offer formal government-sponsored training programs to their members, who can become certified practitioners. This kind of certification gives the employee credibility and it adds authority to any safety-related direction from committee members toward building occupants. In terms of career development, such certification and experience serves as a competitive and transferable skill to almost any large corporation or government entity as the employee not only begins to work with policies and procedures, but also will learn a great deal about the facilities within which he or she works and begin recognizing more hazards and safety issues in the workplace.

Within large facilities, occupational health and safety committees are an accepted reality containing members appointed from within business units in a building. These committees meet regularly with management approval, usually under the guidance of facilities management and/or security and with the participation of unions, management associations, a representative of the facility owner/operator, and anyone else deemed relevant such as temporary representatives of stakeholder groups for special events. Facilities management often provides the meeting place, and the committee usually meets once a month to discuss issues from previous meetings, and to bring up new facility or safety issues with everyone having a chance to participate or speak. The meetings conclude with a selected group doing health and safety tours of the work units in the building to discover new hazards, make recommendations, and ensure previously identified hazards have been addressed. In this cooperative working environment, occupational health and safety committees work very well and achieve their purpose of reducing risk and improving safety in the workplace. Schools, on the other hand, have union-appointed or elected health and safety representatives whose responsibility it is to tour the schools and perform inspections, with the knowledge and participation of school managers. Many of the items noted during school inspections include coffee pots in classrooms, overloaded circuits, paper hazards from teachers posting projects on the walls, improperly stored waste items, and broken equipment, among other issues.

A report is then filed by the OHS representative where hazards may be identified and whereby the school management will be given a chance to fix the issue without penalty. It is a cooperative system that works well with the participation of the union and management.

At first glance one might assume that this kind of legislation gives power to workers over their employers; however, when management and executives embrace the process and participate willingly, they will create a trust and a very positive working relationship with the workers that will serve to protect the employer from litigation and from being blamed for incidents just as much as it protects the workers from being exposed to unsafe conditions. These are win–win situations when implemented as intended and embraced by both sides.

As mentioned earlier, the Occupational Health and Safety Act for the province of Ontario in Canada is a fine example of a well developed piece of legislation that compels employers to conduct their business in a safe environment for the workers' sake and provides workers with a mechanism through which they can identify poor or unsafe working conditions, report them, and have them addressed without the threat of losing their jobs or being disciplined. Corporations and government of all levels in Canada now function with health and safety considered by management and workers as part of doing business. Facility managers across the world should do business in this way—whether there is legislation covering it or not—simply because it is the right thing to do and, in doing it, managers are actually protecting themselves against liability and litigation. A link for this legislation is http://www.ontario.ca/laws /statute/90o01#BK2.

MANAGERS: WHAT TO EXPECT FROM A HEALTH AND SAFETY INSPECTION

"Groan..." is a common first thought in a manager's head when a health and safety representative appears at the door and announces that he or she is doing a health and safety inspection. This is certainly no reason for most managers to panic or to worry about what is going to happen. Most professional workplaces are in relatively good shape when it comes to inspections, which are mainly done to find issues in the workplace and have them repaired or made safe again. The inspector may look for previous issues to ensure they have been rectified; if they have not been, there could be some explaining to do and other penalties, but for the most part the system functions well with managers complying with orders to fix safety concerns. Common issues exposed during health and safety inspections are easily fixed and consist of improper storage of items that are piled in such a manner that they partially block a hallway, violating minimum clearance regulations that are published in the local fire code, or items that have been stacked in a manner in which the pile could topple over and cause injury. Other issues can include improperly stored chemicals, or missing material safety data sheets, use of power bars that are overloading power circuits, and many more. Most of these issues are common-sense items that a manager can solve or even prevent by just being aware of the workplace and watching for shortcuts taken by employees. Managers and supervisors can be proactive in these instances by ensuring employees are following procedures of proper storage, power use, and chemical handling, among others. It is rare for these inspections to reach a disciplinary or enforcement stage as, more often than not, first-level management looks after the problem. However, the regulations are there if they are needed and the inspectors have the power to move forward with enforcement.

Personal Protection

Personal protection is another growing area of concern that has traditionally been ignored by both employers and employees alike in the world of facilities and construction. In the case of facilities management, there are many different types of hazards, ranging from the presence and manipulation of chemicals to significant noise pollution from functioning machinery and construction activity among others at work sites.

As an obscure but very real example, military and police force members face noise hazards from ongoing firearms training sessions when various weapons are fired at both indoor and outdoor ranges, requiring ear protection headsets in addition to soft, pliable earplugs to avoid hearing loss from the loud crack of a round being fired. Although these hearing protection devices are now generally provided by the employers as a standard safety procedure, in decades past it was not acceptable socially to wear protective devices and the result was hearing loss for many now-retired soldiers and police officers. For those brave soldiers and police that have been involved in actual combat or shooting situations, the hearing damage may be unavoidable as hearing protection devices cannot be worn in those types of dangerous operational situations; however, when the opportunity to wear hearing protection exists, it should be taken advantage of.

Other examples of potential hearing loss in industrial or facility applications include the testing and/or use of uninterrupted power supply (UPS) generators where, at times, the diesel engines can be as physically large as busses and so loud in volume that workers can barely communicate to each other standing side by side. This is an example of a controlled situation where hearing protection should be required by the employer and worn by the employee.

Chemical exposure is another potential hazard for which employers must have technology and/or procedures for dealing with accidental exposure. A simple but very common example is the installation of eyewash stations in the basement of a facility where chemicals may be delivered, used, and potentially spilled. In such a case, having a commercially produced eyewash station where the employee can quickly and safely rinse an eye with clean water in a controlled manner might save his or her eyesight.

Well designed legislation will have requirements for personal protective devices and procedures. When there are no such regulations, employers should follow the examples and requirements in a developed system as a course of ethical management and liability protection. In the example of Ontario's Occupational Health and Safety Act, the following regulations have been developed for worker protection:

- **Eye and face**: *Ontario Regulation 851(81)—A worker exposed to the hazard of eye injury shall wear eye protection appropriate in the circumstances.* Employers and workers are then referred to the Canadian Standards Association for the eye protection equipment: CSA Standard Z94.3-92 Industrial Eye and Face Protectors.
- **Footwear**: *Ontario Regulation 851(82)—A worker exposed to the hazard of foot injury shall wear foot protection appropriate in the circumstances.* Employers and workers are then referred to the Canadian Standards Association for the foot protection parameters: CSA Standard Z195.1-02: Guideline on Selection, Case and Use of Protective Footwear.
- **Hearing**: *Ontario Regulation 851(139)(3)—Every employer shall take all measures reasonably necessary in the circumstances to protect workers from exposure to hazardous sound levels.* Employers and workers are then referred to the Canadian Standards Association for the hearing protection parameters: CSA Standard Z94.2-02: Hearing Protection Devices.
- **Headwear**: *Ontario Regulation 851(80)—A worker exposed to the hazard of head injury shall wear head protection appropriate in the circumstances.* Employers and workers are then referred to the Canadian Standards Association for the head protection parameters: CSA Standard Z94.1-05: Industrial Protective Headwear.
- **Limb and body protection**: *Ontario Regulation 851(84)—A worker exposed to the hazard of injury from contact with the worker's skin with*
  - a. *a noxious gas*
  - b. *a sharp or jagged object which may puncture, cut or abrade the worker's skin*
  - c. *a hot object, hot liquid or molten metal*
  - d. *radiant heat*
    shall be protected by
  - e. *wearing apparel sufficient to protect the worker from injury; or*
  - f. *a shield, screen or similar barrier, appropriate to the circumstances*

Employers and workers are then referred to the Canadian Standards Association for the limb and body protection parameters: CSA Standard Z96-09: High-Visibility Safety Apparel.

- **Respirators**: For respirators, employers are referred to the Canadian Standards Association for respirator parameters: CSA Standard Z94-02: Selection, Use and Care of Respirators.

These simple protection devices and procedures should be supplied at work sites by any employer, whether required by statute or not, for the protection of workers and for the employer's protection against future litigation if it can be shown that due care and diligence was applied by the employer at a work site. In the case of facilities, employees should have ready supplies of ear and eye protection, footwear requirements for certain duties, overalls and any other protective clothing appropriate to the duties of the workers, and requirements for head gear such as helmets at construction sites. These should be supplied by the facility manager or individual project managers but, regardless, the protective equipment must be available and its actual use must be enforced as well. It is not acceptable to have protective equipment on hand but not to use it due to shortcuts taken for convenience or because of a lack of procedures.

Supervisors, managers, and executives could find themselves in deep trouble for failing to enforce the provisions of the Occupational Health and Safety Act if, for example, a worker was cleaning gutters on a multistory building and fell to grave injury or death and the investigation found that the employer was negligent in not providing proper scaffolding. Whether the reason is budget cuts, disrepair of existing equipment or anything else, it will not matter when blame is assigned for the accident. The following section of the book deals with what workers can do when they are faced with dangerous situations at work and insufficient or nonexistent protective measures are in place.

Right to Refuse Work

Although workers must be familiar with their own local occupational health and safety regulations to ensure they do not break the law and get themselves into trouble, generally the regulations will or should contain a provision that allows workers the right to refuse work where they feel they are being placed in danger. The following legislated example comes from the Ontario Occupational Health and Safety Act and Regulations Part 5, Section 43(6):

> **Refusal to Work**—A worker may refuse to work or do particular work where he or she has reason to believe that
>
> a. any equipment, machine, device or thing the worker is to use or operate is likely to endanger himself or herself or another worker
> b. the physical condition of the workplace or the part thereof in which he or she works or is to work is likely to endanger himself or herself
>   i. workplace violence is likely to endanger himself or herself; or
> c. any equipment, machine, device or thing he or she is to use or operate or the physical condition of the workplace or the part thereof in which he or she works or is to work is in contravention of this Act or the regulations and such contravention is likely to endanger himself or herself or another worker (p. 53)

The preceding example gives workers the legislated right to refuse to work in an obviously dangerous situation where accident, injury, or even death could result from performing an assigned task. In most situations, supervisors and managers will also recognize the dangers and make appropriate adjustments, but sometimes these types of protections are needed for workers, particularly when jobs are being sped up to meet deadlines or supervisors and managers are not present when a dangerous situation presents itself. Again it is expected that workers will read and understand the occupational health and safety legislation in their own jurisdiction and not rely solely on the examples presented in this book. Workers must recognize dangers on their own and advocate for themselves, starting first with the first line of supervision, as one must always give the local supervisor or manager a chance to rectify whatever issue has been identified. It is expected that most supervisors and managers will act to make a situation safer just out of common sense, but failing that, it may be appropriate to take the issues forward to raise them to higher levels to gain the attention needed. It is not acceptable for a worker to accept his or her fate and work in a dangerous environment when protective equipment and procedures could make a difference.

The Occupational Health and Safety Act also spells out reporting requirements for unsafe situations and inspection requirements by certified inspectors while the workers relocate to a safe location and remain available for investigative purposes. An unsafe situation does not automatically allow employees to leave when they are still accountable to the employer for their whereabouts and behavior. They need to be local and reachable to assist in the investigation and they should remain prepared for reassignment by the employer if alternate duties become appropriate.

Exceptions: Right to Refuse Work

The Ontario occupational health and safety legislation also dictates exceptions to certain emergency services, critical services, and institutions. Police officers, firefighters, corrections workers, hospital workers, and those in other critical institutions such as government laboratories are exempt from this right to refuse to work in Ontario and possibly other jurisdictions. The reasons are that these essential services are trained to operate under dangerous conditions and have first-response responsibilities mandated by government in the protection of the communities. They are the ones that will recognize, respond to, and/or contain any dangerous condition while calling in appropriate resources to deal with the condition. It would simply not make sense to allow emergency responders the right to refuse work when a situation was recognized as dangerous.

Once again, it must be reiterated that it is the responsibility of the individual worker to know and understand the provisions of his or her local occupational health and safety rules and regulations to ensure he or she is operating within the law of his or her state, province, or country. In any jurisdiction lacking such regulations or protections for workers, it would be extremely prudent and ethical for employers to adopt these types of policies to ensure the safety of workers and the ability to address safety issues. A lack of occupational health and safety legislation would certainly not preclude a corporate entity from liability for negligence in the case of a workplace accident where precautions might have prevented a tragedy.

Hot Zones: Welding, etc.

Every facility has hot work performed every now and then to repair plumbing or other metal fastenings or to install new items and appliances. Occupational health and safety regulations often stipulate requirements to make the work safer for workers, especially inside an occupied building. An example can be found in the Canadian province of Ontario's *Occupational Health and Safety Act of 2013*, where it describes the following requirements for fire safety during hot work:

> Section 123: Precautions to prevent a fire shall be taken when using a blow torch or welding or cutting equipment or a similar piece of equipment.

In the case of using blow torches or welding equipment, there are very reasonable, common-sense precautions to take that can vary in form from job to job, depending on the materials used or nature of the work. The legislated requirement is simply to take precautions, which is a best practice whether a particular jurisdiction has legislated regulations or not. Failure to take precautions can be very costly in terms of litigation and damage and it just makes sense for all facility owners/operators to ensure that hot work has appropriate work permits and that the workers take reasonable precautions for safety [1].

Safety Data Sheets

Safety data sheets, or SDSs, are found in all facilities as a safe way of identifying hazardous materials being used or stored on-site. Most of the time the maintenance manager will have the responsibility for receiving SDS documents and ensuring they are kept up to date. These sheets must be made available to anyone wanting to know what is on-site and the potential hazards and they must also be kept handy for the fire department responders, so they can be alerted to any hazardous materials that could pose problems during fire response. In Ontario, regulations require that SDS documents be updated at least every three years, or as soon as possible but within 90 days of any change. Although some jurisdictions may be lacking such legislated regulations, it is still best practice to have such documents describing hazardous materials in any facility so that they can be made available to local fire departments and emergency responders. All potentially hazardous materials must be accounted for during fire or other emergency incidents so that they can be considered in any response plan and also controlled, with any risk mitigated by responding professionals before the emergency is worsened by uncontrolled hazardous materials [2].

Hazardous Material Labeling and Transport

There is an ongoing serious issue in all workplaces and facilities or buildings of all types in regard to the use and storage of hazardous materials, and the potential for misuse and accidental exposure to the general public. Hazardous materials come in different containers and consist of different materials from liquids to solids and gases, and they are generally used to perform tasks related to cleanliness and/or making machinery function. Hazardous materials are not substances to be taken lightly as whoever has brought these materials to a facility will be responsible for what happens with them, including any injuries to people or damages to property.

Currently, the control of hazardous materials is a work in progress around the world, with an initiative called the Globally Harmonized System (GHS) of Classification and Labeling of Chemicals that will standardize control, transportation, and handling of workplace hazardous materials across the world. This has become an increasingly dangerous issue with the globalized economy causing significant increases in international trade and the movement of hazardous materials across international borders. With the increased transportation comes the danger of transporting hazardous materials through multiple jurisdictions, causing the need for standardized terminology and signage so that workers in different countries can instantly recognize and understand the materials that they are encountering on a daily basis, regardless of where the materials have come from across the world [3].

It is useful to look at legislation for worker safety under Ontario's Occupational Health and Safety Act, Ontario Regulation 860: Workplace Hazardous Materials Information System (WHMIS). This requires all employers and workers to have training in handling hazardous materials and it features a standardized system of material identification and signage similar to the GHS so that workers and first responders can instantly know what substances they are dealing with and how volatile the substances might be during an emergency incident (Figure 17.1). As with the GHS, the signage consists of diamond-shaped placards that can be placed on trucks and transport containers of all types and sizes, including small bottles and containers handled by the end user. Canada fortunately is moving closer to the GHS system, as are most developed nations, including the United States, which is much further along in the process.

As most large organizations, such as transportation companies, school boards, and retail corporations, among many others, are training all employees to recognize and properly handle hazardous materials, it is highly recommended that facility managers also seek the training and ensure their employees are trained in the absence of any local program. It is another method of demonstrating professionalism in a company's workforce to outside interests that might be conducting an investigation as a result of an incident within a facility. It also just makes good sense that a maintenance worker—handling potentially hazardous cleaning fluids, for example—is seen by building occupants to be properly handling

Figure 17.1 Representations of hazardous material placards, three with the names of the reactions and three with numbers classifying the substances. These very same types of symbols will be found on containers and bottles at the facility level to advise the maintenance worker or any employee that the substance inside the container is hazardous by being flammable, explosive, corrosive, or even radioactive, although the latter is usually not stored in a work facility or building with occupancy. (From FMCSA Crash Data Collection Resource: http://ai.fmcsa.dot.gov/DataQuality/CrashCollectionTraining/lesson5/placards.html.)

the materials inside a cordoned-off area as required by regulation. On the other hand, building occupants that see a maintenance worker taking no precautions and unnecessarily exposing the occupants to volatile substances may attract a complaint, not to mention an investigation and accountability, as a result of an incident where a dangerous substance caused injury or damage to property. Professionalism in facility management demands that building and maintenance managers and their employees know what they are doing and have the technical skills and certifications to do their jobs properly.

OHS and Restrooms

Having restroom facilities as a convenience for employees and visitors is a very common occurrence in most facilities. As everyone will want to use a restroom at some point during the day, it is incumbent upon the owner/operator to ensure the restrooms are clean and hygienic at all times for the sake of cleanliness and the comfort of people in the building; also, having unsanitary restroom facilities can really affect the reputation of a company or the individuals in charge. Further, unclean restroom facilities in workplaces, and particularly in 24/7 operations, can be a source of worker complaint as most jurisdictions have health and safety regulations requiring cleanliness. It is also a matter of morale and an indication of an owner/operator caring about the people staffing the facility and making the business run. Cleanliness not only includes the cleaning of the facilities but also the provision of a clean water supply. If clean, drinkable municipal water is not available, the owner/operator should consider supplying clean drinking water through an approved filtration system or with bottled water. Again, this goes back to making the occupants and employees feel safe and secure in their surroundings by supplying a basic need without being asked or forced by legislation. Failure to do this also increases the risk of illness in the workplace.

As an example, Ontario's Regulation 213/91 Construction, Section 28—Hygiene legislates that construction projects be supplied with potable water for the use of the workers. It continues by dictating that drinkable water should be supplied by a covered faucet or through a piping system, that workers be supplied with sanitary vessels from which to drink, and that they not be forced to use a common cup among themselves. Facilities are also legislated as necessary within 180 meters of a construction project and available to both male and female employees. Section 29 demands that if water and sewer installed facilities are not available, then chemical flush must be brought in to the ratio of

One portable toilet unit for one to fifteen workers
Two portable toilet units for sixteen to thirty workers
Three portable toilet units for thirty-one to forty-five workers
Four portable toilet units for forty-six to sixty workers
One extra toilet unit for each additional group of fifteen or fewer workers

Cleanup facilities consisting of soap and water or hand cleanser are also required [4].

With such requirements for construction projects, it seems reasonable that facility owners/operators should be providing equal or better facilities in their buildings and that they maintain a similar level of care and cleanliness. This has such an impact on occupants' morale and how they view the employer or owner, or even supervisors that may have control over these issues.

Windows

Windows are found in every building and all rooms and hallways connected to the outside of the buildings. They are a necessary security breach in the square box of a secure building, but people inside need to see out and people outside need to see in (when the owners/operators wish to allow it); windows are a normal part of every person's life around the world. For a facility manager, windows offer a number of challenges that must be met in a manner that reflects what the owner/operator and, ultimately, the user intend. By their very nature, windows are an insecure part of the outside skin of the facility. Most often made of glass, they are easily broken by accident or sometimes on purpose by a person of ill intent, either as an act of mischief or vandalism, but also as a method of entry into the building for other criminal purposes such as stealing and even violent acts against persons.

The following example was used previously to describe facility deterioration and need for ongoing maintenance. It remains an example of unexpected damage and danger to occupants occurred about ten years ago in a major facility where, as the building continued to age, it had shifted enough that inside one of the four floor atriums, a large third-floor interior window popped out of the frame and inward, above the employees working on the floor of the atrium. With thousands of small and very sharp shards of glass held in place by the safety glass coating, the window pane was holding but bowing inward over the open space. The situation forced security person-nel to immediately evacuate the floor of the atrium populated by about 100 employees, who were busy processing the corporate payroll. The security manager and maintenance manager discussed this unprecedented incident and realized their duty was safety of the employees and to get the payroll people back to work as quickly as possible to ensure that pay for thousands of employees was not delayed. They developed a simple but effective plan.

Repairs would take several hours for the glass pane to be removed safely, be replaced with a new section of glass, and set properly before the employees could return. The problem was that the section of window could not be left open as it lined a busy interior hallway on the third floor and was a safety issue to employees walking by. Work could not continue below with replacement work going on several floors above—meaning that the corporation might miss its payroll deadlines. The solution involved agreement from three levels: the security manager, the mainte-nance manager, and the facilities manager, representing the corporation's interests. It was agreed to remove the glass and temporarily replace it with a similarly sized piece of plywood for security, allow payroll employees back to work, and replace the window pane during off-business hours after 5 p.m. This example not only outlines an unexpected incident and how it was handled, but also clearly demonstrates the importance of main-taining good relations and excellent communication between the security unit, the maintenance contractor, and the corporate tenants in order to problem-solve effectively in an emergency.

As such, with unexpected incidents always occurring in facilities, building management must keep track of incidents, and where damage or breakage has occurred, must repair the damaged window as quickly as possible, not only to fix an eyesore but also to resecure that entry point into the building and regain control of the interior atmospheric control by plugging the hole. As explained in the CPTED section of this book (Chapter 5), broken windows and unrepaired damage lead people to believe that the building is not being cared for, affecting the building occupants, who will care less about their environment, and criminals, who may focus on the facility looking for more opportunities to commit crimes. Buildings kept in good repair look professional and well main-tained. Criminals will likely move on to a more opportune target.

In the effort to protect the integrity of the building's security mea-sures, managers must consider how to protect the windows, which are generally the weakest point in the outside skin of the building. Window security should be linked in through the general security system and covered by motion detectors or glass-break detectors that will sense break-age and vibration, alerting security, or in security's absence, the facility manager, to possible intrusion or vandalism. Failing to monitor windows in this respect, leaves them open to criminals and vandals, endangering the occupants. When faced with securing buildings in high-crime areas, some people come up with the idea of putting metal bars in the window, having seen this in other buildings. This solution adds particular safety problems while being a security solution. When bars are installed to keep people out of a building, they unfortunately also serve to keep people in. This violates most fire codes as windows must be kept clear of obstructions that will either stop someone from escaping or hamper efforts to escape. Even the commercial metal bars designed to be opened from the inside present a problem with an evacuating person. Most people caught in real evacuation events are likely in panic or close to it. In that state, people get clumsy and unable to work mechanisms demanding hand–eye coordination, such as a latch on a window bar. For that reason and the violation of most fire codes, it is never recommended to use bars on windows. Security will have to be achieved in another way, in compliance with local fire codes. The best thing for a facility manager to do is seek the advice of the local fire department and local police service to ensure compliance with legislation; this will also let the two emergency response services know what to expect in the building when they respond.

Maintenance of windows also includes cleanliness. The maintenance contractor should always have a means to clean the windows inside and out or have a subcontracted window cleaning company engaged for regular cleaning. Lack of cleanliness in the windows of large facilities can lead to insect problems inside the building and the growth of mold resulting from the condensation of water on the windows with ongoing temperature and atmospheric fluctuations inside and out.

Along with the cleaning of windows comes the accountability for the safety of those engaged in the cleaning. Ontario's Occupational Health and Safety Act stipulates requirements for recording information and registration of those engaged in industrial window cleaning. It also requires the reporting of any fatality or injury connected to window cleaning.

OCCUPATIONAL HEALTH AND SAFETY LEGISLATION

The following topics are covered by Ontario's Occupational Health and Safety Act as a fine example of comprehensive legislation that is designed to protect the worker but also serves as a protection for employers that make a genuine effort to follow the requirements:

- Notice Requirements for Construction Projects—OHS Act, Part 1, General requirements—Sections 13 through 19. These sections contain requirements for posting the name of the constructor and company particulars such as contact information. Also to be added to the list are the names and contact information of the Occupational Health and Safety (OHS) committee members selected for the construction project. Also required are appointments of supervisors, inspections of equipment and machinery, detection of hazards on the site, written and posted emergency procedures to be followed, as well as consultation with the OHS committee, and communications equipment made available for emergency contact capabilities in the event of an accident.

These sections ensure that every construction project must post identification and contact details of the company and OHS committee members and the procedures to follow when something goes wrong. They also require employers to provide reliable communications equipment so that emergency contacts can be made from the site if needed.

- Protective Clothing, Equipment and Devices: OHS Act, Part 2, General construction Sections 20 through 27. These sections require the use of protective gear for workers against hazards and the employer's responsibility to provide instruction on the use of protective gear. Items include safety boots, protective head/eye gear and clothing, safety rails where there is risk of falling, and fall arrest systems for poles and other high locations, including recording of training provided in use of the system. Also specified are regulations where water is present requiring life jackets and persons trained in rescue skills, First Aid and CPR.

Any facility manager must consider the safety of employees and the occupants of the facility when engaging in any construction or reparation project. As managers, they are responsible for what happens to the employees serving with them and, of course, they carry a great deal of responsibility to the building occupants. Ensuring that safety precautions are taken and having training to ensure safety precautions are done properly is professional and prudent, whether local regulations demand it or not (Figure 17.2).

Figure 17.2 A safety issue at an elementary school that is very much something to be handled through the occupational health and safety representative. This is bus time at the end of the school day, and young students, staff, and parents are filing out of the main entrance under a motorized scaffold as a worker continues working above their heads. The work should have been stopped before the school bell rang and the scaffold should have been removed to avoid contact with students and the potential for injury. (Photo by J. Henderson.)

- Hygiene: OHS Act, Part 2, Sections 28 through 30. These sections require human needs, such as drinkable water, to be supplied at the work site as well as the means to drink it using sanitary containers without having to share with other workers. Also required are sewered or nonsewered toilet facilities within designated distances from the work site and that the toilet facilities be serviced and sanitary.

These sections concern the conditions provided by the employer to keep workers healthy and in working condition. It is common sense to provide such necessities as water and access to toilets, and facility managers should be ensuring access of workers to hygienic water and toilet facilities at all times.

Other sections carry on with legislating requirements for bracing structures to prevent injury to employees while they are working; housekeeping, where employers are required to keep the work site clean of debris and have falling materials guided by chutes instead of free falling, moving debris safely and stacking it in a safe manner; and having corrosive and combustible substances contained in storage cylinders, where to place the cylinders for safety, and the warning signage that goes with them. Adequate lighting, ventilation from noxious fumes, and temporary heating where required are also included. Fire safety regulations are present as well, requiring the presence of appropriate firefighting gear for flammable and combustible liquids and open flame or welding operations so that employees can quickly extinguish a spark or flame that gets out of control. Further mandated are traffic and access/egress controls, signage and traffic signals, and buffer zones in high-traffic and highway areas to protect employees from getting hit by vehicles. Stairs and ladders are covered as to size and width, while forms are covered to ensure that a load does not exceed the form's ability to hold it. Vehicles, machines, tools, and equipment are mandated for good working conditions and maintenance for the safety of all.

There is not much that this particular legislation does not touch in terms of safety standards and it is a good guide where a jurisdiction does not have such regulations. If occupational health and safety legislation exists in the jurisdiction where the manager is working, then he or she must follow that legislation as it will be the law in that particular jurisdiction.

The three main examples provided earlier give an excellent preview of how modern employee-centered legislation and policy must be designed in order to protect the interests of the workers and their families. Although it appears costly up front for an owner or employer to buy bracing equipment and to have to provide training in how to use it, for example, the fact remains that a healthy, well looked after workforce will be happier and more motivated. The costs in the end will be far less than having to undergo an investigation, prosecution, and civil suit following a work site incident caused by a lack of safety procedures or equipment.

In conclusion, a good rule of thumb for facility managers to go by when coordinating construction, maintenance, and reparation work in their facility is to consider, as a facility manager, what he or she would want to experience if he or she were doing the work. It is not only an ethical approach to care for your employees in that manner but it also avoids so much needless tension and animosity, and likely money. Happy workers feel cared for by the efforts of the employer to ensure safety and comfort. In return, the workers will show loyalty and hard work, which contribute to higher quality work that will make the manager look good!

Asbestos

Asbestos is a topic that often makes facility managers quake with fear if news reaches them that asbestos exists in their facility. It is a dangerous cancer-causing substance that has been widely used in the past as an insulator for buildings, among other applications. From 2015 and beyond, facility managers will most often have dealt with it as leftover building insulation that was never removed previously and it has become a major project in itself to remove it due to the inherent danger of working with asbestos, particularly when it is disturbed and contaminates the air in its vicinity enough to cause illness. People working with asbestos must wear protective clothing and breathing apparatus to avoid contamination and the Occupational Health and Safety Act covers the details in order to protect all persons who may come into contact with this very dangerous substance.

The standard used to establish the type and content of asbestos comes from the United States Environmental Protection Agency, while the OHS Act prohibits the installation of asbestos-containing materials beyond a very small percentage of content of other material. As such, employers are compelled to advise any worker of any asbestos-containing material that they may be required to handle. Demolition work can only continue when any asbestos-containing material has been removed using specialized procedures and equipment.

The legislation also asserts that owners should know or ought to have known that material in their building contained asbestos. Ignorance is therefore no excuse and questions about potential asbestos should be on the agenda when owners are purchasing older buildings that could contain asbestos materials. If asbestos is known to exist in a structure, it must be documented, and the document should be kept on-site for reference. For workers' protection, owners are further compelled to advise anyone coming in to work in the building that there are materials containing asbestos. The owner must also provide a training package advising workers how to handle asbestos and avoid contamination.

If an employer or—in the case of this application, the facility manager—discovers asbestos material in the facility, he or she is compelled to advise the facility owner, so that he or she may enact his or her notification responsibilities to government. Any handling or removal activity performed concerning asbestos must be completed using the standards enacted by the legislation, which is a typical requirement in all jurisdictions.

Finally, there are legislated reporting requirements to government after the completion of asbestos abatement or removal projects. As a special note for facility managers, if there is any suspicion or actual knowledge of asbestos material in the facilities for which they have responsibility, it is a critical responsibility for them to access the local regulations and legislation of the jurisdiction and to seek guidance from government experts about what to do and how to handle it. Asbestos becomes dangerous when it is disturbed, so it is best to find out what to do in advance and then get it done in accordance with the local legislation [5].

OHS Anecdote

As occupational health and safety contains such a wide variety of potential issues, it is desirable to include an anecdote to illustrate the point of how the unexpected can become a central problem for a group of workers. The following example is just such an incident that happened to be reported during the writing phase of this book. The situation included the workers, the workers' employer (a temporary employment agency), and the client (a chicken farm). No one appeared to have known this was going to happen, but it was handled using OHS committee parameters and members.

Occupational health and safety covers a vast array of different health issues, one of which was illustrated by CBC News on August 31, 2015, where temporary employees in the Midwest of North America were assigned to a chicken farm facility by a temporary work agency and were advised that they might encounter wood ticks at the work site. Much to the shock of the workers, they were inundated with waves of bedbugs that were turning up in clumps everywhere they went in the facility. These bugs were biting the employees constantly on the legs and drawing blood, but the biggest danger was that they would spread the bedbugs all over the nearby city as the workers went home. In this case, the client company had a responsibility to advise the temporary work agency of the particular insect infestation, which in turn had a responsibility to advise, train, and properly equip the workers to deal with the infestation. Local occupational health and safety representatives were called in to investigate and make recommendations to rectify the problem and protect the workers. The situation appeared to have developed naturally without fault to the client, so no enforcement action appeared to be imminent. However, this a good example of a possible workplace issue that no one anticipated but that could have had a huge impact on the community if proper steps had not been taken with the advice of occupational health and safety [6].

No Solicitation?

Vendors/Solicitation

As a security, maintenance, or building manager, you will be faced with ongoing advertising and solicitation in person by vendors wishing to sell goods and/or services to the building management or to occupants.

To maintain control over this often annoying reality of running a facility, it is always best to have a policy and some procedures already in place that have been agreed to by the owners/operators, building managers, and representatives of the occupants. With a policy and relevant procedures in place, people know what to do and how far they can go, with tension being very much reduced. The vendors will also know what to expect, what to do, and how not to annoy the building operators, and both the vendors and end users in the building will achieve what they need from the appearance of these salespersons or solicitors. The policy may consist simply of no solicitation allowed in the building and employees being advised to simply turn the solicitor away. When solicitation or vendor calling is permitted, it must be controlled by a procedure. A procedure could consist of contact with a designated employee in the Purchasing Department, for example, who will generally be cognizant of the types of vendors relevant to the business at hand. This contact would then issue approval and instructions, including limitations to the visit with specific people to meet with and limited access to the facilities. These visits must be sponsored by an employee and recorded, to avoid problems and to allow security or even the police to investigate if something negative does happen. A log should be kept as to when the visitor arrived, the number of the visitor tag issued, and when the visitor left and returned the tag. Where the visitor was going and who the sponsor was must also be recorded for accountability purposes.

Vendors should never be given full access to a facility and, if allowed access into work areas, they should be escorted at all times while inside any nonpublic area. Access control rules should be enforced at all times, and vendors should be screened just like anyone else upon entry. They should **always** be asked to sign in at reception, show photo identification, and give corporate contact information to ensure they are who they say they are and not trying to enter the facility to steal goods and/or proprietary information. Solicitors/vendors should be given a visitor tag and then escorted by a designated building employee wherever they go, even to the washroom. Compromise should never occur in the form of a building employee or sponsor of a visitor deferring responsibility to a nonbuilding person. In other words, unless specifically noted in writing in the service contract as an accountable duty, a contracted person should never be escorting another contracted person or outsider such as a vendor inside a corporate building. This is to maintain the integrity of security in the facility by making escorts assignable only to persons with accountability to the organization. To allow contract workers to escort contract workers or noncontracted individuals, regardless of familiarity, is risky because, at the end of the day, their employment is held by another entity and they will always answer to their employment executives before their contracted managers. This is a shortcut seen often in government as building employees and managers just do not want to be responsible for or spend the time and resources escorting workers around. They will defer to the contracted maintenance manager to escort these workers to avoid this time-consuming duty. When that happens, it inadvertently enables the contracted maintenance manager to make operational decisions and to take shortcuts with that amount of control over who is where and at what time in the midst of another corporation's world. This is also where problems start occurring with critical systems such as elevators, for example, since the contracted worker escort without the accountability to the corporation will eventually start leaving that elevator technician inside the secure zone to attend other mandated calls and just assume or even hope the job will get done properly. In the elevator failure scenario mentioned earlier in the book, the familiarity of the contract workers and non-involvement of the building management allowed the elevator technician the time and opportunity to manipulate his time to his own advantage, to the point where *he started eating breakfast in the cafeteria after signing in*, using the time allotted to elevator maintenance. The elevator technician was in effect being paid by the organization to eat his breakfast instead of maintaining the elevators that were constantly malfunctioning.

A favorite tactic of recently retired or resigned employees who are newly hired vendors for other companies is to attend their former employer's work sites and use their familiarity with staff and their former status to gain entry and full access to the facility, circumventing access procedures for nonemployees. "Can I go in and say hello to my friends in Payroll? I will just be a minute…" is often a story that access control employees will hear from a familiar face. They may find out later that this former employee toured entire floors trying to sell items and services with full access to corporate assets and proprietary information. This type of scenario should never be allowed to happen as the former employee has a new boss and a new agenda and is no longer accountable to this employer. Employees enabling these vendors to enter work sites will be held accountable by the employer if something occurs and the inevitable question is asked, "How did that person get in here?" Employees that casually think, "What is the harm?" or "He is fine; I know him from when he worked here..." often put themselves and their employment in jeopardy by facilitating unauthorized entry for noncleared persons into secure sites. Periodic reminders of this fact are always a good idea for a facility manager to consider.

Electrical

Most commercial facilities have an in-house electrician or at least one on contract that ensures the hydropower (hydro) supply in the building is adequate and in good repair. This is another critical system that must be prioritized above almost everything else since most equipment, fire detection and alarm systems, refrigerators, HVAC (heating, ventilation, and air conditioning), and the furnaces and commercial chillers that provide the cool air, among other systems, will not function without reliable power. Large office buildings, retail centers, sports complexes, academic institutions, apartment buildings, and any large facility can consume enormous amounts of power, which must be monitored on an ongoing basis by a designated professional and certified electrician who can make minor repairs on the spot and knows when to call in appropriate resources for larger problems.

One ongoing problem that facility managers, maintenance managers, and security/safety managers must be on the watch for constantly is the employee use of power bars and other items designed to add electrical outlets to a standard two-plug outlet. As the outlets have been installed by plan to satisfy the building code by a certified electrician, most of them were never designed to give power to more than two items, be they lamps, microwave ovens, audio-video equipment, and so on (Figure 17.3). As users move in and wish to power all sorts of equipment within the same space, they are able to go to the local store and purchase power bars, extension cords and other plug-in power outlet extenders. These items that have been installed by tenants and building users most often do not meet the local fire code requirements and constitute a real fire hazard. Employees and tenants will most often cause a fire hazard by building a maze of plugs, extensions, and power bars to provide hydro to their increasing use of electronics instead of notifying facilities or maintenance of the increased power need. If maintenance know about a need for increased power, personnel possibly could install a new plug connected

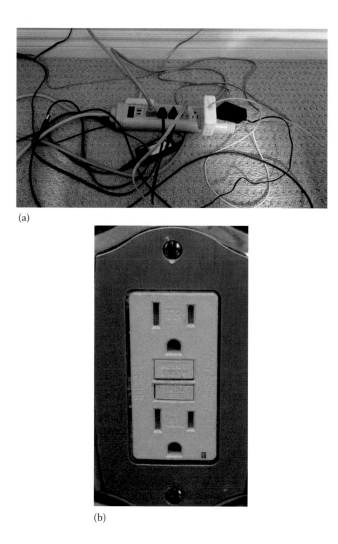

(a)

(b)

Figure 17.3 (a) Light bar with plugs for two computers, a cell phone charger, a makeup mirror, and a laser printer coming out of one plug with one plug still available. This can overload a circuit breaker and cause a fire hazard if all appliances are used at the same time. Advice: Ask a certified electrician about extra power needs. (b) This simple circuit breaker outlet will cut the power if too much is being drawn. It is most often found in washrooms. The reset button is central. (Photos by J. Henderson.)

to an underused circuit, reducing the fire hazard considerably and ensuring that the area remains compliant with the fire code and building code. To do anything other than what the facilities or maintenance department has recommended, based on the sound advice of a certified electrician, is to risk creating a fire hazard to which the person who did not follow the recommendation may be held accountable.

To complicate matters in a facility, any time that extra events are held, such as charity fund-raisers, large celebrations, entertainment for one reason or another, and anything that brings more people than usual and extra functions to a location, the temporary power requirements may rise considerably. Rather than take chances that the existing power system can handle everything at once, it is highly advisable to approach the maintenance manager or the owner/operator of the facility to advise of the power requirements and give him or her a chance to plan correctly in accordance with the fire code.

UPS

UPS in this application is not referring to the well-known corporation that delivers packages around the world. UPS stands for *uninterrupted power supply*. Every facility, building, and even residences should have UPS backing up critical electrical systems. UPS typically comes in the form of batteries, sized appropriately for the amount of power needed. This can be a small battery backing up a single computer, or a large room full of interconnected batteries resembling car engine batteries that can keep an office building working long enough for other measures to occur. Other measures include diesel-powered generators that should be a longer term solution when the power is out for hours or even days (Figures 17.4 through 17.6). The point is that without UPS power backing up office equipment, computers can black out instantly with any slight power bump or surge and unsaved information can be instantly lost. The UPS batteries are intended to keep the equipment powered up fully through those power disruption events to avoid loss of data. The office-sized UPS batteries often come in power bars and contain power surge protection that prevents too much power from the hydro grid from reaching the computer and damaging the components. Power surges can come from both hydro sources and from natural lightning strikes.

Having UPS is a critical part of operating a facility, but parallel and just as critical is ensuring that there is an ongoing program of UPS maintenance and testing. An experience in one major facility of critical

Figure 17.4 A typical diesel-powered generator for the purpose of uninterrupted power supply. This engine is programmed to turn on automatically using diesel as the fuel from storage tanks and to begin producing electrical power almost immediately. The generator in the photo is for a communications building containing about 30 people. Larger buildings often will use multiple units. (Photo by J. Henderson.)

Figure 17.5 Two functional banks of uninterrupted power supply batteries that can power an entire facility for a brief period until the diesel generator comes on. These batteries store power but the main power of the building is siphoned through them, so, when hydro is disrupted, this bank of batteries will keep selected critical systems powered fully until the generators kick in. This particular bank powers the same communications facility of 30 people as the generator in Figure 17.4. (Photo by J. Henderson.)

Figure 17.6 These two fuels tanks contain diesel and are kept full all the time in case of emergency need for power generation. They have fuel lines that connect directly to the diesel generators, so fuel renewal and testing are critical to ensure the generator will function any time it is needed. Note the small, unconnected generators kept as a last resort if all else fails (bottom left). (Photo by J. Henderson.)

importance came about when the building, because it was new, did not have such a program for the three large diesel generators that were each the size of a bus, references to which were buried deep in the maintenance contract for the building with a population of 1700 people.

Because this was a newer building, the UPS had never been an issue and the maintenance company never got into the habit of checking the UPS generators. About five years later, as the new security manager came in just before the 9/11 terrorist attacks in the United States, a facility security review was done, revealing that the generators *were not being checked* as a routine. The security manager requested the maintenance manager, who was also new to the facility, to have a look and ensure the generators were functioning. He came back with a report and sample from the diesel fuel supply tanks showing that the diesel fuel mixture had actually separated in the tanks and a test tube was produced showing exactly what had happened. The diesel tanks had to be emptied of thousands of gallons of separated and spoiled fuel, cleaned, and refilled with new diesel at a cost of tens of thousands of dollars. Once this was done, the generator engines required mechanical maintenance and then testing.

What came about after that experience was a scheduled monthly diesel transfer test whereby the entire building population was to be notified of the test so that they could shut down their computers and allow the diesel engines to kick in and power the facility. This was all in place during the major blackout of the northeastern United States and central Canada of August 14, 2003, when the power grid failed suddenly over a vast area of industrial North America. As the blackout struck instantly, the large bank of UPS batteries in the basement kept the building powered until the diesel generators started up and seamlessly powered the building for five days. If this problem had not been recognized and rectified several years earlier during the review of security, this facility of critical importance would have powered down and gone dark right when it was needed the most, requiring the evacuation of critical staff and their relocation away from all the critical information, supplies, infrastructure, and equipment in the building and adjacent grounds.

The point of this anecdote is that one can never predict when something unexpected is going to happen. Therefore, any basic power system, such as hydro and gas/oil supplies as well as any UPS system, must be kept in good repair and be tested monthly to ensure that it is ready to go when something comes along to require it. Without basic power supplies, chaos will ensue when disaster strikes and it can be the difference between saving lives and losing them.

Diesel generators for UPS systems are meant to be ready to go at a moment's notice and it is the facility manager's responsibility to ensure they are ready to go any time. Power disruptions can occur as follows:

- During thunderstorms producing nearby lightning strikes
- From an overloaded hydro grid when too much power is drawn by air conditioners in the summer
- From accumulations of water, ice and snow overloading hydro towers and lines with weight in the winter

These systems must be tested monthly for reliability in what are termed transfer tests, where the power is switched from the main grid to the generators to ensure the transfer of power works smoothly and reliably. Planning of UPS should always be to have a system that exceeds the estimated requirements by a wide margin. As an example, one of the facilities of critical importance used in this book to illustrate various other topics has a room containing three diesel generators, each of which is as large in physical dimensions as a small bus. The amount of power that officials estimate can be generated when the generators are powered up together would be enough to supply a small city of 40,000 people with electricity when the facility itself actually would never contain more than 2000 people. This over-powering of UPS provides government with much flexibility in a time of crisis and gives authorities options for dealing with chaos. This kind of planning provides redundancy of UPS for other facilities such as hospitals, fire departments, and others. If all facilities over-plan their UPS needs in an organized manner, a community could have a web of redundancy where damage to one facility can be compensated for by the UPS power of another facility without negatively affecting power supply to either.

There is one last point to make about UPS generators. In facilities where they are in place and functioning, they can tend to be quite active during the summer months when ongoing thunderstorms and lightning strikes cause many power disruptions to the hydro grid. The results, when people are working in facilities that feature UPS systems, at times are as small as those minor power bumps that last long enough to make the timers on ovens start to blink, or they can be a bit longer, lasting minutes or even several hours. When these disruptions occur and staff in the building become aware that the UPS generator may have kicked in and run for a period of time, a *report of the UPS activity should always be forwarded through channels to the facility manager at least by the next morning*. The reason is that after any use of the generator(s), someone in maintenance or facilities should be checking the state of function of the generator(s) and fuel storage tank levels to ensure the tanks are topped up and ready to go again at any time. One never knows when the generators may be required for an extended period lasting days or even weeks. If those tanks are not filled and the generator checked regularly for optimal performance, they may fail at an inopportune time. This is a critical responsibility for a facility manager concerning the life/safety system of the facility.

REFERENCES

1. *Occupational Health and Safety Act and Regulations,* 2013 consolidated edition. Ontario: Carswell/Thomson Reuters Canada Limited, p. 160.
2. *Occupational Health and Safety Act and Regulations,* 2013 consolidated edition. Ontario: Carswell/Thomson Reuters Canada Limited, pp. 772–773.
3. Workplace Safety and Prevention Services (http://www.wsps.ca/Information-Resources/Topics/WHMIS.aspx).

4. *Occupational Health and Safety Act and Regulations*, 2013 consolidated edition. Ontario: Carswell/Thomson Reuters Canada Limited, p. 125.
5. Occupational Health and Safety Act Ontario Regulation 278/05, Sections 1–21, pp. 335–372.
6. Canadian Centre for Health and Safety, a government website (http://www.ccohs.ca/products/posters/WHMIS2015/).

18

Business Continuity Planning

Business continuity planning is an important concept brought to the forefront by the September 11, 2001, terrorist attacks on the World Trade Center and the Pentagon, including the flight that ended in Pennsylvania with the bravery of the citizens on board when they brought down their own plane, which was controlled by terrorists and targeting another site. Other incident types that have spurred the development of the business continuity concept include hurricanes, tornadoes, and other massive weather events that cause considerable damage in the community. These often catastrophic events serve as graphic reminders that people must remain ready for all events in facilities management.

What is the responsibility of a facility manager or a security manager when the facility within which he or she works has been compromised, damaged, or even destroyed? The responsibilities of those that operate the buildings do not stop, even if the building has been completely destroyed, and each facility must have in place policies and procedures to deal with shutdowns, partial shutdowns, evacuation events, or attacks on the facility.

Whether damaged or completely intact, facilities contain people, personal assets, business assets, and proprietary as well as personal information. As it is the responsibility of facility and security managers to ensure the buildings and properties under their care are safe and secure during the best of times, it remains their highest responsibility when something catastrophic happens. Although not a pleasant topic to cover, a facility that is being managed can be partially or completely destroyed—for example, the 9/11 attacks and the Murrah Federal Building in Oklahoma City that was initially partially destroyed in 1995 by a terrorist bomb. What is left after all of the occupants not killed have been evacuated from the site?

What is left is a damaged shell of building that still contains people that may have been killed or are injured and may still need rescue, as well as personal assets, business assets, and proprietary and personal information. Facility managers must consider this reality and act accordingly because it is their responsibility to care for the site and the contents, even in damaged and tragic circumstances. It is the responsibility of facility and security managers to work with emergency responders (police, fire department, and ambulance)—most often through the incident response commander—to offer what assistance and expertise they can offer. A secured perimeter is necessary to allow authorities to stabilize the site and to search for and evacuate injured victims and the deceased. The intimate knowledge of the facility becomes a critical piece of the incident response and it is the facility and security managers that possess this knowledge, which can help responders in a positive manner, perhaps facilitating the rescue of people and saving of lives.

Part of business continuity planning involves the initial response to a catastrophic event and being ready for it. This means that a facility manager should have copies of the security and access control databases stored securely off-site as a backup in case the information or computers containing the information on-site were damaged or destroyed. This can be done by securing portable hard drives and laptop computers in other corporate locations or, where there are none, contracting the company that provides security services hardware to securely maintain backup data off-site, so that it can be accessed after a catastrophic event. Having this information at hand can assist first-responders with knowing who was in the facility when the incident occurred by checking card swipe data. It also may enable easier security of the site if the access control system can be quickly repaired, or parts of it repaired using the backup data and card programming. If this information is stored only on one computer on-site and it happened to be destroyed during the incident, that information would be lost and securing the site would be significantly more difficult. Also, the emergency responders might have a more difficult time figuring out who may have been on-site during the incident.

To achieve this state of readiness, policies and procedures must be prepared and approved in advance so that the mechanisms are in place to store backup data and for facility and security managers to have procedures to follow that will maintain the integrity of the system and present credibility to the first responders. The policies and procedures should always be prepared in consultation and cooperation with the local police, fire department, and health care services. This enables all responders to know who is doing what and how the facility management team can assist with the response effort. Being an accepted part of the response effort is a major bonus for the building ownership and their management team as their interests actually become an official part of the response effort. Working together with the responding authorities is a much better strategy than working in organizational silos with different priorities because facility management must be part of the decision making and priorities of responders. Failure of facility management to prepare in advance in cooperation with authorities will result in its being unceremoniously pushed aside or ignored at the most critical point of a disaster and the loss of influence on what is going to happen to the facility, assets, and information at that site. Facility management cannot afford to lose its place or influence during a critical moment of chaos and be officially told to stand behind the caution tape with everyone else. The people or organization to whom the facility and security managers report will expect them to be involved and to have a say in what is going on.

BUSINESS CONTINUITY FOR WORK

The main focus of business continuity planning is for the corporation or entity to be able to continue conducting business in the face of a temporary or even permanent loss of facilities. The loss of facilities, even temporarily, means the business is losing productive time, which in turn becomes financial loss and the loss of corporate influence. These disruptions can also affect corporate decision making at critical times. It is never acceptable for a facility issue to interrupt business and completely unacceptable to stop business altogether. All business, corporation, and government entities should have a business continuity plan (BCP) that can quickly get the corporate machinery back into operation, even at a reduced rate, when unexpected situations compromise the facilities within which it is housed.

The BCP is a tailored and living document designed primarily to move critical functions and management from a disabled work site to a secondary site prepared beforehand where management and operations can resume quickly in a timely manner. As it is being developed, the planners must decide on which functions are the most critical to keep business functioning in a scaled-down operation. A second location, off-site from the main business campus, must be selected and secured by purchase or lease, if not already owned by the entity, and retrofitted to become a temporary substitute to keep the business functioning until the main site is either repaired or replaced if need be. The facility and security managers have pivotal roles in this process as they must ensure the site not only is secure but also has the necessary infrastructure and facilities to support the people and the business functions adequately until the main site is ready and useable again.

Considerations in the selection of a business continuity site can be easy if the corporate entity is large enough and has off-campus buildings already. Government is an example of this, where it may simply be a case of selecting another government building and outfitting it. But most entities do not have this luxury and must budget and otherwise plan, which includes selecting another location to use. Smaller private businesses may even have to resort to using employee homes, with their agreement, when there is no money to establish a secondary site. Otherwise, the owner/operator may have to simply accept the temporary shutdown and plan accordingly for the shutdown to try to minimize the losses by being organized about how the shutdown will be carried out and quickly getting operations going when the facility is accessible again.

The main considerations for business continuity are as follows:

- **Safe location**: a crime-ridden neighborhood is not the place to put a BCP facility. Local crime statistics and observations are necessary to ensure company officials are selecting a safe location. The safety of employees is paramount in getting to and from the BCP site by car, rail, and city bus, as well as in reducing the likelihood of break-ins and vandalism to the BCP facility that can cause further damage to the group's experience. Locating a BCP site near a prison is not ideal, for example, with less desirable people and their families accessing or leaving the prison on a daily basis. The site should also be located far from facilities of critical importance and centralized government facilities that could also become targets of attack or disruption. It is not ideal to have your BCP location shut down as a result of collateral damage from another high-profile site that was attacked.
- **Transportation**: ease of access is essential for the employees to get to and from the location, as well as for delivery and/or shipment activity. BCP sites should be located near highways, rail hubs, and/or airports so that time is not wasted getting to the site and there is a manner in which supplies such as food and goods/hardware can be accessed or delivered. Roads should be in good repair and serviced regularly by the municipality in all seasons.

After the BCP site has been activated during an emergency is not a good time to find out that the road does not get snowplowed in winter because this task was never assumed by the municipality. Such is the research that goes into BCP site selection.

- **Services/utilities**: potential BCP sites should be surveyed for adequate and reliable sources and infrastructure of hydropower (hydro), natural gas, water and drainage/sewers. If uninterrupted power supply (UPS) is not already featured in the site, the possibility of installing UPS hardware and fuel storage, and being able to secure it and keep it serviced and ready to use is essential.
- **Timely response**: consideration must be given to response times for police, fire, and ambulance when selecting a BCP site. Having acceptable response time is gauged by contacting the individual emergency services and asking official representatives about response priority and time for the location in question. After BCP site activation is not a good time to find out that the selected neighborhood or industrial park is a low-priority response area with long wait times during an emergency event.
- **Internal structure/utilities**: the buildings under consideration to become BCP sites should be examined for age, structural integrity, and services such as hydro supply and interior hydro panels to ensure adequate amounts of hydro will be supplied consistently to power all functions required. Also, water pipes and drainage systems should be examined for age and integrity. If a site is ideal with a structurally sound building, there could still be renovations required to replace aging or missing infrastructure. The existence of or ability to install trunk lines for communications equipment is a further consideration for government and corporations requiring high-tech and communications equipment.
- **Security audit? Now?**: security audits or at least Crime Prevention Through Environmental Design reviews should be completed on each site being considered. It must be known up front whether or not the site in question can be secured effectively and with reasonable costs. Questions need to be documented and answered for executives to make their decisions with accurate information. For example, is the compound fenced? What kind of gates are there? Can an electronic access control system be installed combined with closed circuit television? Is there enough bandwidth in the site wiring for communication and data needs? How big a job would it be to physically rekey the site? How many security

officers are needed to secure the site when the BCP site is not being used throughout the year, and then how many security officers are needed when the site has been activated? Are the local police, fire, and medical response authorities prepared to work with and support the BCP management in establishing this site?

- **No site? Working from home**: where there is no BCP site due to the size of the organization and/or budget, perhaps working from home or some other location is necessary. To do this, there must be backup computers and data reliably stored somewhere for the employees to use; otherwise, business will simply shut down until the main facility reopens.

Although this is a long list of considerations to make in selecting a BCP site for an entity, it is far from being complete and does not address specific needs for specific businesses, functions, or government requirements. Facility managers involved in BCP site selection must go into the process with a critical eye and match the potential facilities to the specific needs of the organization. Cooperation and communication with other managers and executives in the organization, as well as their support, are vital to the success of the project, as are communication and establishing relationships with first-response agencies in the jurisdiction of the proposed business continuity plan sites. Without wide support, the proposal, if adopted by the organization, is doomed to inaccuracies and potential errors, none of which the facility manager can accept or for which he or she would want to be held responsible.

BUSINESS CONTINUITY PLANNING: SEVENTY-TWO-HOUR EMERGENCY KITS

Business continuity planning as a concept has been around for decades but has received more attention only recently since the 9/11 terrorist attacks in the United States and widespread severe natural weather events such as the ice storm of 1997, hurricanes that caused significant damage and casualties such as Katrina and Sandy, and earthquakes and ongoing appearances of destructive tornadoes that have forced the issue of business continuity planning into the forefront. The question is, "What happens when infrastructure fails?" This is a serious question as Western society and most developing countries in the world are increasingly urbanized with cities containing hundreds of thousands to millions of people requiring major logistical networks to move food supplies and goods into the cities where they can be distributed to the people. At the best of times, this is a challenge to ensure that sufficient supplies of food and water are transported from the source to the distribution points, which to ordinary people happen to be the grocery stores and municipal water works. Accordingly, what does happen when this system fails or faces disruption?

The obvious effect is that within a couple of days and without resupply, grocery store shelves begin to empty as people continue buying food supplies. In a widespread emergency such as a severe weather event, people will actually accelerate and contribute to the immediate problem by hoarding whatever they can find in the form of food and water, putting further strain on the supply system and emptying store shelves much more quickly. If the municipal water supply is compromised by damage or a poisoned supply, people would be warned to stop using the municipal water supply altogether until the system is repaired and tests clean.

Very quickly, within a matter of days, cities begin to be unable to supply the large urban populations with food and water, requiring assistance from the state or province as well as the federal level to move supplies to where they are needed on an emergency basis. This, however, can take time for situation assessment to occur, decisions to be made, and then to actually acquire and move the supplies to where they are needed. This is the rationale behind governments recommending to families to have 72 hours worth of supplies in the form of food, cooking fuel, water, first aid kits, and medicine among other supplies to bridge the expected gap of a 72-hour response from government. Families must be self-sufficient until government can move appropriate supplies into urban areas during a widespread natural emergency scenario.

The author had a personal experience during the precellular-phone era in 1997 when the large ice storm of Eastern Canada and the Northeastern United States occurred. The storm caught most people by surprise although the population had been warned in advance through the media that an ice storm was possible with precipitation from the south encountering cold air from the north. However, no one predicted the severity of the coming storm and there was no recent experience to draw upon or to predict what was going to unfold. The storm hit overnight and, as huge amounts of rain turned into freezing rain among a plummeting temperature, everything was coated with a dangerous amount of ice. Being in a rural section of the outskirts of a city, I opened the garage door in the morning to be confronted with six inches of ice accumulated on cars, and trees coated in ice, with the crowns of the trees crashing one by one through the forest canopy and smashing on the ground, making it extremely dangerous to go outside. Looking at the lawn, even the individual blades of grass had a coating of ice and, of course, the roads were impassable until road crews were able to get out and spread salt and sand. Along with the weight of the ice came a massive power failure as hydro infrastructure suffered major damage to the lines and stations, affecting widespread areas. Accordingly, everything stopped at once. If there were no batteries, radios would not even function. Toilets did not function and cooking was impossible unless a fireplace or a grill was used. In the author's situation, for five days, life became a routine of sleeping, but waking periodically to ensure the fireplace stayed lit as temperatures plunged toward –20° at night. The day consisted of chopping wood for the fireplace, through which warming certain rooms of the house was accomplished, as well as the cooking, since the propane tank for the grill was out of propane. As the house was by a river, water was hauled up constantly to make the toilets flush, which is a surprisingly regular occurrence when a group of people are together in one place. It was an exhausting five days until the roads were passable and it was safe to drive to the next community to replenish drinking water and buy propane, batteries, and whatever food was available. Although supplies in the house were adequate, it still took several days before the army circulated through the neighborhood to ensure each family had enough necessities.

The experience of going through a natural disaster or severe weather event leaves one with the realization that it actually does make complete sense to have 72 hours' worth of supplies on hand to get through a delay or collapse of the food and water supply systems. Families must be self-sufficient for that length of time until the emergency government logistics can get started and begin moving critical supplies.

Business continuity planning for corporate office buildings, apartment complexes, and retail centers has different considerations than for individual residences. Building managers must have plans prepared in advance tailored to their specific type of facility to mitigate the chaos that might accompany such widespread events as lengthy hydro outages caused by severe weather events or natural disasters. Each type of facility will have a different set of problems and, with differing resources at hand, the manager's differing abilities to assist people inside the facility. Planning must therefore be done in cooperation with local disaster assistance agencies, police, fire, and ambulance to ensure all responders are on the same page with the facility manager.

It is not useful to make plans in advance without consultation, particularly if the aim of the BCP plan is to temporarily set up business in a separate building in a different location and never having advised that manager that his or her facility appears in another facility's business continuity plan. Having five different entities claiming the same space for business continuity during an emergency with no one realizing the other has claimed it only defeats the purpose of the plan and creates more logistical problems, compounding what is already happening. This situation actually occurs when organizations attempt to tackle business continuity planning for the first time. Thinking in silos, many managers will come to the same conclusion and all list building A on site B as their primary BCP site. It is often only during practical exercises when the plans are put to the test that the managers realize with some embarrassment that multiple managers had selected the same building A on site B to set up temporary operations, but no one shared that information among themselves or even with the manager of the selected site. BCP planning must consist of consultation and, if managers are selecting another building for temporary operations, not only should they notify their own colleagues and consult with the building manager in charge of that building, but they also should do a site visit as well to ensure that the building has sufficient room, sufficient types of spaces, proper hydro supply for the expected use, and any other concerns of leaving an established workplace.

WHAT SHOULD A BUSINESS
CONTINUITY PLAN CONTAIN?

A business continuity plan should be tailored to the type of facility it is protecting. It is a method of continuing business when a disruption occurs to the facility within which the business is located and a way to keep business flowing, rather than to have to shut down operations for a period of time. Accordingly, a BCP should be planned for relocation to a preselected site and equipped in advance to allow the business unit to seamlessly enter and very quickly begin operations. Considerations include the following:

Similar facility with similar floor plan and desk space
Similar electrical requirements, plugs, and computer stations
Communication facilities
Designation of space per person in advance so that employees know
   where they are going

Washroom facilities, adequate parking, transportation options
Loading dock and mail room where necessary
Supplies and stationery; computer cables
Food stores and water (these should be rotated periodically and refreshed)

The BCP facility should reflect the regular facility as much as possible in order to have as little negative impact as possible on the workers who have been forced to relocate. Advanced planning is necessary to ensure a quick and easy transition from the regular facility to the BCP location. If a lunchroom and workout facilities exist at the regular site, it would be a good idea to incorporate them into the BCP plan as much as possible to keep morale as high as possible, given that the entire exercise of using the BCP may upset some workers, particularly if they are there because of a natural disaster or some other upsetting event. The BCP site must be ready for rapid adaptation to replace the production lost in the original facility. It is not realistic to expect production levels to approach those of the regular facility when a BCP location is activated, but doing it properly with the right equipment and environment will help.

Other kinds of business continuity planning will include the following:

1. **Residential apartments**: Apartment buildings will become cold blocks of concrete without hydro and gas services. The people residing inside these buildings will have to be advised to maintain their own 72-hour survival kits; however, the facility manager must plan for the fact that the lights may be off, requiring emergency lighting in the hallways and hopefully a diesel generator to provide hydro. Elevators will not function, requiring all tenants to use the stairs, which increases the risk of tenant injury and overexertion of the sick and elderly from climbing stairs. Consideration must be given to the physically challenged, and the building manager must know where the physically challenged are located in the facility to ensure they get the help they need during a crisis. A good idea is to form a building committee to identify and address these and other building-specific issues, perhaps by using volunteers who can help patrol and manage the building to increase security when the access controls are shut off and to help those in need during the crisis. Having these and other issues addressed in advance will greatly reduce risk and chaos when actual emergencies occur. It will also foster a feeling of community among the building population to know they will

be looked after during a crisis. Having intimate knowledge of the people in the facility will also be of great assistance to emergency responders when they enter the building on an emergency call.

2. **Retail centers**: Malls and retail stores, including restaurants, will likely have to be self-sufficient during a business continuity type of crisis. However, some advance planning, such as the engagement of a diesel generator for power, may enable these businesses to stay open and continue providing service to the public unless, of course, the supply of goods runs out before the crisis is over. Owners of these facilities must be aware of the possibility of crime and looting directed at their establishments during a crisis and may want to consider locking down their premises depending on their location and circumstance. Planning advice from local police and state or provincial emergency services agencies should be sought for specific situations in order to get the best advice possible.

3. **Sports stadiums and arenas**: During a major emergency, it is not supposed that sports venues are going to be open for business; however, they could provide emergency shelter if required by municipal business continuity planning in certain circumstances, just as the New Orleans superdome provided shelter to local residents during the highly destructive Hurricane Katrina in 2005. These possibilities should be discussed and arranged in advance since being organized and prepared is always better than sorting out chaos in the middle of a crisis. Any use of a sports venue for emergency shelter purposes is going to require owner and government support, logistical structure, food and water supplies, sanitation and disposal of waste on a large scale, and, of course, first aid and medical support as more and more people seek shelter.

Once a BCP has been designed, it should be tested for effectiveness and to ensure that unexpected problems are minimized in advance. This testing should never be done in isolation, but rather with other entities and local responders, if possible, to be able to detect issues and unexpected problems so they can be repaired before a real event strikes, requiring activation of the plan. Annual testing is an excellent practice to incorporate, but an employee must always be designated to keep track of the ongoing movement of people and to ensure that positions of responsibility in the emergency evacuation and BCP are filled with committed pcople. This must include replacements when these volunteers are absent so that there is always someone with the knowledge available. Completed BCPs should be considered living documents, always subject to updating as better ideas or facilities materialize with time.

Business continuity planning is one of the most important aspects of security and facilities planning with which managers will be faced. It is always a challenging exercise that requires patience, negotiation, good ideas, and the ability to communicate ideas. A good plan will keep the wheels turning in the midst of a crisis and, for that reason, BCP must always be a priority in any corporation or building.

19

Concluding Topics

ETHICS AND LEADERSHIP

The subject of ethics always makes for an interesting and often misleading discussion as so many people will pull out manuals, carefully constructed definitions, and studies to support their views and arguments about what ethics mean and how to implement leadership correctly. Many organizations actually teach ethics as a subject and the instructors usually miss the mark by misunderstanding the topics and failing to inject the ethical standards into leaders that organizations need for continued success. Often the executives at the top simply do not understand what is going wrong and, at times, they are part of the problem. Discussing ethics and leadership is very important for managers and people that wish to become managers because it is so important to have an ethically based relationship with subordinates in order to get the most out of them and to gain their support when things go wrong.

To start with, the primary role of both managers and supervisors is to support their subordinates and set them up for success, which in turn will foster trust and enable better production. This identified role is in opposition to those leaders and managers that feel subordinates are not to be trusted, requiring them to crack the whip and punish people in order to get better production and obedience out of them. Often, the word *accountability* appears in the organization's behavioral competencies at the supervisory and management levels. Many ambitious workers simply misunderstand what accountability actually means and set about looking for situations where they can hold people accountable for errors, in order to articulate to hiring boards how they have fulfilled the behavioral competency of *accountability* by writing people up for mistakes and creating work improvement plans to "get them back up to standard." This is not only unfair to the workers, but it also creates a poisoned work environment that the managers cannot see developing.

In most cases, errors made by staff can be corrected with understanding, some patience, and perhaps a little bit of educational counseling. Most workers come to work wanting to do a good job and are not expecting to make mistakes. They are generally open to being told that they made an error and how to do it correctly. The supervisor can make some private notes about how it was handled, which provides the basis for going the next step in discipline if the situation repeats. This is a prime example of holding someone accountable and working through it. It is a major mistake for a supervisor or manager to take that same situation, write negative documentation for the worker's file, and then create a formal work improvement plan because by then the supervisor or manager has lost the employee's enthusiasm, trust, and even work ethic using an unnecessary, negative process. Most employees and those around them figure out quickly enough what is going on anyway and realize they have an ambitious supervisor or manager who is "developing" himself or herself on the backs of the employees. This becomes a poisoned work environment, and once this happens, a poisoned work environment is very difficult to repair without the outright removal of the offending party. This kind of situation is an abuse of supervisory/management authority and reflects a dramatic failure of leadership with long-range negative effects for the organization.

The discussion in this book is experience based and does not come out of textbooks and studies. It is from someone who has not only studied leadership theory but also served at the bottom of organizations. The author has enjoyed the privileges and status of rank, as well as the responsibility of leadership, but have never lost sight of real ethics and leadership and the effect those topics have on those working in the lower end positions.

The word *ethics* suggests to people that honesty and integrity are the way to go, and most people will always count themselves as being honest and full of integrity. Even those that get away from ethical practice over time will still view themselves as ethical and then qualify the statement with "but at work, that is how you get business done." That excuse makes it easy to sway from ethics to "get it done," but soon these people start using the tactic all the time and their ethics have disappeared. What these ethically compromised people do not realize—or what some do not even care about—is that others are watching. The people working hard at the bottom of the organization see what is going on and experience the results of unethical practice from those racing to climb the ladder of corporate success. This is where ethics and leadership collide, and the lack of ethics actually compromises leadership and turns otherwise functional organizations into inefficient bureaucratic nightmares.

Despite how people define ethics and how they loosely apply them, to have ethics is to operate honestly and with integrity. This does not include parking ethics at the curb in certain situations because "that is how business gets done." That approach may garner some success, but it always catches up to people eventually and their reputation suffers as a result. With whom does the reputation suffer? Not with like-minded people who are doing the same thing and using that approach as a way of doing business, but rather with the people under supervision or management that see what is going on and lose respect for the people and the organization. This is the cornerstone of leadership that all supervisors and managers must make decisions about as they go about daily business.

A real-world definition of ethics and leadership is important to the management of facilities, given that proper facility management only occurs when overlapping services cooperate and can depend upon one another. This means that ethical behavior and leadership are critical to relationship-building between Security, Facilities Management, Maintenance Management, and the first responding emergency services such as police, fire, and ambulance personnel. Any of the managers or supervisors engaged in this work must always be truthful, even when the truth is not good news or may cause a problem. To not be truthful instantly erodes trust and, quite often, the person receiving the untruthful information either already knows it is not correct or will figure it out soon enough. Most of the time, the person receiving the flawed information will not even let on that he or she realizes the information was not truthful, but the relationship is damaged from that point on.

This kind of trusting relationship between the different entities that are managing buildings was quite evident during the previously mentioned double-alarm event in two different buildings during a Christmas tree festival. As the volunteers intended to act as parking attendants and assisting inside the building failed to materialize, the pressure was on the paid security staff to not only respond to the alarms but also continue to staff the festival. When the first alarm came in, each employee was fully tasked to maintain the event coverage and investigate the alarm source. When the second alarm came in only minutes later, there were no more security officers to make a response. However, that close working relationship between security and maintenance enabled the use of the maintenance department workers, who immediately jumped in and said, "What do you need us to do?" Some maintenance workers were dispatched to the other building, while several relieved security officers, who were then able to perform the response at the second building. Without the familiarity and close working relationship between the two entities, such cooperation might not have materialized as quickly as it did and the result of the crisis might have gone the way of full evacuation of the building staff and the general public attending the festival. The fire department also rolled in and knew enough about the building two-stage alarm system and response protocols that their response went smoothly as well. They were soon off the premises with the main building containing the festival being completely cleared of fire hazard, while the second building across the road had to be temporarily closed due to a sprinkler system problem. In all, there was only a disruption of about half an hour to the festival, which can be attributed to the close working relationship of the units involved, united through familiarity and a wonderful initiative called the emergency planning committee.

EMERGENCY PLANNING COMMITTEE

Communication between entities remains a critical aspect of managing facilities and getting the main entities and controlling interests working toward common goals. One way to ensure a constant communication flow is to establish an emergency planning committee for the building or complex of buildings in a compound. The implementation of such a committee can bring to the table all of the sectors that are deemed to be stakeholders, in that they all share common interest in responding to emergencies efficiently in the community of the building. The emergency planning committee should consist of the building owner or a representative; building operator; maintenance manager; security manager; representative of the tenant population or workforce occupying the space; occupational health and safety committee representative; local police, fire, and ambulance services; and anyone deemed to have a stake on how problems are solved within the building community.

As an ongoing feature of the committee, guests should be invited as representative stakeholders for upcoming events or contracted renovations, etc. The committee should have a regular appointed or elected chairperson, who should be from the facility itself to ensure the needs of the facility always come first. In the name of transparency, someone on the committee should be appointed to take minutes, and the minutes should be published and distributed to stakeholders as a way of tracking discussions and decisions and helping to add accountability to those on the committee.

The committee should meet as regularly as deemed necessary, but at least once a month to ensure ongoing and timely coverage of upcoming events and construction projects or just to discuss problems within the facility or complaints from the building occupants. This type of committee not only brings the important players together but also fosters a spirit of cooperation that will pay dividends when a major emergency does strike, such as a region-wide power failure, a real fire evacuation event, or an unexpected natural disaster such as a tornado, an ice storm, or seasonal flooding. The emergency planning committee can become a decision-making body in times of crisis as it will most likely have executive- and management-level participation from the first-response organizations in the community. This idea should be developed and included in the facility emergency response policies to establish legitimacy and to ensure it is officially included in disaster training scenarios and recognized by government.

GENERAL CONCLUSIONS

The essence of most facilities and buildings is the same in terms of a protected space containing walls, doors, windows, and human necessities such as plumbing, running water, heating and ventilation systems, restrooms, office space or living quarters (or both in some cases), and a myriad of uses, each with its own specific set of variables. Aside from those variables, facilities have enough commonalities to produce a general skill set for facility managers where the same concerns and activities seem to permeate any facility regardless of the reason for its existence or the functions performed therein. This book is an attempt to bring those commonalities together as a guide for facility managers who will see what typically happens in community-sized buildings and what a manager may expect as he or she carries on with day-to-day operations.

The main theme to think about is that a facility manager not only keeps the machinery and systems of the building running, but also manages a microcommunity within the facility where many or most of the functions of a small town might be concentrated. The facility manager finds himself or herself as the central figure among different corporate entities, government or retail facilities, and/or tenants. The manager represents the building owners on-site and, as such, needs to know what is really going on in the building as opposed to what the general reputation may be among certain executives or management who may have an entirely different idea of what is going on compared to the maintenance technician, janitor, or tenant who accesses a basement locker on a daily basis and sees illicit activity going on where none was thought to exist. The facility manager is the person to whom most people turn when something goes wrong in a building; therefore, the facility manager needs to have relationships developed and resources at hand to engage whatever resources are required to mitigate problems and keep the facility functioning as it should be.

Facility managers become broadly skilled not only in ensuring the mechanics and machinery of the building function seamlessly, but also in becoming financial managers who handle budgets, contracts, and subcontracts as well as hire staff and lead the group in the daily effort to achieve the goals of the facility.

Facility managers must also get to know the population of the building and build relationships with the various entities populating the building. They must collect information on an ongoing basis to properly analyze the situation and equip the facility with proper access controls and security/safety measures to protect the building community that expects some measure of protection while on-site. An effective facility manager will find himself or herself to be the central cog in the middle of a thriving, active community where a little relationship building through discussions and committees can connect relevant people to the current issues affecting the building and the community. This makes problem solving a cooperative venture through the stakeholders and produces effective solutions for the betterment of all.

In times of crisis, facility managers may find themselves to be a critical central figure to whom not only building occupants look for leadership, but also to whom first response providers look as the local expert on how the facility functions and as the evacuation leader, suddenly in charge of moving hundreds or perhaps thousands of panicking people out of the building and away from danger. Being a facility manager requires a broad base of skills and it is a position of trust and leadership in the community. The facility manager must also have a good team around him or her that will keep on working when required in the interest of the building population and the facility itself. Being ready and being able to anticipate are two elements that facility managers can rely on as being critical to success as *anything can happen at any time in a facility*. These are words to frame and put above the office desk.

REFERENCES

Reid, Jason D., founder and senior advisor, National Life Safety Group: Fire, Life Safety and Emergency Management, speaker and author. Permission given by telephone (416)770-8005 on September 16, 2015, at 1353 hours.

Workplace Safety and Prevention Services http://www.wsps.ca/Information -Resources/Topics/WHMIS.aspx.

INDEX